The Book of the Courtesans

The Book of the Courtesans

A Catalogue of

Their

Virtues

Susan Griffin

BROADWAY BOOKS   NEW YORK

Library of Congress Cataloging-in-Publication Data

Griffin, Susan.
The book of the courtesans: a catalogue of
their virtues/Susan Griffin.—1st ed.
p.   cm.
1. Courtesans—History.   2. Courtesans—Biography.
3. Mistresses—History.   4. Mistresses—Biography.   I. Title.
HQ1122.G75
306.74'2'09—dc21   2001025768

Art credits appear on page 271.

FIRST EDITION

Designed by Chris Welch

ISBN 0-7679-04508

1   3   5   7   9   10   8   6   4   2

for Odette Meyers

HER MEMORY

AND FOR FRIENDSHIP AMONG WOMEN

Acknowledgments

LET ME ESPECIALLY thank Leonard Pitt, who has been generous with his time and his extensive library on nineteenth-century France. I am also grateful to the late Odette Meyers, not only for her friendship, but for teaching me so much about the French language and French culture as well as for having what Leonard Pitt has called such a *belle intelligence.* My dear friend Edith Sorel has provided guidance, wisdom, invaluable knowledge, and her brilliant wit. Odile Hellier of the Village Voice Bookstore in Paris was helpful, as she is with so many writers. The Baron du Cassagne kindly gave me several interviews as well as an indispensable perspective on events in the nineteenth century. The Baroness Liliane de Rothschild was kindly helpful with reference to Marie Duplessis. Let me again thank Marlotte Reinharez for accompanying me to the Château du Monte Cristo and Raphael Balmes for accompanying me to the Musée Gace devoted to Marie Duplessis. Carol Spindel helped me with more than one difficulty in Paris. Daniel Meyers, too, has been helpful to me in Paris. Thanks to Madeleine Barcheuska for sending me a tape of Sarah Bernhardt playing La Dame aux Camélias. Thanks also to Lea Mendelovitz for her helpful knowledge of Paris. Thanks also to Alberto Manguel for the reading list he gave me, his generous insights, and for helping me at the Bibliothèque Historique de la Ville de Paris. Thanks to Randy Conner for his marvelous manuscript on Baudelaire and Jeanne Duval and for his suggestions. Thank you to Joanna Bernstein for her encouragement and for giving me an invaluable reading list. I thank the Théâtre de la Ville, which was once the Théâtre Sarah Bernhardt, for allowing me to see Sarah's dressing room, and Micheline Boudet for her book *La Fleur du Mal.*

Margot Hackett supplied me with two books difficult to find, and her wry sensibility gave me courage. I thank Moira Roth for reading bits of the work in progress and for her encouragingly whimsical perceptions. I thank Anita Barrows for her friendship, her reading of the manuscript, her generous and fine mind. Daidie Donnelly, too, has been a wonderful friend in this period, reading my manuscript with sensitive, delicately intelligent encouragement. I thank Jodie Evans for her passionate friendship, her encouragement, and profound understanding of this book. Sandra Sharpe, too, has been a wonderful friend in this period, laughing with me at the right moments, making me laugh at the right moments, reading and listening with great perceptiveness. I thank Bokara Legendre, too, for her friendship and help.

Thank you to Beverly Allen for immediately grasping what this work is about on the deepest level and for her helpful knowledge of the Italian Renaissance and Venice. Thanks to Gudrun Icsimo for her kindness in Venice. Thanks to Georgina Morley for a day and evening in the courtesan's Paris. Thank you to Joe Wemple for his friendship, his playful encouragement, as well as several helpful references. Thanks again to Isabel Villaud and Christian Roy-Camille for their help with Marie Duplessis. Thank you to Monique Saigal for helping me extend my research into a wonderful cyberspace network of French scholars. John Levy helped me find a valuable reference, as did Dan Church, Jim Allen, and Yvonne Bayer at Vanderbilt University Library. Lise Huerelle helped me from time to time with French translation.

Let me thank my daughter, Chloe Andrews, for asking about this book and listening, for encouraging the work and responding with great clarity to what she read. And I thank my editor, Lauren Marino, for her intelligent reading, her warm encouragement, and her perceptive editing. Thank you to Cate Tynan for managing so many details. And to my agent, Katinka Matson, for her care, understanding, and humor.

Contents

The Book of the Courtesans

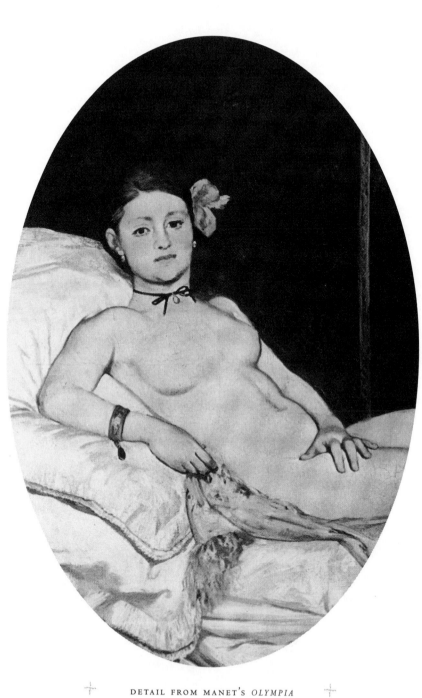

DETAIL FROM MANET'S *OLYMPIA*

A Legacy of Virtues

She had charm, a dazzling complexion and wit. It was the
last great heyday for courtesans and she made hay.
—JANET FLANNER, *Paris Was Yesterday*

Goodness had nothing to do with it.
—MAE WEST

COURTESAN. AT FIRST glance, the word seems to sit almost coyly on the page. But first impressions can be misleading. The slightly risqué connotations which come to mind hardly reveal the abundance that is hidden here. What was a courtesan, really? As with any tradition that was once alive, the meaning is far too rich for a simple answer. Dictionary definitions will hardly suffice. Where one edition says the courtesan was a prostitute who associated with wealthy men or aristocrats, another refers to her as a kept woman. Yes, she shared characteristics with both. But she was neither.

To claim that courtesans were prostitutes would be deceptively simple. It is true that Madame du Barry, favorite of Louis XV, was once patronized by upper-class men who paid nightly for her favors. And we know that Céleste Mogador, who eventually became a countess, worked in a brothel when she was very young. But their stories only make what may seem a subtle distinction on paper more clear. To become a courtesan was a promotion of great proportions, a fortunate leap into an unimaginably better life. Unlike a prostitute, a courtesan did not live in a brothel, never walked the streets, nor did she, strictly speaking, have a pimp to control and bully her.

On occasion, usually early in their careers, some women did have procurers, but it was their mothers who played this role. Sarah Bernhardt, for example, was given her first liaisons by a mother who, being a courtesan herself, looked to her daughter to provide for her in her old age. This arrangement was common in sixteenth-century Venice and Rome, where mothers who had once been courtesans would, as a matter of course, procure for their daughters. The relationship between mother and daughter is entirely different from that between pimp and prostitute in many significant ways, including the fact that unlike the prostitute, who enriches a pimp more than herself, while she supported her mother, a courtesan could benefit from her own success.

But the distinctions are far greater. With some legendary exceptions, the agreements made with courtesans were hardly quid pro quo. It is probably true that la comtesse de Castiglione was given 1 million francs for a twelve-hour orgy with Richard Wallace, natural son of the fourth Marquess of Hertford. And the rumor may be justified that Liane de Pougy was given 80,000 francs by Henri Meilhac, the librettist for Offenbach's popular operas, just to see her nude (or so Edmond de Goncourt writes in his *Journal*). But the usual arrangements were like those made with mistresses and even wives—longer lasting and more subtle in nature. And in distinction to the support given mistresses, who were often modestly kept, these relationships were far more lucrative. Soon after their liaison began, for instance, Louis XV presented Madame de Pompadour with an estate, one of several she was to receive in her lifetime, including the mansion known as the Palais Elysée, now the home of French presidents. A hundred years later, following the same tradition, in addition to giving Marie Duplessis a splendid coach, a team of the finest horses, and a monthly allotment to pay for a maid and a cook, le comte de Stakelberg bought the courtesan her fashionable apartment on the boulevard Madeleine.

The splendor in which the great courtesans lived is fabled. At times their riches grew to exceed those of their protectors. They accumulated town houses, châteaux, villas, all decorated with frescoes and sculptures by important painters, with wood embellishments carved by the best craftsmen, endowed with precious materials—gold gilt, silver, crystal, marble, and onyx—and furnished with the finest antiques, silver services, porcelain vases, the most select china, and priceless tapestries. Their coaches rivaled those sported by the elite. Their wardrobes, made from the most luxurious fabrics and by the most celebrated designers—Charles Worth, for instance, or Paul Poiret—were envied by respectable and titled women who copied the styles they wore. And above all, courtesans collected jewelry: strings of diamonds and pearls, diamond tiaras, sapphires and ruby rings, emerald brooches, which they displayed with a good measure of pride and also canniness. In a memorable scene from Colette's novel *Gigi*, the daughter of a courtesan is carefully taught to tell the difference between a canary diamond and topaz; a *cocotte's* cache of gems served both as an emblem of success and as a fund for her retirement.

The rivalry between courtesans over jewelry had occasional dramatic moments. A story is told about the competition between Liane de Pougy and the Belle Otero which is true, though the setting is disputed. Some say it occurred at Maxim's; others, such as Janet Flanner, the correspondent to *The New Yorker* in the early twentieth century, place it at the Opéra; and still another, Pougy's recent biographer, places it at Monte Carlo. But the essence of the action is always the same. First, Otero makes her entrance, dripping with diamonds and precious gems in every form: necklaces, bracelets, earrings, anklets, layered and piled in a glittering display of astonishing abundance. Then, shortly after, Pougy enters, wearing only one very elegant diamond necklace, but she is followed by a maid who carries a high pyramid of her priceless jewelry stacked on a red pillow.

The goods would have come from many sources. If, as with a mistress, an affair with a courtesan was rarely just a one-night stand, that is where the similarity ends. Courtesans could be both less and more than mistresses. Less because they were by no means always faithful. Usually, they had several lovers, some who contributed to the household expenses and some who did not. Like other Venetian courtesans, Veronica Franco had many protectors. Sharing in her support, each was pledged a different night of the week in her schedule.

And unlike the mistress of a married man, who is often kept hidden, just as the courtesan was proud of her jewelry, she too was proudly displayed. She was expected to accompany her various lovers to public places and events, cafés, restaurants, balls, parties, the theatre, the opera, even hosting gatherings of her lover's friends at her own home. In sixteenth-century Rome, when the powerful banker Chigi entertained at his villa near the Vatican, his lover, the courtesan Imperia, was usually the hostess. It is thought that her beauty inspired Raphael's famous fresco of Galatea that still adorns one wall there. During the Belle Epoque in Paris, among the wealthy playboys, aristocrats, and businessmen who belonged to the exclusive Jockey Club, it was considered de rigueur to keep a courtesan—so much so that even homosexual men felt they had to do it for show.

But perhaps the greatest distinction we must make here between kept women and courtesans is that the latter were personages. They were, indeed, what we call today celebrities. Friends of kings, regents, emperors, statesmen, financiers, famous writers and painters, they were the constant subject of columns printed in weekly journals, gossip about their romances, what they wore and what they did providing continual fodder for public curiosity. Flaubert, Zola, Balzac, Colette, the Goncourt brothers, all based major characters on the lives of courtesans. And of course, from Praxiteles to Titian to Manet, they were favored as subjects by painters and sculptors.

For this reason, a courtesan had to be highly cultivated. Often born to poverty, with no education and lacking upper-class manners, a young woman would have to be taught many skills in order to play her new role. As in Shaw's play *Pygmalion* (or the musical that followed, *My Fair Lady*), she would have to learn to speak with an upper-class accent, dress well if not lavishly, arrange her hair fashionably, walk gracefully, dance, and play the piano. She would be required to know table manners, of course, but also different protocols, including at times the protocols of the court. A woman who may not even have been able to read very well would now be expected to know the plots of operas, recognize literary references, and have some familiarity with history. Only the brave and intelligent would be able to survive the course.

Many courtesans exceeded these requirements. Some, such as Céleste Mogador, who wrote novels, or Tullia D'Aragona, three hundred years earlier, who wrote a philosophical text on Eros, were writers. Veronica Franco was a respected poet. A great many wrote their autobiographies. More than can be counted were notable actresses, dancers, singers, music-hall and circus performers. A few, such as Sarah Bernhardt and Coco Chanel, became far more famous in other professions. An even smaller group, the comtesse de Loynes for instance, gained titles when they married their aristocratic lovers, then having learned to behave well enough and after acquiring sufficient wealth, they slipped past the arbiters of class into high society.

But if these women were remarkable in their accomplishments, they were exceptions among the already exceptional. Altogether, there can be no doubt that courtesans were extraordinary women, not only considering their talents but because, as Simone de Beauvoir writes, they created for themselves "a situation almost equivalent to that of man . . . free in behavior and conversation," attaining, "the rarest intellectual liberty." For centuries courtesans enjoyed more power and independence than did any other women in Europe. To understand why this was so, we must consider the history of women in Europe, a history that is by no means always the same as the history of men. The consideration is crucial, especially because outside the context of the larger narrative of women's lives, the word "courtesan" loses much of its meaning.

For the several centuries during which courtesans practiced their skills, women were far more confined and regimented than they are today. Except among courtesans, if a woman had wealth, it was almost never her own, but hers to use only through the beneficence, permission, or parsimonious allowance of a father, brother, or husband. Thus it was rare even for women born to wealthy families to be financially independent. Though a luxurious dependency may sound attractive, economic dependency implies a loss of freedom. An upper-class woman did not own the houses she inhabited, could not in fact purchase a house if she wanted to, nor even furniture, china, jewelry, clothing, or food without approval, nor could she travel by her own choice or alone. She was controlled by those who controlled the purse strings.

This circumstance was coupled with still another condition that served to keep upper-class women dependent. They were not fully educated. According to the century in which a lady lived, she might be taught to embroider, to sing, to play the piano, and to dance; she would be instructed in religion and given the rudimentary skills of reading and writing, but what she knew of history, literature, philosophy, or politics she would have had to glean by inference from listening to the conversations of the men in her family. And until the latter part of the nineteenth century when, because of the influence of feminist movements, a few women were admitted to universities, medical, law, and art schools, women were denied the training they would need to enter a profession. Thus the ways available to upper-class and respectable women to earn an independent living were very few. Lacking either inheritance, a family wealthy enough to sustain her, or a husband, an aristocratic or bourgeois woman might become a governess. For the most part, her only other option was to join a convent.

The purpose, therefore, of a young girl's life was to prepare her to attract a husband. She was taught to dress and dance and curtsy so that she might be presented at court or at a debutante ball, where it was hoped she would meet her future husband. But though she was required to enter the rituals of courtship, neither her feelings nor her preferences were considered relevant. Most marriages were not made for love. They were, rather, thinly veiled financial agreements, arranged to benefit a young woman's family or the family of her future husband, while conferring prestige on one or the other or both.

Even the instructions she was given to be pleasing to men had unnatural limits. Given almost no sexual education except the advice to behave with a modestly flirtatious deference to men, her efforts to catch a husband were supposed to be innocent, just as her limited knowledge of the worlds of finance and politics was thought to add to an air of innocence, lending her an attractive naïveté. We might say that, paradoxically, by the rules of this social world, her dependency was her chief asset.

But this state of being could also easily prove her downfall. A descent of this kind has been painfully captured by Edith Wharton. In her great novel *The House of Mirth,* Wharton depicts the financial and sexual naïveté of Lily Bart, a young woman who is upper class by birth, with only a small inheritance, whose ignorance leads her to commit several social follies that leave her both penniless and unmarriageable. By painful degrees of descent, she meets the worst fate imaginable for a woman born to privilege—she is forced to begin life as a working woman.

The fact that throughout centuries of European history the majority of women had to work is often omitted even from accounts that purport to focus on women's lives. Peasant families depended on the labor of women and children alike to eke out a living. And among those who lived and worked in the city, apart from the nobility or the wives of the professional classes and the bourgeoisie (who only began to grow to significant numbers in the eighteenth century), whether women took in laundry, worked as chambermaids, charwomen, seamstresses, or weavers, they were wage earners. Married or not, the income they earned was necessary to their own survival as well as that of their families, yet they could earn only a fraction of what men could. In Paris in the early nineteenth century, for example, when peasant economies in France began to collapse and the cities, especially Paris, were flooded with refugees from the countryside seeking employment, even the salaries of workingmen were barely sufficient for survival. Though they worked long hours, often sixteen hours a day, many women could not live on the salaries they were paid.

Thus the word for a woman working in the garment industry, the most common form of employment for women, *grisette,* which derived from the dull gray of the muslin dresses she wore, acquired a second meaning. Even into the mid-twentieth century, dictionaries still defined the *grisette* as "a woman of easy virtue." Earning 1 to 1.5 francs a day for work that was seasonal, the garment worker had to turn to other sources for her income. Some walked the streets; some lived with casual lovers, oftentime students, who helped to pay the bills; others attended the many public balls that were popular then in Paris to search for wealthier men who might pay for their favors for a night.

It was for this reason that so many courtesans began as *grisettes*. If they were lucky enough or extraordinary in some way, they could climb the rungs of a ladder that could lead them further and further away from penury and a grueling schedule of hard work. At a public dance hall, a young woman might meet a man who would set her up in an apartment. A woman who had this good fortune was called a *lorette*, the word for a would-be courtesan, a woman who was kept only modestly. She did not habituate the elevated circles in which courtesans traveled, though she was a social fixture of the bohemian world. Mimi in Henri Murger's *Scènes de la Vie Bohème* was a *lorette*. But the story is better known as Puccini's opera *La Bohème*.

Only the few who were the most talented among *lorettes* would ever become courtesans. The heroine of another famous opera, Violetta Valéry in Verdi's *La Traviata*, was modeled after Marie Duplessis, a real woman who started as a *grisette*, became a *lorette* soon after, only to ascend with remarkable rapidity to the rank of courtesan. Her story is typical of the rags-to-riches ascent that was both as desirable and improbable then as is the dream of becoming a sports hero today. Born to near poverty in Normandy, Marie's mother died early. After a period in which her alcoholic father, an itinerant salesman, hauled her with him about the countryside, offering his daughter at least once as merchandise, and after being abandoned by the same father to distant and unwelcoming cousins in Paris, she began work as a *grisette*. That she was poverty-stricken during this period is verified by the testimony of Nestor Roqueplan, director of the Opéra, who spotted her a year before she became famous, on the Pont-Neuf, dressed in dirty, ragged clothing, begging for a taste of the *pommes frites* that were sold on the bridge. It did not take her long to meet a restaurateur who established her as a *lorette* in her own apartment.

But this tenure was equally brief. She rose quickly to become one of the highest-ranking courtesans of her time. Well fed and housed, considered to be the best dressed woman in Paris, the woman known as "the divine Marie" had acquired great fame, not to speak of a title, before her death from tuberculosis at the age of twenty-three.

Class is an essential ingredient in the history of courtesans for many reasons, including the dramatic transformation that occurred in the life of a woman who was elevated thus. According to accounts from the eighteenth century, Madame du Barry, who herself experienced a spectacular rise from *grisette* and sometime prostitute to become the favorite of Louis XV, spoke far better French than his previous mistress, Madame de Pompadour. Since the celebrated Pompadour had been educated by her bourgeois family, she spoke a French that was at least passable at court. But because Barry's working-class language was entirely unacceptable, she was compelled to learn an upper-class grammar that was far more correct than that of her predecessor.

Still, the plot thickens. The issue of class cannot be understood apart from issues of morality. For several centuries in European cultures, with some variations, it was thought that a woman should be chaste before marriage, and if not absolutely faithful, she should at least behave with enough discretion to protect her reputation. The requirement was not uniform. In certain periods and places, especially those in which the poor were driven to desperate measures, a woman's chastity had less significance among working people than it did for the aristocracy. But this division of sentiments was not consistent. The peccadilloes and open liaisons of nobles, kings, and emperors were known to incite wrath from the less privileged public.

What remains relevant to this history, however, is another condition that fostered the tradition of courtesans, the simple fact that as with Edith Wharton's character Lily Bart, a wellborn woman could fall, and in falling not only lose any chance for marriage but be shunned by society as well. In that case, one of the better options open to her would be to become a courtesan. There were so many women who chose this solution in Paris at the turn of the century that a special word was used for them: they were referred to as *demicastors*. Because of a scandal that had ruined her reputation, one such woman, Laure Hayman, was ostracized until she made her way back into society in another role, as a courtesan. She counted among her lovers many powerful men, including Louis Weil, the uncle of Marcel Proust. It was probably because Proust had known her since he was a boy that he took Hayman as a model for Odette Crécy, the fictional courtesan whose story threads through *A la recherche du temps perdu*.

The tangled skein of double standards regarding both sex and money, gender and class, creates an interesting controversy over whether or not certain historical figures ought to be classified as courtesans. Agnès Sorel, favorite of Charles VII of France, is generally not considered a courtesan, nor is Alice Keppel, longtime mistress to the Prince of Wales, though both were given financial aid by the monarchs who loved them. One might answer that they did not take money from any other lovers. Except that Pompadour, who took remuneration from no other lovers either, is called a courtesan by almost everybody, probably for the sole reason that she came from the bourgeoisie. Rather than probe the justice of this reasoning, the hope is that these controversies might be resolved by the chapters to follow, which in general use the term "courtesan" as a favorable designation.

Yet it should not be construed that *The Book of the Courtesans* attempts to argue that its subjects were virtuous in a moral sense. No effort will be made here either to defend or condemn their behavior. Rather, the virtues in the title take their definition from an older usage—one that was once applied exclusively to men, but which, though it has been out of fashion since the Renaissance, this book revives and applies now to women. In this older definition, virtue has nothing at all to do with chastity. It refers rather to the strengths and attributes that characterize as well as distinguish a person.

Though circumstances must and will be summoned so that these stories can be better understood, the emphasis here will be on the creative response each woman showed to the conditions she confronted. For this phenomenon to be entirely explained, we must explore the considerable magic of human ingenuity here. There are so many kinds of genius to be found in these stories that were we not to place our focus on virtue, we would be squandering a treasure that belongs to all those who are the inheritors of this history.

For history it is. Although the many virtues that courtesans possessed were employed to defy circumstances, the role they played depended on the same circumstances over which they triumphed—conditions which today, fortunately for modern women, no longer exist. At least within modern European cultures women are not expected to be virgins before they marry, nor do they have to be dependent on husbands, brothers, or fathers for their economic survival.

And there is still another reason for the disappearance of this tradition. The temper of the times has shifted, too. Technically speaking, many women today do what courtesans did; it is quite common still for a married man to support his mistress, and a whole population of highly cultivated and elegant women serve today as escorts, call girls, and modern hetaerae. But just as surely as the role of the courtesan was created by historical conditions, she was also inextricably linked to a historical mood that had come to an end by the third decade of the last century. In 1948, after visiting La Belle Otero, Anne Manson wrote: "When Otero departs there will depart with her the last symbol of an epoch, superficial, light and at the same time virtuous and cynical, covetous toward others yet madly extravagant in its pleasures, full of faults but not without its splendors."

To become a courtesan, a woman required a setting. Though she was center stage, she was not alone. Nor was she hidden. Almost by definition, she was surrounded by scintillating activity. She was inseparable from the *demi-mondes* she inhabited—slightly rebellious, risqué, or naughty worlds, alternate societies where a certain sophistication, including carnal knowledge that was banned from proper society, was allowed to thrive. The Belle Epoque, the period that Otero symbolized, was famous not only for its writers, artists, playwrights, and actors but also for the glittering social scene which was staged almost continuously on the Grands Boulevards in Paris, the epicenter of the atmosphere, and the stage on which the courtesan played a vital and charismatic role.

In this, she was part of a tradition that stretches back over centuries. The Belle Epoque may have been the last period in which the courtesan reigned, but it was by no means the first. For at least a hundred years before the end of the Belle Epoque, Paris had been a magnet for courtesans, would-be courtesans, and men seeking the magic of their company. Indeed, the Second Empire, earlier in the century, was so dominated by this presence that Balzac seemed almost to be stating a simple truth when he wrote, "Paris is a courtesan."

But what took place in the Second Empire was also a continuation. In the seventeenth and eighteenth centuries, the alternative life with courtesans that aristocrats, princes, and kings conducted at the courts, places, and fine houses of France was called *galanterie*. Several famous courtesans from this period are still remembered, among them Ninon de Lenclos and La Pompadour. And in turn, French *galanterie* was inspired by an even earlier history. Venice during the Renaissance is the only place and time that can be said to rival nineteenth-century Paris for its courtesans. Just as Balzac likened Paris to a courtesan, the seventeenth-century English poet James Howell took this figure as the metaphor of Venice. "Syren-like on Shore and Sea, Her Face," he writes, "Enchants all those whom once she doth embrace." The reputation of Venice's courtesans was once one of its chief attractions. "So infinite are the allurements of these amorous Calypsos," another Englishman, Thomas Coryat, wrote of the courtesans he encountered when he visited the city, "that the fame of them hath drawn many to Venice from some of the remotest parts of Christendom." At one point among scarcely more than 100,000 inhabitants, there was said to be over 10,000 *cortigiana*, or 10 percent of the population, though only a portion of these would have been courtesans for whom the honorific title *cortigiane oneste* was used.

Among those who were honored in this way, 210 women were listed in a catalogue (*Catalogo di Tutte le Principali Già Honorate Cortigiane di Venezia*) available for the more affluent visitor.

The antecedents for the word "courtesan" first appear in fourteenth-century Rome, where *cortigiano*, or "courtier," evolved into a female form with a somewhat different meaning. It was from this Italian word that the French *courtisane* developed, the term that finally inspired the English "courtesan." But by a different name, centuries before courtesans appeared in early Renaissance Rome, the tradition of the *hetaera* was a fixture in ancient Rome and Greece.

The reappearance of this tradition in fourteenth-century Italy was partly a consequence of the revival of antiquity that was so crucial to the Renaissance. A lineage of courtesans can be traced from antiquity through the great masters into the modern period. We might begin, for instance, in Greece, with Praxiteles, whose most celebrated *Aphrodite of Cnidus*, modeled after his mistress the courtesan Phyrne, initiated the tradition of the female nude in sculpture; then move on to Italy during the Renaissance, when portraits of Venus and other goddesses, for which courtesans often modeled, were painted by Veronese, Titian, Raphael, and Tintoretto; then go to eighteenth-century Paris, where Boucher's frothy images of frolicking goddesses recalled the rosy likenesses of the Pompadour he painted; and end finally with the famously frank portrait of a courtesan, *Olympia*, by Manet, which was intended both as a copy and a parody of Titian's *Venus of Urbino*.

Not only did many artists in the Renaissance, among them Cellini, Raphael, and Titian, frequent courtesans, but friendships were often forged between the members of these two professions. Veronica Franco was a good friend of Tintoretto, just as Raphael and Imperia were also friends. The rapport is understandable for many reasons. The revival of antiquity benefited both, restoring an honored place for courtesans at the tables of noblemen and intellectuals alike, at the same time as it elevated artists above the position of artisan to which they had been relegated before. Moreover, since the amorous Greek and Roman gods belonged now to the vocabulary of art, artists found themselves free to explore the erotic life in their images.

The greater accumulation of wealth that characterized the same period meant that artists could sell their works more frequently and for higher prices. This abundance did not always help women. Since greater wealth meant that the price of dowries was suddenly higher, women from less fortunate backgrounds could not afford to be married. For this reason, more women were forced into becoming courtesans. And yet, paradoxically, the same wealth that had prevented a woman from marriage benefited her greatly once she became a courtesan. And finally, both courtesans and artists, being newly and only provisionally accepted into society, shared an ambiguous terrain, a world of salons and parties, taste and wit that, skirting established power, existed just past the edge of the respectable world. Together, through their association and the connection they were making between art and sexual liberty, they were resurrecting and reshaping the tradition that would lead one day to the *demi-monde* in Paris, the Gay Nineties, if not to several contemporary movements of a different nature. It is a history that has affected countless lives, in ways both obvious and subtle.

A catalytic spark travels back and forth between each life and the spirit of an age. The mood of an age affects the choices that those living in it make. What is equally true is that the unique choices made by those who live in any period create a particular atmosphere. No tradition can remain the same for very long. A living tradition is dynamic. Just as with a great epic poem that is passed down orally from one generation to the next, some lines repeated and others slightly changed, so by minor increments of change, gradually major shifts will inevitably occur in every tradition.

Though courtesans depended on the maintenance of a double standard, as they became more popular, the eventual effect of their transgressions was to liberate women from the strictures that had sexually confined them. At the same time, the economic independence of courtesans served as a model to women, making the feminist vision of eco-

nomic parity seem more possible. First gradually, and then like a house
of cards, the whole edifice of values that had nurtured the existence of
courtesans fell. Braving scandal, upper-class men began to marry the
women they loved. Soon upper-class women insisted on marrying for
love, too. The idea of the virgin bride began to seem antiquated. Finally,
when the old way of life had changed forever, a long tradition came to
an end.

But though the great courtesans no longer exist, we still have their
virtues. Of course, nominally these virtues have always existed. But if
beauty, grace, and charm have long been considered feminine virtues,
with creative ingenuity the great courtesans expanded these attributes,
sometimes simply adding a new tone or texture to them, at others reversing the meaning of them almost entirely. Indeed, since any movement outside conventional roles can create considerable erotic energy,
this reversal accounts for some of the appeal courtesans once had—an
appeal that their virtues have for us still. Despite changing conditions,
the effect can still be felt in the gritty aura of bravery that surrounds the
images and stories, phrases, songs, and dances in which their influence
remains.

That we are remembering courtesans whenever these vestiges of their
existence come to mind, however, has until very recently been obscured.
The idea of scandal outlived the tradition long enough to erase our
awareness of the crucial roles the courtesan has played in history and in
art. This amnesia is especially strong in America, where, in the first pro-
ductions of *Camille*, the heroine was changed from a courtesan into a
chaste young woman who was innocently betrothed and cruelly jilted. By
contrast, if in mid-nineteenth-century France the first production of
Dumas' *La Dame aux camélias* was temporarily halted by state censors, by
the time of the Belle Epoque, Liane de Pougy was affectionately called
"our national courtesan," as now in countless ways this history is still remembered and honored there.

It is wise to remember this history. Without it, any reading of our
cultural heritage must be somewhat shallow as well as naive. We need

only think of the familiar term "Gay Paree" to grasp the significance of this forgotten dimension. At the end of the nineteenth century, the word "gay" was used to describe women who were courtesans, as "the gay life" referred to the world of the *demi-monde* that was built around them. Understanding the reference throws light in two directions, past and present, illuminating both Paris at the turn of the century and the homosexual identity for which the word is used now.

Not only Renaissance art but modern art is filled with images of *demi-mondaines*. The faces and figures of courtesans appear throughout paintings by the artists who have shaped contemporary vision: Courbet, Manet, Degas, Béraud, Renoir, Toulouse-Lautrec; they are gracefully present in the posters made by Mucha, humorously depicted in the caricatures by Daumier and Sem; in sculpted form they adorn more than one grand building, and even today dance in a sculpture that flanks the entrance to the Palais Garnier, the old Opéra in Paris.

Neither modern literature nor the modern sensibility would be the same had courtesans not existed. They people the poems of Baudelaire, the novels of Balzac, Dumas and Dumas *fils*, Zola, Flaubert, Colette. Proust's great novel, *A la recherche du temps perdu*, the work that more than any other has defined the aesthetic of his age and perhaps also our own, places a courtesan at the center of the narrative. A whole repertoire of plays, operas, and films has been based on stories and legends of *cocottes*, including Franz Lehar's *The Merry Widow*; much of Offenbach's work; Verdi's *La Traviata*, of course, and the great film by George Cukor from the same plot, *Camille*; Pierre Renoir's *Lola Montes*; and Howard Hawks's *Gentlemen Prefer Blondes*.

The great fame of Maxim's, where the second act of Lehar's light opera is set, is due in large part to the fact that this was once the restaurant favored by the *grandes horizontales* and their escorts. The fabled Grands Boulevards of Paris took their sparkle from them. They invented the cancan at the Moulin Rouge and provided the most celebrated acts at the Folies-Bergère. From these women a dazzling lineage can be traced that leads from the *cafés chantants*, public dance halls, and music halls where they performed, to cabaret life, and the modern French song as it came to be sung finally by Edith Piaf, Yves Montand, and Maurice Chevalier. Indeed, the wonderful singer and comedienne Minstinguett, who was Chevalier's partner, was encouraged at one point by the Second Empire courtesan named Alice Ozy. Fréhel, the working-class singer who preceded Piaf as a great favorite in the public eye, wore a gown in her first performances that was given to her by La Belle Otero. Laure Hayman introduced Marcel Proust to contemporary artists and gave him an education in worldly ways at the salon she hosted in Paris.

The lineage continues. The good timing and cheekiness of courtesans, the graceful way they leaped and slinked and kicked their way past boundaries, their implicit and explicit androgyny, their wit, their luminescence, their aesthetic sensibilities, their capacity to fascinate and enchant, all have been continued by a lineage of actresses, film stars, comediennes, singers, dancers, who though not courtesans, studied and learned their virtues. Josephine Baker, Greta Garbo, Marlene Dietrich, Mae West, Gracie Allen, Elizabeth Taylor, Susan Sarandon, Madonna, and Chloë Sevigny reshape and continue what is even now a living legacy, an inheritance which has been handed down to all of us.

If the role the great courtesans were supposed to play was to please the lovers who sustained them, within the seemingly narrow compass of that task they discovered a kind of magic. In the unpredictable realm of eros, that which pleases most is not simple submission. The secret they discovered is a paradox: Those who would dominate are soon bored by their own powers. And correspondingly, desire is excited by the presence of a spirited soul—independent, unpredictable, incandescent with the mysteries of a separate being. Perhaps in this way desire mirrors the incandescence of life, which is by nature submissive only to an inner order, an order quickened by changes of every kind, tuned to a mandate of transformations beyond our powers to fathom or command.

Here, then, are the virtues.

CORA PEARL

Chapter One

Timing

Ripeness is all.
—WILLIAM SHAKESPEARE

T IS ALWAYS wise to begin with a mystery. Translucent, invisible, continually in motion, timing is difficult to discern and just as hard to describe. Nevertheless, the appeal of anyone who possesses this virtue is certainly palpable. Let us suppose, for example, that in the bare beginnings of the twentieth century, in say 1906, you chance to attend a party given at the country estate of Etienne Balsan. You may find yourself smiling at a woman who passes you on the stairs. And though you have not met her yet, you realize you are wishing that you will soon. Later, when you see her talking with a small group across the room, you are almost embarrassed at how often your eyes wander in her direction. What is it about her? She is good-looking but not extraordinarily so. No, it is something else that draws you. An air of indefinable excitement that seems to radiate out in waves around her.

You see that her presence affects those who are standing near her. The atmosphere in that part of the room is distinctly electric. The way she is dressed gives you a clue. She is wearing what looks like a man's riding jacket, only cut to follow the lines of her small body. Though the look is eccentric, the style seems to place her at the very edge of the present moment. And the look in her eyes, almost mocking, gives you the intriguing impression that she is seeing just past the precipice of what is happening now, that she is, in fact, fully aware of (and more than ready for) the moment which has not quite arrived yet. Still, she has not given herself to the future. Fully here, her movements and gestures are perfectly syncopated with the soundless rhythm to which you suddenly realize the whole room is moving. As the air fairly crackles around her, you begin to believe that she is helping to bring new possibilities into being, including the new worlds that seem to have emerged in your own imagination since the first moment you laid eyes on her. Only at the end of the day do you learn that she is your host's lover, a young woman named Gabrielle. When, later, you hear her name spoken all over Paris, you are not so surprised. What was it about her that was so extraordinary? Her timing was brilliant.

Still, as compelling as a woman with good timing is, the question remains: Why should this virtue be placed first in our catalogue? Asked what could make a woman so attractive that a man would be willing to spend a small fortune to keep her, one might in all likelihood think of beauty first, to be followed quickly by wit, or that talent indispensable to the art of seduction known as charm. As appealing as it is, timing may not even be on the list.

Yet, of all the virtues a great courtesan had to possess, good timing was perhaps the most crucial. Indeed, her very existence depended on it. Had she not been able to move in perfect synchrony with history, no woman would ever have been able to enter the profession. Whether it was poverty or scandal that she faced, her genius was to turn difficult circumstances to immense profit and pleasure. She did the right thing at the right time.

Regarding survival, the best choice to be made at one moment will, in another period, not even be a good choice. All things considered, it would not be a wise choice for most women to become courtesans today. Indeed, the ingredients required to become one no longer exist. A courtesan occupied a precise place in society; as independent as she was, circumstance defined her. If, in the middle of the twentieth century, Helen Gurley Brown, future editor in chief of *Cosmopolitan* magazine, was kept by a wealthy movie producer, she was not called a courtesan. Like the atmosphere that created the tradition, the word had already become an anachronism.

Just as Venus arose from the sea instead of a lake or a river, the courtesan emerged from a very particular medium. The waters of her birth, salted by the bitter tears of women who were condemned to penury and by those of wealthy and poor women alike who lamented the rules that limited and constrained their erotic lives, were made up of a perfect blend of injustice and prudery. The genius of the courtesan was in how she turned the same ingredients to her advantage. Considering the distribution of power between men and women in the times during which she lived, to say that she turned the tables would be an understatement. If we ponder very long the fact, for instance, that La Belle Otero, the famous courtesan of the Second Empire, successfully demanded from one of her lovers the priceless long diamond necklace that had once belonged to the former queen, Marie-Antoinette, we may begin to appreciate the dimensions of the reversal. Yet exactly how this stunning victory was achieved remains a mystery.

Some clues are given to us in a story that Colette tells about a conversation she had while she was still performing in music halls with La Belle Otero. Thinking the young woman somewhat green, Otero offered her some advice. "There comes a time," she said, "with every man when he will open up his hand to you."

"But when is that?" Colette asked.

"When you twist his wrist," Otero replied.

Like many courtesans, Otero was known for her wit. Doubtless, that is why Colette remembered the dialogue. Indeed, the key we are seeking to the mystery is less in the content of Otero's answer than in the way it was given. She delivered her last line with consummate timing. And looking further at what she told her young protégée, it becomes quickly evident that the crucial phrase in her advice is not in the last line but in the first phrase, "There comes a time." The secret of her success was that she chose exactly the right moment to twist her lover's wrist.

We cannot know, but only surmise, that Otero would have been glad to tell Colette exactly how to recognize the right moment for doing anything. But those who have this talent rarely understand themselves how they know what they know. Rather than a technique that can be analyzed, the ability for good timing must be the product of a particularly intense relationship with the present. To speak of having an awareness of the present moment may seem strange, as if such an awareness should be commonplace. But in fact, since most of us, much of the time, are focused more on the past or the future than on what is here now, the ability is unusual.

This uniqueness may explain why courtesans were so often found at the cutting edge of new sensibilities. While she used time to her own advantage, the courtesan expanded the terrain of the imagination. Indeed, the fact that so often whenever culture made a daring turn, breaking old boundaries, flying in the face of convention, courtesans have been part of that history illustrates how time moves forward. In contrast to the conventional view, it is less by aiming yourself in the direction of the future that you will affect the tenor of your times than by immersing yourself in the present.

How did she develop her unique presence? At this point, we can only guess. But our guesses are educated. Early deprivation and fear for survival would have played major roles in the unfolding drama. Traumatic events, losses, and miseries can make every moment of life seem like a precious substance, not a drop of which should be missed. At the same time, narrow escapes and fortunate breaks can loosen the hold that well-laid plans have on the mind, serving to free events from any narrative plot that is too constricting.

And from this perhaps we can also begin to grasp why, aside from any efficacy, good timing is so attractive. Though you would not have been able to name the seemingly ephemeral effect she had of enlarging your consciousness, a courtesan's awareness of time might make you long for her in the same way that a mystic longs for God. Or, if you are devoutly secular, for what is still nascent in yourself.

Yet, as ephemeral as it may seem, this virtue means far less in the abstract than it does in the concrete example. So let us proceed, if not methodically, bit by bit, through many of the simpler expressions of good timing that are more plainly manifested in the lives of courtesans. This is, after all, hardly a dreary task. Known as a "good-time girl," the courtesan had to be able to make men laugh, which called on comic timing. To dress well, she had to know what to wear—and when. And for flirtation, of course, essential to all her other accomplishments, she had to have exquisite timing. There is almost nothing she did that did not require this virtue. But we begin with the activity most often associated with courtesans, perhaps because it is the one with which so many began their careers: dance.

The Way She Danced

Then I started to dance, the way I have always danced.—Josephine Baker, *describing her debut at the Johann Strauss Theatre*

The moment was legendary. Before the music began, no one had heard of her. But as she circled about the floor, her body moving up and down with a vitality memorable even today, every eye in the dance hall was on her. As the polka beat out its inexorable rhythms, the heat of attention only increased. When she and her partner stopped dancing, the inevitable crowd of men surrounded her. Because of the way she danced that night, her life would never be the same again.

Why was her dance so powerful? Philosophy pauses here. Though time is a fascinating concept, it pales when you think of this scene. Even to begin to answer the question, we will have to expand our vocabulary. Timing may serve to describe the ability to coordinate desire and circumstance, yet it fails to illuminate the mysterious bodily process by which these effects are achieved. For this purpose, we must explore the concept of rhythm, too.

Yet even this word needs some resuscitation. Perhaps because of the clock and metronome, in contemporary thought we have come to mistake rhythm for a simple mechanical activity. Even the dictionary makes this error, calling rhythm "a procedure with the patterned occurrence of a beat." But buried deeply within the entries, you can find the word "cadence," an older term, with an appealing gloss and a far more sensual patina. And listed third or fourth in the definitions of cadence there is an entry that serves this exploration well: "the pattern in which something is experienced."

Just think of the beat that underlies all that we do. Breathing, of course, is almost too obvious. As is lovemaking, abundantly clear. But there are also walking, eating, and even seeing, as the eyes dart about the room, or speaking, as impulses and desires swim past and through consciousness, surface, and slide away again. Whether by the subtle starts and stops of a conversation or the inescapably loud punctuation provided by a pair of cymbals, rhythm shapes and inspires every moment.

The rhythm at the heart of dance is the same as the one that informs all experience. The only way to move with a piece of music is to feel the rhythm as it expands into your hips, your legs, your arms, your feet. Think for instance of a line of Rockettes, or better yet, since many dancers from the Folies-Bergère became courtesans, a circle of chorus girls from that show. If one of them were to be off step, we would quickly sense her failure to feel the music. Her performance would lack more than tempo. The spirit of both the music and the dance would be missing, too. Her dance would be lackluster.

The great French actress known as Rosay, who studied music as a child, referred to rhythm as a form of energy. She used the word to describe the way actors go beyond merely pretending to feel what the characters in a play are supposed to feel. Instead, she said, an actor must actually experience the feeling. If the courtesan was, to some degree, always acting, her success depended on how well she could act, that is, on whether or not she actually experienced the feelings she radiated. But this must have been what Rosay meant. When you find the right tempo for any activity, whether it is eating or walking, talking, or making love, you have also found the capacity to feel.

In her *Mémoirs*, Céleste Vénard, the dancer known as Mogador, claimed that she never wanted to be a courtesan. Even so, she must have played the role with feeling. The way she danced was so inspiring that when she performed the polka in the crowded dance hall called the Bal Mabille, she made her reputation in a single night. Though we can only imagine this famous dance now, several clues to the charm it must have had remain for us. There is, for instance, the series of etchings and paintings that Toulouse-Lautrec did of dance-hall life. He often depicted a dancer and courtesan known then as *La Goulue*,* who was famous for dancing the cancan. At public dance halls, women would compete with each other over who could kick her legs higher and thus reveal more of what was underneath her skirts. La Goulue became famous as the undisputed winner. The thrill was, of course, to be able to see so far beneath the skirts of the dancers, who were not always wearing pantaloons. The ardor of the revelation was only increased with the progressively rapid, excited beat of the music to which each kick was timed.

In one of the posters Toulouse-Lautrec designed for the Moulin Rouge, he portrays La Goulue with an expression that is neither bawdy nor frivolous. As she balances on one leg and lifts her right leg high, she stares intently into space, as if concentrating on her art. She is clearly a woman serious about her work. Of course, even if at other moments she laughed, she had to be focused at this moment. She was earning her living. But Lautrec has captured another energy altogether in the lower half of her body. La Goulue, whose name means "glutton," was known for her appetite. Below her waist, a froth of lace and lingerie gushes forth, as if out of a hidden source within her, threatening to fill the room.

Perhaps had we been at the Bal Mabille, we would have been able to detect waves of energy from Céleste's dance filling the crowded room. It was a force that seemed to belong more to working-class women than to the refined and wealthy men who sought them. Even the dances they performed, like the cancan or the polka, seemed to be wilder, part of an earthier past that most Parisians had left behind. Imported from Bohemia, the polka conjured images of beer barrels and peasants and hay.

* "The Glutton."

To perform it took a great deal of raw physical energy; the word that comes to mind here is "robust."

Before Céleste began to attend the Bal Mabille, a woman known as *La Reine Pomaré* was the most favored dancer. She was named after the queen of Tahiti, whom she was thought to resemble. Given the reputation she had for energetic dancing, it is surprising to learn that during the years she reigned she was suffering from tuberculosis. In fact, TB, at least until its terrible final stages, did not prevent the afflicted from dancing. "It's not me who is dancing too fast," Marie Duplessis once said, "it's the violins that play too slowly."

This is understandable from the point of view of the one who is ill. As your energy waxes and wanes, life itself seems to appear and disappear. Released once more from the confines of the sickroom, side by side with gratitude a kind of hunger arises, the urge to gobble every possible morsel of experience before the inevitable returns. Certainly this desire would have given La Reine Pomaré's polka an evocative quality, as if she were dancing away death and sweeping up life with each wide and forceful step.

From this short exploration, perhaps we can begin to imagine something of appeal of her dance. Since it was the lower half of her body keeping time with the music, her movements would have been especially erotic. Added to this would have been the desire to survive, which is of its nature erotic, too. The wish to forget every fear of privation, which remained nevertheless as if in every fiber of her body, would have made her dance especially vibrant. And all this would have been harnessed like a giant horse to the tempo of the polka, a horse that seemed to be able to fly.

Pomaré's illness, however, finally outpaced her formidable spirit. When the effects began to be visible, Brididi, her dance partner, the man who had both masterminded and profited from her career, started to look for a replacement—another hungry young woman who might fill the Bal Mabille with gentlemen eager to see her dance the polka. That was how Céleste got her start.

On the night that Brididi asked Céleste Vénard to dance a quadrille with him, there must have been many hopeful young women waiting at the popular dance hall on the allée des Veuves hoping to be chosen. During the ninteenth century, countless young and single women who were looking for sugar daddies and lovers flocked to the public dance halls scattered all over Paris. Wealthy or titled men, young and old, came to the same places, looking for partners for the evening, perhaps to take home for the night, or if the desire was strong enough, to set up in an apartment. Dancing well would command the right attention and thereby increase a woman's chances. And if, through talent and good fortune, she were among the elect, chosen to be elevated as a mistress, she would have to cut an elegant figure at the parties and balls to which she would be ushered by her new protector.

When at last Brididi ushered her onto the dance floor, Céleste knew she was being auditioned. There would have to have been a brief moment of timidity, a fainthearted feeling. So much would be riding on her success. But again a good sense of timing would have saved her. *Don't think of anything else but the music,* she could tell herself, and then let the music convey her where it might, her fear, her own resolve to survive, her lust for life, transformed in the alchemy of rhythm. Brididi was convinced enough by her talent to spend five hours over the next day teaching her the polka. It is not only in fairy tales that good fortune can arrive swiftly with almost no forewarning. Céleste had her debut the same night.

What must La Reine have thought while she watched a pretender to her throne capture the attention of the ballroom? Céleste was given a new name that evening, a formative event in the life of a young courtesan, the christening that signaled her arrival in the fashionable underworld of Paris. As men crowded around her, eager to ask her to dance, Brididi cried: "It would be easier to defend Mogador than my new partner." From that moment on, Céleste Vénard would be known by the same name as the Moroccan fortress that had just been captured by French troops.

For a while, Pomaré and Mogador were a double attraction at the Bal Mabille. Should it surprise us that they became good friends? Who else would have had so much in common? In 1845, when Pomaré died at the age of twenty-one, Mogador was one of the few who attended her burial in the cemetery of Montmartre. It was she who paid for the marker, which bore a farewell to her friend chiseled in stone. From this we can begin to guess how important the preservation of memory was to her. Perhaps we might even say that she valued history (which is, of course, simply another facet of time). This conjecture seems almost self-evident when we read of the anger that Mogador expressed years later toward Zola for creating a portrait of Pomaré as an old and wretched woman selling second-hand clothes. "Is this what Naturalism is?" she asked angrily of her friend Georges Montorgueil. "Is this their idea of precise detail?"

The passion Mogador had for setting the record straight must have helped her with her memoirs. This remains true even if the tone of her autobiography takes a decided slant of regret. "I was defending myself," she said later. "I did not want to excite poor creatures to copy me, to follow in my steps; I wanted to show them the perils of this kind of life. . . ." Though this regret may have been hard to detect as she fought her way to success in the *demi-monde*, like truth itself, autobiography is fluid. It depends as much on a sense of timing as does dance. Whatever ideas you may have about yourself and your history are, of necessity, always shifting. This is not due to dishonesty so much as the creative nature of what is called "the self." Over time, the stories you tell about your life will alter slightly, reflecting the attitudes of whomever you have more recently become. During the time that Mogador wrote her *Memoirs*, she had fallen in love with a young man, the comte de Chabrillan. As gradually it seemed more likely that she would marry him, she came to regret her past.

But it was not only her past that she would end up regretting. The fact that she had written about it caused her grief, too. On the eve of her marriage, she tried to retrieve the book from publication. Yet her publisher, knowing he had a great literary success within his grasp, refused to relinquish the book. Mogador's fears were not unfounded. The book came close to preventing her marriage. In this sense, we might say her timing was not good. Yet we could also say that in a larger sense her timing was perfect. The *Memoirs* were a sensation. They quickly joined that pantheon of notable works filled not only with great literature but also with books that capture the spirit of the time in which they are written.

Among children who have been abandoned or endangered, it is often the case that when they come of age they find a home in history. After all, it was Mogador's prominence in the public eye that had allowed her to survive, flourish, and meet the man she loved. Céleste could have remained silent and written no memoir at all, thereby if not erasing her past entirely, at least avoiding so much scrutiny. Or, if the urge to write was irresistible, at least as the prospect of marriage grew more real, she could have refrained from submitting the manuscript to her publisher. Yet, though she was in love and longed for a more respectable life, she must have found it difficult to discard altogether the fame that had saved her. Even under the influence of a great and tender passion it is difficult, if not unwise, to give up all that has sustained you in the past. Especially when what has sustained you is as precious and rare as the gift of celebrity—a gift which, in Céleste's case, had come to her in much the same way as the miraculous reprieve that saves the heroine of a fairy tale from the direst circumstances. In a part of her soul that was perhaps less visible to herself at this moment, could it be that Mogador knew her story belonged to time?

If this is so, we can only be grateful, for time has given us her story, a compelling tale, which depicts her rise from rags to riches, filled with the grimmest circumstances along with glamour and romance. Because she rose from a perilous position as the illegitimate child of a working woman to become first a famous performer, then a countess, the two poles of her life—splendor and misery—could not have been further apart, although in another sense these opposites cannot really be disentangled. Misery was there in her memory, along with splendor, in its nascent form the night that, under the many beautiful gas lamps in the famous gardens that belonged to the Bal Mabille, she incited fire in the eyes of the gentlemen who watched her dance, just as splendor and misery are present in our minds most of the time, if only as fear and desire.

Céleste never knew her father. He abandoned her mother, Anne, before Céleste was born. Soon after this, because of the shame she brought on them, Anne's parents turned her out of the house when she was still carrying Céleste. If, after this fateful decision, the story of Céleste's childhood is in any way predictable to us because we can look back and say calmly, *Yes, that is how it was in that time*, to Céleste these events must have been as unpredictable as they were harrowing. Since in that century without welfare, when wages for working women were so low a single woman could not survive on what she earned, it is easy to see why Anne would stay with the man who was the first lover she found, even though he would often drink until he could hardly stand and then return home to beat her. It was only when he beat her so badly she had to be brought to the police station on a stretcher, and after he threatened to kill her along with her daughter, that Anne finally decided to leave him.

She managed to get as far as Lyon, where she took a job in a milliner's shop; but he followed her there, and while he was searching for her, found Céleste alone in the street one day. He kidnapped the child and brought her to a brothel, where he held her hostage. She was saved only because a kind and quick-witted prostitute locked her in her own room and secretly sent for the mother. Together, all the women in the brothel held him at bay, while mother and child made still another escape.

It must have been a terrible time in Céleste's life. But hearing the story, we should take note of the rush of energy that fills these two episodes. There are so many narrow escapes in her story. She is so often rushing with her mother through the streets of Paris or Lyon, around the corner, or to a railway station, moving breathlessly to the sound of doors slamming and cries of threatened violence, barely eluding capture. As, years later, Céleste whirled about the dance hall to the insistently jubilant sounds of the small band that accompanied polkas and quadrilles, the exhilaration of these two escapes must have livened her steps.

The exuberance might have been dampened but still not erased when Anne's lover finally caught up with them once again. He promised to behave better when Anne, probably as much from exhaustion as love, took him back. Soon she found out he had joined a gang of thieves, but before she could make still another escape, fate stepped in with an unpredictable ending. He was killed suddenly in a riot in Lyon. With some money that her father had sent her, Anne returned with her daughter to Paris, taking a room on the boulevard du Temple.

But now, even while destiny was robbing Céleste of any sense of safety, like the careening rise and fall of the polka, it also conspired to tempt her with something grander than simple security. A glittering life, sparkling with the same celebrity to which the young girl was soon destined, dominated the boulevard du Temple. All the great popular theatres were nearby: La Gaîté, L'Ambigu, the Variétés, the café-theatre Bosquet. Peddlers and showmen set up booths outside, and occasionally, actors performed in the street. Inside the Théâtre des Funambules, on the same bill that also featured acrobats and animals, the great mime Debaru performed as the sad-faced clown Pierrot. In the Variétés there were vaudeville acts, comedians, dancers, and musicians following each other onto the stage.

The melodrama to be seen at the Ambigu or the Théâtre de la Porte Saint-Martin was perhaps the form that was most beloved, by common audiences and critics alike. Because of the great many scenes of murder and mayhem acted out in the neighborhood, the boulevard du Temple was also called the boulevard of crime. According to Dumas *fils*, Frédéric Lemaître was capable of inspiring real cries of terror among the members of his audience. For a small fee, you could sit in the highest balcony of the theatre, the place reserved for the poor that was called, ironically, "Paradise," perhaps to watch the woman who was George Sand's favorite actress, Marie Dorval, perform a suicide with such alarming accuracy that while she was sinking to her nightly death, the members of the audience scarcely breathed. Indeed, she was not breathing either. To achieve the effect of realism, she nearly asphyxiated herself for each performance.

Is it surprising then that very soon Céleste began to dream that one day she would perform on a stage herself? It was not just the proximity of the theatres, but that, along with many others among the poor of Paris, she saw the melodramatic events of her own life reflected there. Even today, on any given night in the theatre, a pulse can be felt to vibrate back and forth between the stage and the audience, as the players strike a chord, a situation or a feeling that members of the audience recognize and to which they respond. The resonance of their feeling rebounds to the stage, inspiring the actors to even greater intensity.

In Céleste's life, this pulse would have continued after she left the theatre, as she realized that the heroism of the players reflected her mother's heroism and her own when they were confronted with violence and the threat of death. The images she saw would have dignified this victory, giving the spirit within her a new strength. In this way, imagination must have played a crucial role early in her life.

Perhaps it was the ability to imagine herself as heroic that helped her survive the next chapter in her life. Her mother soon took a new lover, a fair-haired, blue-eyed young man from whom her daughter was to face still another peril. Almost from the beginning, Céleste disliked Victor. Rough and moody, he was at times resentful of her, and perhaps she sensed, in the way that children can, the side of his character that was to emerge later. It was after she became an adolescent, the beginnings of a woman's body newly visible, during a period when her mother was visiting her own father in Fontainebleau, that Victor attempted to rape her. Céleste fought him off, and for the third time in her life escaped. But now, alone in the streets of Paris, without her mother, she had nowhere to go.

Yet here is where her history began to form another pattern, one that could easily have given her the illusion of predictability. For again a prostitute was to come to her rescue. Céleste had slept for four nights in a hayloft and wandered the streets of Paris by day in search of food when finally she broke down weeping. There, just in front of the massive entrance to the Eglise Saint-Paul, a streetwalker named Thérèse found Céleste and took her home for the night to her own room. It was an act of extraordinary kindness, especially since a prostitute caught keeping a child on her own premises could be sent to jail for six months. In fact, when they were walking together in the streets a few days later, a policeman took Céleste away from Thérèse, incarcerating her, as was a common practice for the protection of homeless girls, in the women's prison named after St. Lazare.

Soon afterward, Thérèse found Céleste's mother and told her where her daughter was. But a month passed before Anne came to bring her home. In that time Céleste began her education, an introduction to another world, one that for most working women was always perilously close to their own. A world of last resorts, but also a world of dreams. Her time in the jail was softened by the friendship she made with a girl called Denise, hardly older than herself, who would tell her about the fine clothes a young prostitute would be given in a brothel and the good money she could earn there. "I saw myself rich and covered with lace and gems," Céleste wrote later in her memoirs.

When she finally returned home, nothing had changed. Her mother did not listen to her when she tried to tell her why she had left. Victor kept trying to molest her. In the way that it can only for an adolescent, her life seemed hopeless. Another girl might perhaps have waited, languished in the atmosphere that was eating away at her. But from the two earlier escapes she had made with her mother and the one she had made herself, Céleste had learned well the lessons of urgency. And though later she would come to regret bitterly the decision she made, the logic of association is clear. Since she had already been saved twice by kind prostitutes, it makes perfect sense that at the age of sixteen she would have become a prostitute herself.

In jail, Denise had given her the address of one of a handful of the very fashionable brothels that catered to a wealthier clientele. Madame welcomed her with ample sustenance and the finery Céleste would need to ply her new trade—clothes, perfume, jewelry. It was only later that Céleste began to understand the consequences of the agreement she had made. All that she was given, including her room and board, was to come from her earnings. She would not be able to leave until she had paid what she owed. As she sank deeper and deeper into debt, she realized she would never be free. She had simply fallen into another trap.

"To have to laugh when you want to weep," she would write later; "to be dependent and humiliated." In the brothel, nothing belonged to her, not even her own body. When even the beating of your heart, the breath you take, is not simply under surveillance but summoned and marshaled, continuously made to march according to someone else's rhythms, you will lose touch with the pace of your own soul. The spirit that sustains you will begin to die.

Perhaps her despair made her more susceptible to illness or perhaps it was simply contagion, but soon Céleste fell very ill. Yet she was to be rescued once again, this time by a client who, alarmed to see her so sick, paid off the debt she owed to Madame and took her to his own apartment. But the story of this escape does not end here, for a doctor was soon summoned, who diagnosed smallpox. Though he said she could not be moved, as soon as she was left alone, she dressed and descended to the street, where she called a cab to take her to the Hôpital Saint-Louis.

Thinking of the force of will it must have taken to drag her weakened and fevered body into the streets brings to mind the way she danced the polka. In the structure of the music, within each four beats, every third beat will be emphasized. It is not hard to imagine her moving to this pattern, landing hard on the third beat, and afterward rising higher with great emphasis, as if she were taking the great galloping force of the music into her body and making it, in every instant, her own.

But the will Céleste exhibited was not simply the will to survive. She was proud. And that this quality was reflected in her dance can easily be deciphered from the rest of her story. As she tells us, it was in the hospital while she was recovering that she fell in love with a medical student called Adolphe. Yet though he appeared to be in love with her, she soon discovered she was naïve to trust him. He invited her to attend a ball with him at Versailles, but when they arrived she found he had another mistress with him, a woman well known as a *lorette*. In the sexual economy of nineteenth-century France, the *lorette* existed somewhere between a prostitute and a courtesan. She was kept, but only modestly so. And though she could dress well enough to attend some public balls, she was generally neither educated, mannered, nor celebrated enough to mingle with high society as courtesans did.

Chances are Adolphe would have set Céleste up as a *lorette* were not the mistress he already had too jealous. Seeing him enter the ball with Céleste, Louisa Aumont ridiculed her—the unsuitability of her dress, her manners so clearly lower class. In a loud voice, in front of Céleste, she harangued Adolphe on his bad taste for having brought this embarrassing young woman with him. Céleste walked back from Versailles alone, a journey that took her all night. The incident was etched in her memory. After she became famous as Mogador, and the wayward Adolphe began to pursue her again, it is understandable that she would be quick to score her triumph. She promised to take him back only if Louisa Aumont would apologize to her in public.

You would have been able to see the quality in the posture and the timing of her dance, a robust assertion of pride punctuating every step. And something else less easy to name would have been present, too. Something she knew—what she had learned, in a sense, from dancing with the many unpredictable events she encountered in her young life. The brutality of her mother's first lover, his attempt to kidnap her, his sudden death, her return to Paris, Victor's attempts to rape her, the nights she spent homeless in the streets of Paris, the weeks in the prison at St.-Lazare, a nearly fatal brush with smallpox. Whether dancing with fate or a mortal partner, she had learned well to perceive even the smallest alterations in a pattern and respond quickly with a brilliance of her own to the most subtle signals. And eventuating from this knowledge that life is always in motion, that nothing ever remains the same, there must have been an aura, invisible to the eye, but even so a halo of a kind, surrounding all her movements; she had witnessed the constant change that lies at the heart of the universe.

The unpredictability of Céleste's life continued. After the summer months, the Bal Mabille would close. Soon she found work performing at the Théâtre Beaumarchais. But as luck would have it, after acting there for a few weeks, it, too, would close. Yet, by another turn of chance, she was hired again, this time by one of the Franconi brothers, who had just erected the new Hippodrome. Appearing in a horse race with five other girls on Bastille Day, July 14, 1845, at the opening of the circus, her timing was superb again. Winning the race with the same exuberance and pride with which she had executed the polka, her equestrian feats became the toast of Paris.

Now Mogador could enter the prestigious world that glittered nightly at certain cafés and certain addresses in Paris. She was welcomed and celebrated at the Maison Dorée and at the Café Anglais, where newly wealthy bourgeois men, aristocrats, and royalty came, amid the flotillas of courtesans who hung on their arms, or flitted and flirted about the tables, making the atmosphere flutter with their presence. Soon she became the mistress of the duke of Ossuna, who set her up in a comfortable apartment on the rue de l'Arcade, not far from the Place Vendôme, where the extravagant jewelry could be purchased that she wore when she visited the cafés on boulevards nearby. She took many lovers, including an Italian tenor, before her felicitous career came suddenly to an end. She had fallen from her horse, and unfortunately the fall was bad. One leg was broken. There would be weeks in bed. It was too dangerous for her to ride ever again.

But the unpredictable nature of events did not fail her. Just around the bend of this disaster, only days after she was allowed to go out again and had made her return to the high life, as she was leaving the Café Anglais, Céleste chanced to meet a young man, Lionel de Chabrillan, descended from one of the most illustrious families in France. They fell in love. That first meeting did not, of course, end the whirlwind of events that characterized her life. After several more quick turns of fate, during which Lionel showered her with jewels and horses and cashmere shawls, exhausting his inheritance, he decided to leave her because of scandal. Mourning his loss, she came close to marrying another man, in the meantime profiting from the scandal when, because of her newly aggrandized fame, she was given a role in a production at the Théâtre des Variétés. Still, when all was said and done, she landed well. She married the man she loved, and finally became the comtesse de Chabrillan.

Her Surprise

Prince Gortschakoff used to say that . . . he would have tried to steal
the sun to satisfy one of her whims.—Gustave Claudin, prominent
Boulevardier

Comic timing, which depends on surprise, is an ineffable skill, difficult
to teach or even describe. This is an appropriate quality if you remember that laughter itself, being made of mere air and fleeting sounds,
weighs almost nothing. In accordance with its ephemeral nature, there
are even some who associate mystical experience with laughter. The air
of laughter is, as Barry Saunders writes, "risible," and according to the
Greeks, who believed that laughter could make the soul immortal, it rises
toward heaven. The route, however, was reversed during the Christian
centuries during which laughter was thought of as a sure path to hell.
No wonder then that it was during the Renaissance, when classical ideas
were embraced again, that courtesans should come into vogue. Women
from this profession have always been associated with mirth.

If, as the Greeks believed, laughter buoys us on toward timelessness, we
might question why timing should be so critical to humor. But it is.
Whether you are hearing a joke or witnessing a prank, just a fraction of
a second in the timing can determine whether or not you will laugh. But
once you are laughing, it is as if you have been transported, instantly lifted
out of your present circumstances into a larger realm. The experience can
be intoxicating, as while you laugh, the moment expands until finally both
the past and the future have, at least for a moment, disappeared.

This must be why laughter ameliorates suffering. It is hardly a coincidence therefore that courtesans, most of whom began life facing difficult circumstances and who thus knew well what it was to fear the future,
seemed to be so good at inducing laughter. Cora Pearl, courtesan of the
Second Empire, is a case in point. She was known to have a particularly
earthy humor. Some of the social commentators who wrote about cour-

tesans even found her crude. But this opinion did not lessen her popularity at all. Among her many illustrious lovers was Prince Napoléon.

One evening during the height of her powers, Pearl played a prank on her dinner guests that has become legendary. Like many courtesans, she entertained frequently, to quote one version of her memoirs, "in the finest style." One night, after all the courses had been served except dessert, she excused herself, telling her guests that she wanted to supervise the presentation of the final dish. She went to the kitchen and, shedding her clothes, stepped onto a chair and positioned herself on a huge silver platter she had borrowed from the prince d'Orléans. Then, "with that deftness and artistry for which he is so famed," her pastry chef, Salé, began to decorate her "naked body with rosettes and swathes of creams and sauces." After placing a single unpeeled grape in the dint of her navel, he surrounded her with several meringues and then gave her a generous dusting of powdered sugar before lowering a vast silver cover over her. Then two footmen carried her down the passage to the dining room and set the platter on the table.

The hilarity of the prank, of course, depended on good timing. For one thing, her guests had already been fed and so they were not distracted by hunger. Then, by saying she wanted to supervise the presentation of the dessert, she had inspired anticipation. And finally, because the platter was covered, her presence was discovered suddenly, creating an element that is indispensable to comedy: surprise.

It may be interesting and more than a diversion here for us to consider another story from the annals of humor. This one is about Gracie Allen. Indeed, Burns and Allen started in vaudeville, which was once a popular venue for courtesans, and thus, though Gracie was by no means a *cocotte*, it is more than possible that the comic timing of courtesans was still part of the atmosphere in which she learned her art. So it is significant in more than one way that in 1940, when Gracie Allen mounted a comic campaign to become the president of the United States, she announced she was running as the head of a new political party called, she said, "the Surprise Party." Asked the provenance of the name, she replied that her mother was a Democrat and her father a Republican, but she had been born a surprise.

Like all humor, the joke reveals a deeper layer of meaning that is not immediately evident. Surprise is at the heart of sexuality: not only the surprise of conception, but the unpredictable nature of arousal itself. And lurking close behind conception, the surprise of mortality is due to appear soon, too, because like it or not, the arrival of the next generation signals the demise of our own. But laughter, since it whisks us off toward immortality, redeems the prediction.

And there is this, too. If the conversion of mortality into immortality is confounding, it might be helpful to know that according to the Greeks, comedy returns us to the timeless center of existence, a place of mystic nothingness in which all that we habitually believe and practice is reversed. Which is important here because in a sense, Cora Pearl's dessert constitutes a reversal of many events and conditions, including the story of how she fell from grace, the fall that led her to become a courtesan in the first place.

Cora was not born to poverty. Still, she claimed that she was forced into her profession by what, according to modern standards, would be considered a rape. The story she cites in her memoirs as determining her fate resembles the cautionary tales told to young girls during the Victorian age. Though if we are to understand her decision, a few facts from her childhood will be necessary, too. It is not insignificant that when she was still a child her father abandoned the family. Nor that shortly thereafter, her mother sent her to a convent in France. The pattern of abandonment continued when, after graduating, she returned to London. Instead of taking her daughter back, her mother sent her to live with her own mother. Though Cora's grandmother was kind, she was overprotective. Following the years she spent in the French convent, where Cora claims to have received a very liberal education from the other girls, this atmosphere must have felt stifling. Made to read books aloud to the old woman for hours on end, Cora seldom went out, except to go to church on Sunday. But one Sunday, when the maid who always accompanied her home did not appear, she set off into the streets of London by herself. Soon she discovered she was being followed by an older man named Saunders, who eventually persuaded her to go with him into a "drinking den" where after tasting what he gave her, she lost consciousness, regaining her awareness only the next morning when she found herself in a bed upstairs.

There is no way now to determine the validity of this tale. The memoirs of courtesans were often embellished with fantasy and fiction. Generally, Cora Pearl was known to be very honest. Indeed, during the Second Empire, when a certain kind of deception was thought preferable in women to frankness, she was often described as vulgar. And there is also the fact to consider that the practice of spiking a young woman's drink, thus rendering her an easy prey to rape, is still in use today.

Decades later, when she told this story in her memoirs, she said that as Saunders helped her to her room, she was aware of his intentions and hoped "that at last I might be about to discover the pleasure of lying with someone of the opposite sex." The next morning, however, she remembered nothing, which, in one version of her life story, she claimed was her only regret. In another version, she wrote that the incident left her with "an instinctive horror of men."

Whatever the truth was, on the first morning she woke up in his bed, she knew she could never go home again. Though the modern reader may simply shrug her shoulders at this slightly sordid initiation to sexuality, in that period, Cora was ruined. Which is to say, she would never be able to make a respectable marriage.

Whichever version we read, she must have felt at least a moment of fear, when waking disoriented in a strange room, she realized what had happened to her. Both versions of her memoirs, written to raise money, have the exaggerated style of a book written to be salacious. But there must be a seed of truth in each description. She was spirited even as a young woman. Which is to say that she would not have let the moment grow into despair but instead moved within herself, in a timely fashion, to leaven her despondency with humor and resolve. If on seeing the five pounds Mr. Saunders had left her she felt tempted toward shame, she did not allow the mood to take hold, but swiftly calculated instead how much more income she had just gained, more than a milliner would earn over several weeks.

The young courtesan managed the new profession that fate had thrust upon her with a vengeance. Her first lover, Robert Bignell, who was the owner of the Argyll Rooms in London, a "notorious pleasure haunt," supported her well. But she was not satisfied. And from the day that Bignell suggested she accompany him to France, her life was to take on a momentous change. Masquerading as husband and wife, they toured Paris and the French countryside, traveling afterward to the spa at Baden-Baden in Germany, where she spent 200,000 francs of Bignell's money. Still, at the end of the trip, she sent him back to London alone. She preferred life in Paris, where she quickly became a favorite of the most powerful and wealthy men; soon she was wealthy herself, her private collection of jewelry alone worth a fortune. Over time, more than one man exhausted his inheritance for the love of her. If once a single man had had the power to ruin her, now she was coolly ruining many men.

That she served herself as dessert could easily be read as an extreme form of servility. But this reading of the event would be too simple. As she records the incident in her memoirs it is clear that she took enormous pleasure in her seductive powers. She tells us that even as the prank was being prepared, one of her servants was taking great interest in the chef's work, "and the state of his breeches proclaimed that his attitude to his employer was one of greater warmth than respect." She reveled even more in the awe she struck when her footman raised the silver lid that concealed her body. "I was rewarded," she wrote later, "by finding myself the centre of a ring of round eyes and half open mouths." Her memoirs make the power of her presence evident. "M. Paul," she tells us, "was the first to recover," after which her dinner guests, in the posture of petitioners paying homage to a goddess, kneeled "on their chairs or on the table . . . their tongues busy at every part of me as they lifted and licked the sweetness from my body." The reversal is clear. If once she had been abandoned by her father and mother, now she was the undisputed center of attention. If she had been seduced by a gentleman, now she was the seducer of many; if once she had been fed a drink that made her lose her better judgment, now she herself was the libation that drove men to a frenzy of desire, while calmly she enjoyed the effect.

Her Blue Dress

Nana dazzled him and he rushed over to stand on the step of her carriage.—Emile Zola, Nana

I was able to start a high fashion shop because two gentlemen were outbidding each other over my hot little body.—Coco Chanel

Let us return to the party of 1906 with which our exploration of this virtue began. This was a pivotal moment in the life of that woman with such good timing, called Gabrielle. Like many courtesans, she was born poor. Abandoned by her father, she was raised in an orphanage. And as was also true for many *cocottes,* she began her life as a *grisette.* But though she liked trimming hats, she did not want to live out her days working long hours in the cramped quarters of a dimly lit room. So eventually, she began to sing in cafés, which is where she met her lover, the very wealthy Etienne Balsan. He was in the audience when she performed. The simple fact that he kept her would in another time have immediately classified her as a courtesan. Indeed, when she lived with him on his estate near Compiègne, she shared both his bed and his mansion with another woman who was already attracting public attention. Usually dressed in raspberry pink, witty, and often outrageous, Emilienne d'Alençon was a famous courtesan during the Belle Epoque. Far from jealous, the two women admired each other, though more for their differences than what they had in common.

The difference was clear in the way they dressed. While d'Alençon, one of the last *grandes horizontales,* had a lavish style, Gabrielle wore simple, almost boyish, clothing. The choice was less accidental than portentous. Instead of developing a career as a courtesan, she went into another business. Convincing Balsan to lend her his apartment, she set up a hat shop in Paris. Emilienne did her friend an inestimable favor when she appeared both at Maxim's and the races in the Bois du Boulogne wearing one of Gabrielle's creations.

At the turn of the century, Longchamps was well established as a pre-miere showplace for new fashions. Zola, who well appreciated the sig-nificance of fashion in the lives of courtesans, describes in exacting detail what his heroine, Nana, wore to the Grand Prix there. She was dressed in blue and white, he wrote. The silk bodice she wore, cut close to her body, was blue. And even for an age of enormous skirts, her crinoline was exaggerated. Over this she wore a white satin dress. The white sash that stretched diagonally across her chest was adorned with silverpoint lace that seemed to glitter in the sunlight. And finally her hat, a toque, was also blue except for the single white feather she had placed on top.

The outfit, of course, was designed not only to please the eye, but to be read for meaning. The colors she chose belonged to the stable owned by her benefactor's family. Her toque resembled a jockey's cap. The size of her crinoline, which was daring, emphasized the size of her hips (or, read another way, libido). The sash implied that she was a conqueror (which, in a certain sense, she was). Silk and satin served to remind everyone who gazed in her direction of her wealth as well as the way she had made it. The glitter and shininess of it all reflected the powers she possessed to attract and fascinate. And the feather? On the one hand a bird, wildness itself, the voluptuousness of nature, and on the other, the hunt—the urge to capture, ravish, possess.

Clothing is not just practical. What we wear on our bodies speaks to others, expressing intent and mutual understandings, while acting as a public calling card, telling others, even strangers, who we are, or at least who we pretend to be. But that is not all dress does. Aside from protec-tion and expression, clothing can also be read as a sign that reveals the *Zeitgeist* of a culture, a spirit that is always changing. Indeed, fashion is one of the principal signatures of time. What is desirable at one mo-ment will not be acceptable at the next. To know what color to choose, at what length to measure your hem, which shoes you should wear for what occasion, requires an acute awareness of the present moment.

It should not surprise us then that the word *chic* came into use in association with courtesans. For these women, not only was it imperative to be à la mode, the successful courtesan had to stand out among fashionable women. She could never afford to be boring. Her timing had to be such that she was always just a few steps ahead. Perhaps this is why the great courtesans were known for having set styles. If in the eighteenth century, Madame de Pompadour, the mistress of Louis XV, was so skillful at making alterations to the designs of her tailors that she entered the history of couture, the courtesans of the Second Empire followed suit. It was Alice Ozy, for example, who introduced the custom of wearing all one color. Collectively courtesans popularized the crinoline. Indeed, all through the nineteenth century and two decades into the twentieth, *grandes horizontales* set the style in Paris. Charles Worth, who inaugurated the tradition of *haute couture*, was eager to design dresses for women who were courtesans. His clientele included not only the Empress Eugénie and the most prestigious families of France, but Cora Pearl, Païva, and the Countess de Castiglione. The notoriety of these clients made his designs even more notable. Since, as with the clothes film or rock stars wear today, what the *grandes horizontales* wore was news; columnists who wrote weekly about their exploits included detailed descriptions of their wardrobes. And there was another reason for their popularity among designers. Like movie stars or rock stars, as outsiders they could take more risks, a bravado that allowed couturiers to be more creative.

The subject of style is often looked upon as trivial, but it is no less so than any art. Clothes announce the changes in society that are yet to come. By the time Cora Pearl was having her dresses made by the same couturier as the Empress Eugénie, as power moved with a steady pace from the hands of the aristocracy to the newly rich bourgeoisie, a great shift had already begun. The drama was perhaps at its most intense during Holy Week at the opening of the races when, as a parade of carriages would make its way down the avenue de L'Impératrice toward Longchamps, the cabs that carried courtesans were indistinguishable from those belonging to the ladies of high society. Though, as with all members of the *nouveaux riches*, courtesans could be revealingly ostentatious. Cora Pearl, for instance, shocked the sensibilities of the socially well positioned when she dressed all her livery men in yellow suits she had tailored to copy the style of British jockeys. During the Belle Epoque, Cornelia Otis Skinner describes another courtesan who stepped slightly over the line of modesty when she festooned all her horses' bridles, her footman, and her driver's hats with cockades of pink carnations. Still, like the cabs of those born to high society, a *cocotte*'s carriage would usually be signed by one of the most sought-after Prussian carriage makers.

But though they arrived in the highest style, once inside the arena, courtesans were constrained by the old class distinctions. It is often the case that when a social system is waning, the old order will be asserted at certain sites with an almost vengeful rigidity. At Longchamps, the barrier between the terrain of those called the "proud elect" and the "impure" was, as Amédée Achard wrote in *Paris Guide*, "insurmountable." Here, the sanctity of bloodlines was asserted not only in the stables but in the galleries. Courtesans were not allowed into the enclosure near the jockey stand where titled and wealthy families watched the races.

The courtesans, however, met this defense with a campaign of their own. Through weapons as flimsy as silk and cashmere, the old barriers were not only challenged, they were seriously compromised. More than one competition took place at Longchamps. While thoroughbred horses were readied to run, the track became a "battleground of dresses." One by one, women with no pedigree, but who were nevertheless kept and dressed by the gentlemen sitting in the enclosure that excluded them, entered the amphitheater in full regalia, dazzling the excited crowds with an array of luxurious fabrics, deep and luminous colors, ribbons, lace, rich embroidery, feathered hats, and blazing jewelry. Every eye was upon them. And though some thought it scandalous that these outcasts dressed as well as, if not better than, ladies from high society, despite their disapproval, wellborn women felt compelled to study the detail of the courtesans' apparel carefully, for what the *grandes horizontales* wore would dictate fashion for the coming season.

The triumph was more than sartorial. Mirroring the social revolution that already was in the making, through the splendor of her clothing a courtesan could attract the kind of attention formerly reserved for royalty. Thus Zola describes the arrival of Nana to Longchamps, "When she had made her appearance at the entrance to the public enclosures . . . with two footmen standing motionless behind the carriage, people had rushed to see her, as if a queen were passing."

The crowds were already the new arbiters of taste and power, and they belonged to her. It was as if into this arena ruled by speed and the stopwatch, time marched in, riding on the hems of flamboyant skirts, feathers, and glitter, providing evidence of the constant motion into which all are eventually swept.

Change was only to continue in the same direction until finally, when Gabrielle arrived on the scene, the style she invented symbolized the new independence women were seeking. After the great success of her hat shop, a second lover, Boy Capel, bankrolled a dress shop. Nearly a century later, the name of the legendary house she established still has the power to evoke the old excitement. It is called, of course, Chanel.

Flirtation

(THE FIRST EROTIC STATION) ✛ ✛ ✛ ✛ ✛ ✛ ✛ ✛ ✛ ✛ ✛

I assisted at the birth of that most significant word, flirtation,
which dropped from the most beautiful mouth in the world.—Earl
of Chesterfield

WE CAN SEE all the elements of timing, not only rhythm but also a
talent for both comedy and fashion, at work in flirtation. This is an art
that relies far more on good timing than one would ordinarily suppose.
Let us go to still another party, the one held in 1841 at the old opera, la
Salle Peletier in Paris, on the night that comte Edouard de Perregaux met

Marie Duplessis (the courtesan on whose short life both *La Traviata* and *Camille* were based), to illustrate the process. Though Duplessis was born to a poor peasant family and, like Chanel, had worked for a short while as milliner's assistant at wages too low to keep anyone alive, she was at this moment already a kept woman. She had learned how to dress and do her hair, how to speak correct French with a Parisian and not a Norman accent. She was popular with the Jockey Club, that aristocratic organization devoted both to horse races and to chasing women. But she was yet to achieve the even greater heights of elegance and luxury which for a great courtesan was both the mark of having arrived and her reward.

Of course, once again we can only try to imagine the scene between Duplessis and the count, the man whom, just five years hence, in 1845, she would marry. History has not given as much detail here as the observation of the courtesan's skill requires. But that is why fiction exists—so we may see the undocumented moments that would otherwise pass out of history, and thus out of our understanding, unwitnessed.

Yet good fiction also requires much that is accurate surrounding it. Thus, it is important to know that a few years before this period in Paris, a ball at the Opéra was a very exclusive event, which only members of aristocratic or very wealthy families attended. They were dazzling affairs at which one looked forward to being seen and to seeing. To remain *au courant* (or as we say now, in the swim), one had to attend. But during the reign of Louis Philippe, that ruler who, while trying to be both a monarch and a democratic man, was called "the Citizen King," the balls were opened up to every level of society. And now that almost anyone could come, this particular party was no longer so prized. Many upper-class ladies stayed home. But the courtesans came, along with hopeful *lorettes* looking for a chance to inch their way higher into society or find a new protector. There were still plenty of successful entrepreneurs in attendance, as well as barons, and, as we have already mentioned, at least one count.

As was usual for such gatherings—and still is—at the sidelines of the ballroom floor the crowds settled into small groups and chatted. During the conversation, as also was and is still usual, the eyes of those who conversed would wander the crowd. Ladies would be scrutinizing each other's dresses. Everyone would be curious to know who arrived on the arm of whom. New faces were being scrutinized. And of course, by means of a glance or a stare, whether with subtlety or flourish, countless flirtations crossed the elegant rooms, filling the air with excitement.

It was thus while Marie Duplessis was no doubt chatting with a group of friends and acquaintances that she began to feel the heat of attention fall across her shoulders like a light cloak or a hand brushed in passing against her spine. Just as in the song written almost a century later about a similarly enchanted evening, comte Edouard de Perregaux was standing across the crowded room, or rather, the crowded *Grand Salon* (a salon which everyone in Paris complained lacked elegance), when his gaze chanced to settle on her.

Here is where her timing transformed chance to good fortune. Aware that she was being scrutinized, Marie did not turn quickly, as someone too eager might have done. Though of course we are forced to fill in this part of the narrative, the story is true to the many accounts that we have of her character, all of which, with only one fleeting exception, describe her as refined and kind, two qualities that together would have prevented her from turning abruptly away from the conversation in which she was already engaged.

And of course there was another element that should have slowed down her response—the precise quality of her gaiety. She loved to laugh and laughed often, but her smile had an intriguing chiaroscuro not unlike the mysterious mood of the *Mona Lisa's* smile, a trace of a rather sad boredom just beneath the surface, as if she were saying, "I've seen it all." And this is how the story unfolds further, toward the great complexities of timing together with the many histories that can be sensed at the fringes of frivolity.

First, because she was suffering from tuberculosis, the courtesan believed she would die young. On the one hand, this gave her a great and unceasing appetite for life. And yet, in the strange way that contradictory emotions marry in experience, every morsel of life she tasted was seasoned with the knowledge of death that can give the soul of even one so young—she was just seventeen when she met Perregaux—a philosophical wistfulness. Feeling his eyes upon her, she waited to turn, waited attentively while the moment seemed to expand inside her infinitely.

Second (since there are always many causes for any virtue), she had known desperation. And while desperation causes the kind of hysteria that can make you fall out of step, it can also give you the blessedly carefree attitude that leads to perfect timing. *I have seen the worst life has to offer and nothing surprises or frightens me,* is the mantra. *I have nothing left to lose.*

Which brings to mind the single exception to the many descriptions we have of Marie Duplessis as refined. We have already told the story. It occurred when she was still just a working girl, probably no more than fifteen years old. She stood on the Pont-Neuf on her one day off from the sweatshop where she worked every other day for at least sixteen hours, for starvation wages. That was why she was hungry and that was also why she was standing so near a stand that sold fried potatoes and why she did not buy what she wanted. But as luck would have it, a gentleman happened along the bridge at this moment who responded to her wish and answered her wish. The man who did this, Nestor Roqueplan, would come to know Duplessis later in her life when she had become the best-dressed woman in Paris; they traveled in the same circles. But what he noticed on this first meeting was that she was unkempt, dressed in filthy ragged clothing, and that she grabbed and devoured the *frites* he gave her without any delicacy at all.

To have experienced extreme deprivation before her ascent to luxury would also have given her a covert assurance beneath her refinement, a confidence that came from having survived on the streets, which not only delayed the advent of her decision to turn toward whoever was staring at her but gave the gaze that she did finally return the leisurely air of a queen. She did not bat her eyes. She was neither rushing to please him nor slipping away from his eyes in modesty. She simply stared back.

You can see that look today in the many portraits of courtesans that riddle the history of art. Sometimes they are dressed in clothes more risqué than proper ladies and sometimes not. But what usually gives each woman away is the frank quality of her gaze. Staring directly out of canvas after canvas, the eyes do not flinch or shrink or apologize but instead meet you with unremitting candor.

Now meeting such a gaze, is it not possible that the count lets out an almost involuntary laugh as his attention is discovered and returned? He has been startled to see that this young woman places herself on an equal plane with him. That she is a woman born to a lower rank vanishes in the fresh air of her presumption. The count laughs at himself, at the rules he has grown up with and at the delightfully casual way that this stranger is breaking them all.

Immediately, and in a pace that is at this instant appropriately quick, she grasps the humor, lets him see that she has gotten the joke with a brief smile, and then—but this is what will capture his heart forever— she turns away. And here it is important to note that although this makes him want to follow her, to know more of her, her retreat is not motivated by the false modesty that society requires of women, but from the depths of the character she acquired over a childhood full of loss, including at an early age the disappearance and death of her mother, the profundity of experience that in almost every public situation compels her to reserve part of herself.

The example is inspiring, even now. Knowing that the count will invite her with him to a private party at the Café Anglais and that she will accept, that they will become lovers. That (along with many other men) he will contribute to her support, that they will eventually enter a brief marriage a year before her death, and that he will accompany her body to her last resting place on earth. Still following Marie's exemplary reticence, let us reserve the rest of her story for a later time.

APOLLONIE SABATIER

Chapter Two

Beauty

I look at you and a sense of wonder takes me.
—HOMER, the *Odyssey*

THE VIRTUE MOST commonly attributed to courtesans is beauty. We think for instance of Madame de Pompadour, that delicately pink blush, reminiscent of certain exquisite rose petals, which colors her cheeks in the portraits Boucher painted of her. Or one of several women rendered by Titian comes to mind: Flora, for instance. No matter that the abundance of her flesh is no longer in style. The way her shimmering hair cascades over her corpulent and presumably soft shoulder gives pause.

That beauty would have been a virtue of courtesans is hardly unexpected. It is common knowledge that this attribute excites desire. But beauty is more than a prelude to sexual pleasure. It is a pleasure in itself. In the presence of a beautiful person, man or woman, the eyes, even at times as if unwilled by any thought, but moving instead as if solely of their own volition, will wander toward that face, that body, not simply to record the fact of beauty but to rest there, absorbing the very substance of it. Whether you are moved by the loveliness of luminous eyes or the deeply carnal colors of a portrait painted by one of the Venetian masters of the Cinquecento, or the calm of an elegantly proportioned square framed by eighteenth-century architecture, or a canyon cut through red rock that is so immense the dimensions seem to strain the capacity to see, you seldom turn away from beauty easily.

This is true even though beauty is not a simple pleasure. The experience can, in fact, be hazardous. While beholding beautiful eyes, for instance, you may become suddenly vulnerable to seduction. Encountering an old painting, you are forcefully pulled away from the familiar toward a sensibility that can be, at times, menacingly foreign; entering the square that seems so elegantly balanced, you will feel suddenly off balance, even dizzy; and as for the canyon, its grandness will probably push you toward the edge of awe, a territory of annihilation, where whoever you thought you were momentarily vanishes.

No wonder then that beauty was once considered sacred. Despite whatever danger the desire for beauty involves (the thrill of which may sometimes be appealing), the attraction seems almost inevitable. And if in pursuit we throw caution to the wind, perhaps this is because beauty seems to infuse the whole of existence with a new sense of meaning. This is not a significance that belongs to the world of logic. Even language falters at the task of defining what in the end seems inseparable from life. Beauty is in itself a quaesitum, the solution that lies at the end of a search, the answer to a longing that shapes our lives with a force that rivals even the strongest spiritual aspiration.

Ancient Recipes

Rarely do we appreciate the creative talents of women who are thought to be the great beauties. Beauty is usually described as a passive virtue—an attribute bestowed by nature with no effort on the part of the recipient, who is supposed to be more fortunate than able. The contradictions of this thinking become apparent, however, when it is argued that beautiful women endanger men. In these arguments, the accusation is common that beautiful women use artifice to deceive and entrap their admirers. The idea that beauty is only "skin-deep" usually accompanies this argument. Though in truth, since "wayward" women were accused in such strictures of wearing too much makeup, the beauty in question would have been even more superficial.

But the morality of constructing beauty is less relevant here than the simple fact that the courtesan's beauty was not just given, it was also made. Even what was given, whether it be a beautiful face or body, would have needed to be enhanced as well as properly framed. For this reason alone, if we are to grasp the true dimensions of the second virtue of courtesans, we must understand that legendary beauty is created with considerable skill.

The arts women have employed to create beauty are ancient. The hetaerae of Greece, women who were priests and courtesans at the same time, were also healers. They were known to use herbal formulas devised to nourish skin and hair, as well as sustain the vitality which is so much a part of beauty. That during the Renaissance courtesans also used such recipes must have contributed to the perception that, like many women who were herbalists, they were practicing witchcraft. Among courtesans, the recipes were often handed down from mother to daughter. Pietro Aretino depicts this transmission in his *Dialogues*, in which he renders a fictional account of a Renaissance courtesan he calls Nanna. Though he wraps his description in misogynistic judgments, he has preserved a portrait for us of an old craft. By his own account, he was well familiar with courtesans and their skills.

Before Nanna makes her debut in Rome, her mother, who had once been a courtesan herself, takes great care preparing her daughter for her first appearance. Aretino tells us that Nanna and her mother were Tuscans who had recently moved to Rome for the express purpose of launching Nanna's career, and that in anticipation of this event, Nanna's mother had applied a formula daily to her daughter's face, known to make the skin soft. And since Nanna's hair is described as golden, a color rarely natural in this region, most probably in the weeks before their departure, her mother would have been employing another procedure, too. After using a wash of honey, citrus, and marigold petals on Nanna's hair, she would have given her daughter a hat without a top but with a wide brim over which her hair could be spread before she sat in the sun for hours until it turned blond, the color preferred in this period.

Doubtless the other strategies Aretino describes would have been handed down through generations, too, including the way Nanna's mother staged her daughter's first public appearance. Because word had traveled about the city that a great beauty had come to Rome, men began to congregate outside the house where the mother and daughter were staying. But Nanna's mother would not let her appear in public, nor even stand where she was visible in the window. Instead, she let anticipation grow until she judged the moment efficacious. Only then did she begin to braid her daughter's hair into encircling strands so that it came finally to seem like spun gold that had been plaited.

Choosing what her daughter should wear, the older courtesan knew well how to heighten the drama of this effect. Like many artists of the period who understood the powerful repercussions of placing gold next to red, she dressed her daughter in a gown made of crimson satin. From this detail alone, her talent is evident. Satin, with a subtle gloss, one that did not outshine Nanna's hair but still had the compelling luminosity of a precious stone, would have been the right fabric.

Here we should remember that recognizing beauty is crucial to enhancing it. Thus, knowing that her daughter's arms were beautiful, Nanna's mother chose a design that was sleeveless. And as with the completion of any art, Nanna's mother also knew when to leave well enough alone. Thus, Nanna wore no makeup, which served to accentuate her youth. Still, the dramatic impact of her natural coloring was heightened by another formula, handed down through generations of women, designed to make the skin seem very white and fresh, with which her mother washed her before she dressed.

The labor of preparation went on for several hours—and all to create a particularly ephemeral result. Because carefully washed, coiffed, and costumed as she was, Nanna stood for just a minute or two in the window until she caught the eye of a young man who soon came searching for her. The beauty he glimpsed had fired his imagination. Her gold hair blazing almost like a vision in the lowering light, the deep luster of red following the mysterious curve of her hips, ignited a strange but powerful alchemy in him. Certain in his heart that he had to have this treasure for his own, he hardly had time to realize that he himself was already possessed.

The Pleasure of the Eyes

What poet would dare, in depicting the pleasure caused by the appearance of a great beauty, separate the woman from her dress.
—*Charles Baudelaire*, The Painter of Modern Life

Although conventional wisdom tells us that courtesans made themselves beautiful in order to attract wealthy men, the reverse was also true. Many sought wealth precisely because they wanted to create and possess beauty. Given the profundity of the experience, it is no wonder that regardless of circumstance, whether male or female, educated or not, we all seek what is beautiful. No wonder then again that when, as a small child, Marie-Ernestine Antigny was summoned by her mother to leave the beautiful countryside around Mézières-sur-Brenne, the little girl hid in the attic. At the age of ten, she must have known the subterfuge would not work. But a desperate longing to stay in the country propelled her to try nevertheless. Ever since she was seven, when her mother departed in search of her philandering husband, she had lived with her aunt in this region famous for its lushness that is fed by tributaries from the Loire. She spent long hours wandering in the fields or riding on horseback along a web of trails that wound with slow charm and sudden drama through this stunning landscape filled with wide open spaces, punctuated by lakes, heather, and chestnut forests.

Paris in the middle of the nineteenth century could be a cold, dark place for the poor. But very soon the child found consolation. Her mother did housework and sewing for some of the most prominent families of Paris, including the Gallifets. The marquise de Gallifet, who must have been uncommonly kind, helped to send Marie to the very prestigious Couvent des Oiseaux, a convent school where she was exposed to the wealth and sophistication of her classmates while she learned to speak and carry herself like a lady. But what Marie loved best about the school were the Catholic services—the organ music, the singing, the intense drama of the rituals and the prayers.

Even today, throughout Paris, the beautiful churches are as great a draw for travelers seeking beauty as are the fashion shows. The splendors of even the more modest chapels are at least equally if not more sensual. The changing hues of daylight streaming through ancient cut-glass windows alone are stunning. And then there are the paintings in each alcove; the soaring buttresses of central naves; the altar of course, dressed lovingly in lace and velvet; Jesus' tortured body also beautifully composed along the lines of a cross. And here the golden robes of priests, the red-robed choristers, the smell of incense, the incantatory poetry of the Mass—all would have fused together, as in a countryside, into one experience of beauty that was more than the sum of its parts.

Marie dreamed of becoming a nun. But that was not to be. Still another disappointment, another loss, was in store for her. When the marquise died suddenly, Madame Antigny, having no means to continue her daughter's education, sent Marie to work as a salesgirl. Just as the fields and the chestnut trees had before, the church and its rituals vanished from her life. From now on, she would be allowed to immerse herself in this beauty for only two hours on Sundays. For the rest of the week, she dutifully appeared at a draper's shop on the rue du Bac, where for twelve hours a day she measured and sold bolts of fabric and clothing.

Yet beauty was not entirely absent from the new life into which she had been thrust. These were the first years of the Second Empire in France. Though poverty was still evident, certain neighborhoods in Paris were newly filled with the evidence of wealth. Luxury shops were opening everywhere, with sumptuously arranged windows, rivaling the work of any artisan. There were windows filled with Kashmir shawls, intricately woven in India, or with hats piled with the feathers of rare birds, windows with embroidered bed linens, with lacy corsets, with beaded evening purses, filigreed fans, with scented candles, dozens of roses and bouquets of violets, exquisite perfumes in crystal bottles, pairs of elegant gloves cut gracefully from brown or red or black or white leather, with tiny ivory buttons at the wrist. There were windows displaying hundreds of varieties of chocolate, moving in precisely calibrated range from strong and bitter to milkily sweet.

And because of its location, the rue du Bac had its own charms. Even now, the quarter has the patina of old wealth. Curving from the rue de l'Université to the rue de Sèvres, it crosses two streets lined with elegant old mansions. Built in the eighteenth century, these impenetrably elegant white buildings with neoclassical facades seem to loom over you as you walk by, as if chastening you into submissive silence with that air of unassailable pedigree that only a certain kind of beauty can confer.

"It was a quiet quarter," wrote Edith Wharton, who herself lived for a period on the rue de Varenne, "in spite of its splendor and its history." The splendor was not lost on Marie, who by now had adopted the name her schoolfriends had given her, Blanche, because of her radiantly white skin. She knew the power of her own beauty. And day after day, as she handled bolts of damask and silk and velvet and tulle, she dreamed of how she might augment the effect.

The story is of course open to interpretation. But here, where convention would point out how well Blanche began to use her beauty to her advantage, we can also see that the lustrous fabrics she handled must have captivated her, channeling her dreams in an aesthetic direction. She would not have been the first to be so affected by handling beautiful cloth. The great designer Charles Frederick Worth, the man considered the father of *haute couture*, began his career as an assistant in a draper's shop.

For different reasons, Blanche was soon to become just as famous. Though her elevation was relatively swift, it was more perilous. Like many dreamers, she was far from calculating. She was instead almost alarmingly naive. One night, she accompanied a young shop assistant to the Closerie des Lilas. There, under the flickering light of gas lamps, a new world opened up to her. Laughter was as profuse and scintillating as the abundant champagne she was offered while she sat with a table of young men, caught up as they were in the music. Perhaps because she lost herself in a particularly lusty execution of the cancan, she did not take much notice when her companion left. Since the man who eventually seduced her that night was a Romanian, a few weeks later she found herself in Bucharest.

It was because her Romanian lover brought her to a seedy hotel where they lived a somewhat sordid life that she decided to leave this arrangement to travel and perform with a band of Gypsies. We can easily see why the art of Gypsy music and dance appealed to her. But she was badly treated, and hence chose to escape this life, too. What followed was a short period of despair during which she contemplated joining a convent. But instead she became the mistress of an archbishop. From there she advanced to a prince, who introduced her to the cream of Romanian society, who found her beauty, adorned now with a splendid wardrobe and the glittering gems conferred on her by her distinguished lovers, irresistible.

Though she was at the pinnacle of this world, it was not her own. She began to feel weary, then ill, and all the while her longing to return to Paris grew more intense. It was not just homesickness, the desire to be surrounded by the language of her childhood, or to walk under the chestnut trees in the gardens of the Luxembourg Palace, or to stand on the Pont-Neuf and look back toward the great cathedral of Notre Dame which, from that vantage point, seems almost like a majestic ship, floating in the Seine. Bucharest of course had its own beauty. Even its foreignness would have been exhilarating, at least in the beginning. But just before she left Paris, she had begun a new life there, entering for only the briefest time the world of sparkling wit, late night champagne, rousing dances, glittering gowns and gaslight, which, though it was known as the *demi-monde*, must have seemed more alive to her than any world she had witnessed before.

Once in Paris, she would have to find a livelihood again. Should it surprise us that, not wanting to live with her mother, she moved in with a friend who sold used wardrobes? The match was perfect. Ambroisine, sharing Blanche's love of extravagance, urged her on toward what now with the advantage of hindsight we can call her destiny. If in the beginning she may have been somewhat guileless, within the means available to her and in her own way Blanche was already composing a life for herself—a life in which her ideas for creating beauty would have little restraint.

Like Mogador two decades before her, she started her journey by dancing at the Bal Mabille. She well knew, as did any young woman in her position, that this was a good place to be noticed. Her moment came when, with the encouragement of a journalist she met that night, she broke out into the popular dance called, appropriately, a *galop*. The sight of her flouncing around the ballroom floor caused a minor sensation. In just a few days she had signed a contract to appear in a play at the Théâtre de la Porte Saint-Martin. Since she performed the part of a living statue of Helen of Troy, she neither moved nor spoke. But it hardly mattered. The casting was appropriate enough. The beauty of the woman she portrayed was said to have launched a thousand ships.

During a career of many such performances, in which, if and when she actually spoke any lines, her acting would be forgiven for other qualities, what she launched was wave after wave of an almost orgiastic enthusiasm. While Jules Janin once spoke of her harmonious form, others were more heated with their praise: "[H]er sensual lips are made to be kissed and to empty glasses of champagne." It was almost as if she had the power to evoke fields and grass, rainfall, sunsets, the river Seine itself, together with the good wine and food to be had along its banks. "Under the electric lights and the trained opera glasses," wrote one admirer, "she represented the apotheosis of Matter."

One can see why, a few years after Blanche's death, when Zola was looking for a life on which to model the character of his heroine, Nana, he settled upon this courtesan. The sheer corpulence of her presence suited his purpose, which was to cast a cold eye on the corruptions of the Second Empire. But he never knew the real woman, and those who did felt his portrait to be nothing like her. Unlike the icily calculating Nana, in the early days of her career, Blanche was as naive as she was guileless. She would, for instance, fall into such a sound sleep after making love that any man with whom she spent the night could easily slip away without leaving her any recompense at all. The solution she finally adopted to this problem is symbolic; it points in the direction of the real focus of her labors. Before she fell asleep, she would sew her lover's nightshirt to her dressing gown.

She was not unique among courtesans in her love of clothing. A lavish wardrobe was required for the daily round of events (many of which seemed almost as if they were staged like small fashion shows) that punctuated a courtesan's life. Like society ladies, *demi-mondaines* were expected to wear a different dress for each occasion, and this meant that they might change their clothing as many as eight times a day. For some women, the requirement must have seemed tedious. To return to the closet time after time in the course of the day, peeling off layers one after the other, first a cloak or coat or shawl, then a dress, and then shoes. Perhaps stockings would have to be changed to go with a new dress, and all the accessories: different ribbons, bracelets, rings, even requiring at times, if the skirt were fuller or the bodice shaped differently, for instance, a change of lingerie, all with the aid of a maid, and then finally the hair restyled to match the whole. The necessity would have prevented some women from going out much at all. But to Blanche, this was not just a duty. What she wore was a source of pleasure and perhaps, at times, the very reason she wanted to go out. To show off her wardrobe.

There were peignoirs she could put on for receiving at home, dresses and shoes suitable for walking in the Tuilerie Gardens, clothes to wear at cafés along the Grands Boulevards in midmorning, when, for instance, she would meet her first lover of the day, and the dresses she would wear for what Joanna Richardson has called "the regulation drive" in the Bois de Boulogne. She would perhaps want to change into still different clothes if she chose to take an apéritif in the early evening, and then change yet again, this time into diamonds and furs, if she wanted to attend the theatre. But she was glad for the requirement. Every occasion gave her one more opportunity to display her talent for dressing.

The stage provided a perfect arena for her extraordinary ability. Not only her beauty but her costumes compensated for the talent she lacked as an actress. They were usually extravagant and hence monumentally expensive. In one production, *Le Château à Toto*, she entered the second act to the accompaniment of Offenbach's music wearing a dress that cost 15,000 francs (a small fortune in the nineteenth century); this creation was followed in the next act by a transparent peignoir trimmed with Belgian lace valued at 6,000 francs. In another performance she was so thickly covered in diamonds that one critic wrote: "This is not an actress we see on the stage before us but a jewelry store." The size of her personal wardrobe was legendary, too. The journalist Callias tells us that her departure for a tour to Baden caused a traffic jam when the thirty-seven coaches required to carry her dresses and hats obstructed the rue Ecuries-d'Artois.

But size and expenditure were only part of the story. The fabrics and gems, the colors, cuts, flounces, and feathers that she draped, pinned, and arranged around her body touched and moved a nascent spirit in her audience. You can sense this in the enthusiasm with which Théodore de Banville describes the dress Antigny wore in the brief comedy, *On demand des ingénues*. "Green, the color of waves ... it does not seem to have been cut and stitched ... but trimmed and tossed into shape by the delicate hands of a fairy." By his account, the dress excited perception itself to action: "[I]n every little corolla of green crepe ... a diamond shines and glitters and sparkles in sidereal whiteness, and the light audaciously comes and kisses it." Of course, gowns and jewels cannot create such effects by themselves. Blanche's passionate love for beauty was behind it all, an insatiable desire that against so many odds was fed again and again in increasingly lavish proportions.

If de Banville was to write after her death that she "wore fiery diamonds and rich clothes like the natural accessories of her triumph," the triumph was collective. Using the magic of couture and her own elegant carriage, she created a beauty made to be shared and shared bountifully. Her decorated body offered and gave "all that could be desired," as de Banville wrote, "for the pleasure of the eyes." A cup overflowing with sweet salaciousness, she embodied a fantasy of realization, of wishes immediately satisfied—one that was cherished by many successful men during the prosperous days of the Second Empire. She became, in the words of another critic, "the Venus who characterized an age."

The character in question, however, was given multiple readings. No matter how fervently satisfaction was sought, still the age was ambivalent about its pleasures. In a famous painting for which she was the model, though Paul Baudry partially revealed her lush body and captured the opulent style of her clothing by draping her hips in a swath of shiny azure fabric, he fashioned her as a repentant Magdalen, newly awakened to the holiness of chastity. Zola went in the other direction. As depicted through his heroine, Nana, the courtesan became a femme fatale, leading one man after another to financial ruin.

But Blanche was neither. She did not repent. Nor did she have cold blood running in her veins. In the end, she ruined her career for passionate love. Which should not be entirely surprising if we consider how much erotic love resembles the love of beauty. Like eros, beauty opens the heart, softening not only the gaze but intent itself. Under either the influence of beauty or love, induced to linger, as we sink into the realm of feeling, we forget to calculate our losses.

When she fell in love with Luce, a tenor who performed at the Folies Dramatiques, Blanche dismissed her most wealthy benefactor so that she could spend all her time with her new lover. He was a short, round man, described by one observer as resembling a small ball. Perhaps it was the beauty of his voice that drew her to him. Yet their time together was to be brief. Already ill from consumption, he died within two years.

She was stricken then not only with grief but with poverty. During the period when she was faithful to Luce, and therefore without benefactors, Blanche lost her savings, her credit, her extravagant collection of jewelry, and every one of the carriages that had once transported her in style along the Champs-Elysées. She tried with some success to regain her career in the theatre, until soon after her mother died. She fell seriously ill and found herself alone in a hotel room while her fever rose dangerously. But she was not the only courtesan with a heart. It was because of the kindness of another *cocotte*, Caroline Letessier, who dispatched a carriage to carry her to her own luxurious mezzanine apartment on the boulevard Haussmann, that Blanche lived out her last days in relative comfort. She was still beautiful when she died at the age of thirty-four.

We might be tempted here to make death itself the moral of the story, if it were not for the fact that all of us die. This is a peril that beauty promises us, even with the first sight of a tree in blossom, a green field, an innocently beautiful face; though we may not be fully aware of the thought, we consider time, and the effects of age, of death. In the contemplation of beauty, no matter how quickly the knowledge of mortality passes through consciousness, a thread of subtle and almost sweet sadness will be embroidered there.

A Collaboration

Against a background of hellish light, or if you prefer an aurora borealis—red, orange, sulfur yellow, pink (to express an idea of ecstasy and frivolity) . . . there arises the protean image of wanton beauty.—Baudelaire, The Painter of Modern Life

*I have come to recognize that in Baudelaire's work, Jeanne [Duval] is often depicted as a mirror of the Voudou goddess, Ezili. . . .
—Randy Conner,* Mirror of My Love

As with everything that is fabled, the famous beauty of courtesans continues to haunt us today. Even when no image remains, the words of witnesses, recorded in memoirs or letters from the times, tempt us with what we can no longer see. In the portraits we have of Marie Duplessis, for instance, where her smiles all have an air of sadness, her mouth remains closed. Thus, we can only try to imagine the dazzling white teeth that were so often mentioned in the descriptions we have of her.

Yet some of the words which have been written about courtesans far outshine any physical likeness. Think for instance of the sculpture of Madame Sabatier that can be found on the ground floor of the Musée d'Orsay. It is called *La Femme piqué par un serpent*. From the expression on her face, it is easy to guess what kind of snake did the deed. She is in a swoon. But as successful as the sculpture may be, Jean-Baptiste Clésinger's stone is no match for the lines Baudelaire wrote about Sabatier in *Les Fleurs du mal*:

> *Your head, your mood, the way you move,*
> *With a beauty like the beauty of the countryside*
> *As laughter plays across your face*
> *Like fresh wind in a clear sky.*

If it is in the epistemological nature of all perception to be subjective, this is especially so where the perception of beauty is concerned. When he wrote those lines, Baudelaire was obsessed with Sabatier. He would have a friend leave the poems he addressed to her at the door of her apartment.

Apollonie Sabatier, or Aglaé-Joséphine Savatier, as she was named by her mother, was the natural child of a vicomte and a seamstress. It was because the vicomte, who was also the prefect of the Ardennes, was able to arrange a marriage between her mother and a sergeant in the 47th Infantry, André Savatier, that she was christened with his name. The family lived in Mézières and Strasbourg, before finally moving to Paris, where, since Aglaé showed promise as a singer, she was sent to study with a great performer, Madame Cinti. Indeed, she seemed destined for a career as a concert artist or opera singer, until at a charity concert she was introduced to a former Belgian diplomat, the industrialist Alfred Mosselman. Captivated by a beauty soon to be legendary and by her light, charming manner, he set Aglaé up as his mistress in an apartment on the rue Frochot, in quartier Bréda, on the slopes of the hill that rises up into Montmartre, an area thick with artists, writers, and courtesans. (There were so many *lorettes* living there that they were named after the local church, Notre Dames des Lorettes.)

Because Mosselman was married, he used Fernand Broissard as a messenger between himself and his lover, and it was through this man that the young woman met a wider circle of friends. Broissard invited her to the monthly dinners he gave at the Hôtel Pimodan, where he lived on the Ile-Saint-Louis. Soon she was also attending meetings of the *Club des haschichins*, which met at Théophile Gautier's apartment in the same building. Balzac, Gautier, Flaubert and Maxine du Camp, and Baudelaire are only a few among those who have become illustrious who attended these events. By then, Aglaé had changed her name to the more elegant Apollonie Sabatier. And because of the electric effect of her presence at these gatherings, which seemed to fuse all who were present into a more generous body, she was also given another name: *la Présidente*. Soon she was entertaining the same men, together with Delacroix, Berlioz, Gérard de Nerval, Henri Murger (whose novel inspired *La Bohème*), and Arsène Houssaye at her own apartment.

Sabatier's presence also contributed a distinct aesthetic pleasure to the gatherings. Like Blanche d'Antigny, *la Présidente* loved fashion. She dressed with such a striking originality that the artists she knew began to involve themselves with her wardrobe. As well as making creative suggestions regarding her apparel, some of them even designed clothing for her. Both dressed and undressed she was sculpted by Jean-Baptiste Clésinger twice; Ernest Meissonier did several paintings of her. Ernest Feydeau made her the central figure in his novel, *Sylvie*.

The love affair she had with Baudelaire was notoriously short. In the beginning, Sabatier did not return the poet's love. But after *Les Fleurs du mal* was published, she offered herself to him as an homage. They spent only one night as lovers, after which she fell in love with him and he fell out of love with her. Though she came to love the poet as well as his words, Baudelaire, as it turns out, loved the ideal he had created of her more than the breathing reality. "A few days ago," he wrote, "you were a deity, which is so convenient, so noble, so inviolable. And then there you are, a woman." Instead of lovers, they became friends.

There were many bonds between them, but perhaps the strongest was that they were both captivated by beauty. Just as Baudelaire, who wrote a great deal about the images being created by his friends, collected and studied art, *la Présidente*, who had been a singer and still loved music, also surrounded herself with artists and their work, even painting, herself, in her later years. They both loved literature. In the beginning it was above all Baudelaire's poetry that had impassioned Sabatier. And in different ways they were both creators of beauty. What he described in words, she knew how to embody. Sharing the love of beauty as they did, they were collaborators in the creation of an aesthetic sensibility, giving shape to the astonishingly fecund atmosphere of the nineteenth century.

Gustave Courbet captured a moment in the process of this creation with his celebrated painting *L'Atelier du peintre*. In the middle of the canvas, a half-finished painting sits on an easel. Before the easel stands a model, who watches Courbet paint a landscape in which, curiously, no likeness of her can be found. Aligned with her and witnessing the process, too, Sabatier is prominent in the circle that, surrounding the work, seems almost to generate the painting. She is dressed in black, a Kashmiri shawl draped over her shoulder, her back turned to Baudelaire, who, sitting, turns his attention to the pages of a book.

In Courbet's mind, all those who had contributed to the chemistry of his art must have been there, even if only symbolically. Was it a conscious decision on his part to make the shawl Sabatier wore so prominent? With this article of clothing he had included much that, though absent in one sense, was present in another. Of course the Kashmiri shawl, being such a critical part of a lady's wardrobe, would have recalled the world of fashion. And since this coveted item of clothing cost more than a working woman could earn over a decade, in a subtle way, as with the presence of Sabatier herself, the existing difference between classes had been conjured. And then there was the provenance of the scarf itself, made by women paid very little for their labor, in another country, India, which signified, as well as the exigencies of the empire Europe was building, all the worlds and even world views to be found outside Europe.

The original painting contained one more figure, the woman who more than any other had evoked the exotic realities described by Baudelaire in his poetry. Yet for some reason still unknown to us, Baudelaire requested that Courbet excise the image of Jeanne Duval from his painting. Perhaps she did not like her portrait, or perhaps he feared the jealousy of Sabatier, who, after being rejected by Baudelaire, referred to Baudelaire's mistress sarcastically as "his ideal."

The remark was laden with an unstated prejudice. Jeanne, whose skin was lightly brown, and who was born in Santo Domingo, had been the object of disparaging remarks that slyly referred to race more than once. Even Baudelaire, who loved her passionately, was not entirely free of the attitude which penetrated his culture. Yet in his case there is far more to the story. Between the lines of his poems and letters, we can sense a struggle between the world view into which he was born and the one that drew him to Jeanne. Although she was described by many, including Théodore de Banville and Nadar (who was her lover for a period) as very beautiful, there is every reason to believe that it was also the way she saw the world that Baudelaire found compelling.

As Randy Cooper suggests, it is easy to see the mark of African philosophies, particularly Voudou, in the poems Baudelaire wrote to Jeanne. Can it be an accident that in *La Chevelure* in which Baudelaire tells us "Africa burns," Jeanne's hair is described as blue, the color of the Voudou goddess Ezili? Reading "Sed Non Satiata" the influence is wrapped in a subtle ambivalence:

> Strange deity, obscure as nights
> > that smell of musk and smoke from Havana,
> work of some obi, Faust of the Savannah,
> > sorceress hemmed by ebony, daughter of every dark midnight.

Yet though his ambivalence is sometimes stronger (when for instance he refers to Jeanne as a "demon without pity"), Baudelaire is perpetually drawn in the direction of her philosophy. We begin to understand more about the nature of this attraction when in "Sed Non Satiata" we read the line "the elixir of your lips where love struts," a phrase which recalls the image of a Voudou priestess.

Perhaps here Zora Neale Hurston's account of an exchange in Voudou ritual will explain the deeper meaning that stands behind the metaphor. As Hurston tells us, at the moment when the priestess is asked by the celebrants, "What is the truth?" she responds by throwing back her veil to reveal her body. A body which, according to the Voudou view of the cosmos, is the source of all life and thus also the answer to all mystery.

But whether or not it is Jeanne's knowledge of the religion of Voudou reflected here, Baudelaire makes it clear that the view of the world he has received through his mistress enriches his own vision, giving him an experience of existence which, even while it feels strange, also seems as if it had always belonged to him. "You return to me," he writes in *La Chevelure*, "the blue sky, immense and round." Though he was frightened and scandalized by her, through her eyes the world could be reborn to him each day with new beauty.

Her Portrait

When he wanted to draw or paint some figure, and had before him a real woman or man, that object would so affect his sense of sight and his spirit would enter into what he was representing so that he seemed conscious of nothing else.—Persio, on witnessing Titian at work

. . . So it seems to me that in Titian's colors God placed the paradise of our bodies.—Tullia d'Aragora, Dialogue on the Infinity of Love

The model for the painting is unknown to us. It is only because the woman portrayed here holds a bouquet of flowers that the work was named *Flora* a century after it was painted. Flora, the goddess of flowers, was a courtesan herself before she became a deity. But that the sitter was a courtesan is clear for other reasons, too. In the sixteenth century, it was fashionable to paint the *cortigiana* in just this manner, torso and head filling the frame, the subject facing the painter, her hair cascading over one shoulder. Each of these details would have been read as a sign. A respectable woman of this period would never have allowed herself to be seen in public with her hair down. And certainly she would not have appeared as this woman does, only half-clothed, wearing a long white undershirt, the ancestor of our camisoles, called a *camicia*, a garment that, with its light-catching folds, is pulled down on the right by the same hand that holds the sumptuous dress the model is no longer wearing.

The painting is famous for the contrasts rendered, thus, the shiny embroidered surface of her dress placed next to the bare skin of her breast, making both textures more intense. You feel almost as if you were gliding your fingers over the fabric and then her skin. Yet the effect is subtle. She is not fully revealed. Is that a shadow cast by her hand or just the upper edge of her nipple that we can barely see above the resplendent fabric? Since we cannot say for certain, after all, whether it is nipple or shading, the uncertainty creates a compellingly sensual mystery. An opacity which mirrors the atmosphere the courtesan knew how to create as part of the practice of seduction. The same subtlety can be seen in the expression on her face. Her eyes askance, she appears almost modest in the way that she avoids the direct scrutiny of the painter. Though he was known for his skill at artifice, the expression must have been one Titian observed as well as created. A quality possessed by the sitter. A certain honesty. You can see it in the complexity of the presence the painter has captured. It is authenticity that makes her expression so compelling. Though reticent, she does not hide the reticence she feels. She lets herself be seen as she is. In this sense, her underdress is symbolic. Unlike those with lesser talents who would conceal or pretend, she is accustomed to using her real feelings in her profession. This is how she achieves the intimate moments for which she is so esteemed. And yet even this presence, like Titian's painting, is not without artifice. Intimacy is her art. And like the painter, she knows well how to create a moving composition from elements of truth.

No wonder Titian chose to paint her. Kindred souls, they both inhabit the space that hovers between reality and artifice, a territory informed by telling details and evocative glimpses. Is it just the hint of makeup with which she adorns herself, the layers of fine clothing so artfully assembled, the rich colors with which she surrounds herself, or is it something else, too, that inspires him as he paints? Perhaps complexity itself. Her modesty, for instance, is not simple. She turns her gaze away in a definitive manner, while at the same time, her strong presence, the luster of her hair, her body, which is neither withdrawn nor fearful but instead calmly sensate, charges the canvas.

Her beauty has pushed Titian past the limits of his art. In order to reflect the quality that so fascinates him, he has had to augment his craft. Like Bellini before him, who turned to oil paints to capture the quality of the courtesans he wanted to portray, Titian, using oil, too, paints one color on top of another before the first is dry. It is all there in the layers—the fusion of seeming opposites, the sense of a history beneath the surface, of a knowledge not exactly hidden but nevertheless a carefully guarded resource.

We might propose that Aretino, who was a close friend of Titian, was aiming at the same complexity when he wrote of his character, the Roman courtesan Nanna, as she appeared at the window, trying to arouse desire, when he said that she affected the innocence of a nun and yet looked down with the assurance of a married woman playing the prostitute. But next to Titian's canvas, this description seems oddly empty. Since Aretino depicts only contrivance, his work seems contrived.

Titian, on the other hand, gives us density. The innocence he depicts seems real. She appears to be young, no more than nineteen, probably younger. Since in that period Venetian women married at fourteen, the age at which Aretino claims Nanna started her career, her youth alone would not have argued innocence. Certainly the stereotypical idea adopted by Aretino toward his subject, a concept that is alive even today, is that women who are not virgins have lost their innocence. Yet most women know that innocence is not entirely dependent upon sexual knowledge. Did Titian know this, too? Or was it simply that he loved what he saw and wanted to capture it faithfully? We are moved even unwillingly by this image.

Of course he captures artifice as well, and here, since he makes no moralizing comment, the power of it to sway us is unabated. It is a mannered honesty he presents us with, inextricable from the beauty that wells up out of his color, the fine lines rendered by his brush, and the light—here dazzling, there somber, here gracefully bright, there burnished but penetrating—soaked into the canvas as it is into our eyes. We cannot separate ourselves from the sitter. Looking, we are lost wherever she is lost, triumphant with her triumph, shaken by her splendor, desirous, calculating and reticent, innocent and wise with worldliness.

And there is this, too. Gazing at her portrait, we are staring into another time and place. You can almost hear the waters of Venice washing against the sides of the canals as, hair streaming, *camicia* billowing, Flora fairly overflows from the canvas.

For some reason not entirely understood, many painters have been able to capture the spirit of an age by depicting the bodies of courtesans. Doubtless there are numerous other reasons why so many painters would have chosen to portray them. Some were practical. What other women besides courtesans and prostitutes would allow themselves to be depicted in such a frankly sensual manner? Certainly, too, the image of the courtesan would have conjured the erotic force that gives birth to social and artistic movements. That the *cortigiana* was not only a transgressor but symbolic of transgression itself would only have increased the effect.

But the paintings themselves, even this painting entitled *Flora*, speak of reasons beyond this reasoning. We need only to think of the desire that often can be found sequestered within the wish to make love to a courtesan. Notice how, though with one hand Flora offers flowers to her beholder and with the other pulls down her shirt, almost revealing a nipple, her eyes tell another story. The message is evident. If you seek a night with her, or even several nights, most likely you will be given what you want. But though you have every success in the world, every means of power, including wealth, though you are a doge, for instance, and have recently built a grand palazzo along the Grand Canal, something in her will still prove elusive, tempting you to try to reach that which seems forever beyond you, though every effort you make to get closer only unravels the garments of your own composure. Until, if you are wise, you learn what the painter already seems to know: what you have found so compelling is exactly this, that in a glimpse of the grandeur you cannot possess, for a fraction of an instant, you can see that beneath the dense patina of appearances, what you have been calling yourself is constantly being created, made from a mixture of art and innocence, of what already exists and what is now just being imagined.

Suggestion
(THE SECOND EROTIC STATION) ✦ ✦ ✦ ✦ ✦ ✦ ✦ ✦ ✦

This is how Jean Lorrain described the image that greeted all Liane's visitors: "Taller, slenderer, more refined than ever, with that transparent complexion and those bluish circles round her great frightened doe-eyes." Liane de Pougy would stretch her willowy frame over the white satin chaise-lounge for which she was justly famous. As if pouring from the glistening satin and fur trimming, the sumptuous dress she wore had wide and flowing sleeves of white brocade, and both the fabric and the lining of the dress were patterned with lilies. Which was fitting, because she herself must have seemed like a fragrant flower, her long neck, encircled with six strands of pearls, bending forward as she received each guest.

She had a talent for creating visual effects. Whether you were the librettist Henri Meilhac, who wrote the lyrics for Offenbach's operas (and who had paid Liane 80 million francs just to contemplate her nude body), or the American heiress Natalie Barney, who was for a time Liane's lover, the various settings Liane arranged for herself would have been irresistibly enchanting.

The color white can create a cold, almost sanitized atmosphere, but it can also conjure fantasies of another kind entirely. Under its influence, worlds of delicacy and grace will arise in your mind, realms peopled with diaphanous beings whose arms (or is it wings?) glow as they rush past your ears. Your dream becomes almost real as you swear you can taste icy strawberries crushed in your mouth, and is it because your eyes are brimming with a child's tears of delight that everything around you seems to shimmer? Then, suddenly returned to the present as Pougy moves just slightly toward you, the sight of her hands framed by filigrees of shining thread suggests a touch so soft and subtle that even in the midst of a snowdrift, you will begin to melt. And while she speaks to you now, it seems that, like the sweet pistils of the thousand lilies that dance over her body, her tongue has begun to flicker in and out of your mouth.

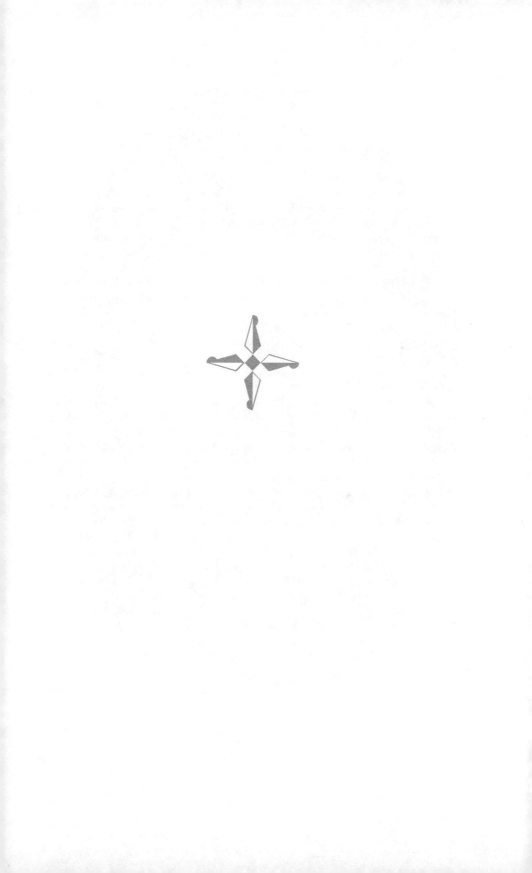

LA BELLE OTERO

Chapter Three

Cheek

I like restraint, if it doesn't go too far.
—Mae West

WHILE TRUE CHEEKINESS contains a mixture of bravado and insolence, it suffers from the drawbacks of neither. Where bravado hints of fear lying just beneath the surface and where insolence can express bitter or even rancid resentments, cheek has none of these shadowy resonances. It has, rather, a bracing but enlivening effect, which even as it startles charges the atmosphere with all the drama of a bolt of lightning.

Though not every courtesan possessed this virtue in the same measure, almost all of them had to have some degree of cheek. A wellborn woman who was no longer marriageable because of scandal would have to navigate an atmosphere filled with whispered judgments, not simply with her head held high but with a kind of sparkling *élan*, a manner whose very force would make what was said against her seem negligible. And for those who were not wellborn there was a stronger current to face, not just passing reprimands over impropriety but the resistance against the implicit challenge their very presence made to society's deepest sense of order.

Yet, formidable as social disapproval can be, it also serves to develop cheek. Partly from desperation, and partly due to solitude, which even if forced upon her, nurtures insight, a woman suffering from the pain of society's rejection might come to detect a certain hollowness in the arguments that she should live under a more strict sexual code than men.

Moreover, once fallen, the spotless conduct and the rules by which she had been carefully taught to behave would now, ironically, precisely because of society's censure, be proven unnecessary.

The harsher circumstances faced by women who were not born to the upper classes only made their perceptions correspondingly more penetrating. It is clear, for instance, that in the seventeenth century, over a hundred years before the French Revolution, the celebrated courtesan Marion Delorme had already seen through distinctions of rank which separated one citizen from another. "Without his biretta and his scarlet robes," she is famous for saying, "a Cardinal is a very little man." She was speaking of Richelieu, a man who virtually ruled France for decades. But that she had been intimate with him would have put the dimensions of his power in a very different perspective.

And there is this to consider. Doubtless, such entitlements were less imposing to a woman whose existence was not recognized by the social order, an order that could easily have seemed a charade to her. Since a courtesan who was not wellborn had to learn late all the manners that aristocratic children are taught from birth, she understood perhaps better than most how much social position is both expressed and maintained by performance. It was a skill which, in the end, allowed many courtesans to surpass all others. When Edwige Feullière was criticized in London for playing the courtesan Marguerite in *La Dame aux camélias* as if she were a *grande dame*, she responded by saying, "The courtesans of France were the only *grandes dames*." Indeed, it was the great actress Rachel, a courtesan like so many women of her profession, who taught the empress Eugénie how to curtsy while scanning an audience with her eyes.

But there was an element Eugénie cannot have learned. Not only were the daily performances the great courtesans gave infused with the delightful humor that can only come from understanding that we are all merely players on the stage of life, but their gestures were fired by the considerable bravura required to pull off the whole charade. Thus we can easily see why, in the heat of such victories, these particular players were found so irresistible.

Wellington's Surrender

When people talk to me about the weather, I always feel they mean something else.—Oscar Wilde

Imagine, then, how it would have felt at the very beginning of the nineteenth century to the fledgling courtesan Harriet Wilson, the daughter of a Swiss watchmaker in Mayfair, when she made her first entrance into high society. Her family was respectable enough, but tradesmen and their children were not welcomed into the circles she had entered. Yet even if she were greeted by a chill, we would find no trembling in her demeanor. Cheek, which she had in great abundance, carried her through as surely as a blazing fire on a very cold night.

In a few short years Wilson became the most popular woman among those who were called "the fashionable impure" of the Regency. Her success cannot be credited to beauty, for which she was not known. Rather, it was cheek itself, which only deepened over time, that made her so attractive. She had, in the words of Sir Walter Scott, "the manner of a wild schoolboy." She was in the fullness of her powers when she met the celebrated Duke of Wellington. And in a sense, so was he. Since defeating Napoléon at the battle of Waterloo, all of England sat at his feet.

However, at least in the account she recorded in her memoirs, Wellington was no match for her. According to Wilson, she sensed the weakness of her suitor immediately. Having paid Mrs. Porter, who was a procurer, 100 guineas to arrange an introduction with Harriet, and promised the same amount to her for a short meeting, he arrived punctually, and bowing, thanked her for agreeing to see him. But as he tried to take her hand, she withdrew hers, chiding him. "Really, for such a renowned hero you have very little to say for yourself."

Elaborately polite himself, cosseted by the rules of polite society, like many great soldiers, the duke was oddly inept socially. But he must have been especially flustered on first meeting Harriet, because after uttering the phrase "beautiful creature," he immediately asked after her current lover, who was also a friend of his. "Where is Lorne?" the duke said.

Reacting to the inappropriateness of his question, which made her feel, in her words, "out of all patience with his stupidity," she asked him directly, "Good gracious, what come you here for, Duke?"

To which, apparently still transfixed and somewhat at a loss for words, the duke blurted out, "Beautiful eyes, yours!"

The compliment did not soften her attitude.

"Aye man!" she answered him quickly. "They are greater conquerors than ever Wellington shall be." To which she added, even more impudently, "But, to be serious, I understood you came here to try to make yourself agreeable."

If then the duke finally lost his temper, demanding, "What, child, do you think I have nothing better to do than to make speeches to please ladies?," still he stayed. Offended as he may have seemed, Wellington was to become one of Harriet's lovers. The affair between them lasted many years, during which time he resolved her debts and contributed generously to her support. Perhaps he was charmed by her apparently effortless ability to insult him, which is illustrated by a brief excerpt from a later dialogue. Trying no doubt to be romantic, the duke told her, "I was thinking of you last night after I got into bed." To which, without missing a beat, Harriet responded, "How very polite to the Duchess."

If the appeal of such rudeness is mysterious, an engraving found in the first edition of her memoirs illustrating her account of their first meeting reveals another side to the story. Here the great soldier is depicted hat in hand, in a lackluster posture, less a bow than an odd gesture of hesitancy and defeat. In sympathy for his plight, he was not known to be handsome. Wilson commented that he looked to her like a rat, and though she was impressed by his accomplishments, she found him essentially boring. He was decidedly not a ladies' man, and this must have made him uncertain of himself, even in the role of a paying suitor. Yet the engraver has captured another quality, less shyness than a curious kind of collapse. His arms hang beside him like dead weights.

Sitting in a straightback chair, Harriet's demeanor is altogether different.

Her arms, one curled in her lap, the other slung over the back of the chair, are relaxed comfortably in an almost modern way. There is a blush to her cheeks. Her breasts seem to fill the room less with size than with the exuberant implication of sexuality. One foot edges forward, not nervously, but instead aware and ready. Though her head, covered with dangling curls, is tilted to one side, this is clearly not, as is often the case with so many women, a gesture of obedience, but rather a teasing pose. In striking contrast to the duke, the consummate effect of her presence is of vitality.

One can only imagine the causes of the duke's relative deflation. Perhaps battle has tired him. And then again, perhaps off the battlefield, without such clear demarcations of danger and victory, life has lost its meaning for him. Confused by domestic intrigue, he only vaguely grasps this terrain, which is why he clings so tenaciously to the manners he performs with rote dullness. And since he is usually surrounded by so many admirers, some of them even sycophants, none of whom will ever risk saying anything disagreeable to him, he is probably used to being bored.

No wonder then that the young woman sitting across the drawing room captivates him so. She does not indulge in small talk. With an easy wit, she cuts through the stuffy air of politeness and the wooden manner of his entrance to tell him exactly what is transpiring between them, even spelling out his own desires. She is, he suddenly realizes, breaking the soporific pattern that has become familiar to him. Far from sycophantic, her words, though amusing, seem more like an assault. Finding himself on the battlefield once more, his nerves begin to quicken and he feels alive again.

We must note here that to be truly effective, cheek must be accompanied by an educated intelligence. It is not just that Harriet is ignorant of manners but rather that she understands the purpose of them very well. And for this reason she never allows herself to be treated without the respect of proper protocol. (She was known to have banished a prince from her presence because he failed to remove his hat.)

Far from ignorant of manners, Harriet is particularly adept at revealing the meanings of protocol. In the world to which the duke was born, where raw power is veiled by title, tradition, and pomp, public events, meetings, and conversations have a strangely empty quality, as if reality had been banished. But Harriet allows nothing to be veiled. It is not only that her gown is cut low across her breasts, nor that she sees the emperor's proverbial nakedness; the empire, too, with every euphemism, and all its secret dealings, seems to shed its clothing in her presence.

Perhaps this is why it is not just Wellington who is drawn to her. Indeed, it seems as if all the great men of the British Empire come eventually to sit at her feet. Along with the Marquess of Lorne, heir of the Duke of Argyll, she has enlisted the attention of the Marquess of Worcester, heir of the Duke of Beaufort; Lord Frederick Bentinck, son of the Duke of Portland; the Duke of Leinster; Lord Craven, Lord Alvanley, and Henry Brougham, a member of Parliament. The poet Byron is her good friend. And along with the most powerful ladies and gentlemen in London, she is invited to all the fashionable parties.

Certainly, such a guest presents a formidable risk. Though polite silence can be fatally dull, even without trying, almost any courtesan supplies a vivid reminder of what everyone knows but cannot mention. Stories of lust and desire, of gain and loss and accumulation, the source of so much significance so carefully hidden now perched at the edge of her tongue. She is like a jack-in-the-box, a flying fish, a roman candle about to burst into sparkling plumes of light. You can never tell what she will say or do next. But you can certainly count on her to deliver you from boredom.

"A Masterpiece of Impertinence"

> Shut your mouths, I'm opening mine.
> —the singer Fréhel to her
> audience at a cabaret in Paris

There is more to say about brazenness itself. The audacity that fuels cheek reveals a spirit not merely willing but very eager to tell the truth. A good example is afforded us by the brief dialogue that took place when the courtesan Esther Guimond, traveling through Naples, was stopped for a routine examination of her passport.

"What is your profession?" the official in charge asked her.

"A woman of independent means," she answered discreetly.

But when she saw that the official, who looked bewildered, did not seem to understand her, she cried out impatiently, "Courtesan—take care you remember it."

To which, probably fired by the energy of her own speech, she added, widening her audacity. "And go and tell that Englishman over there."

We do not know precisely how she came to be so brazen. The history has been lost. But it is clear that once she crossed the barrier against using the word "courtesan," she accelerated her transgression with a kind of glee. In this she was part of a larger insurrection against propriety in language, the same joyous revolution that can be felt in Rimbaud's "Chant de Guerre Parisian" where he writes "Oh May, What delirious bare asses."

Like Rimbaud, Guimond's verbal rebellions were not only defiant but talented. The sharpness of her tongue was remarkable enough that, in a Paris full of famous wits, she was famous for her repartee. A lover of the journalist Emile de Girardin for many years, she was known to have contributed more than once to his work. And when, after the popular revolts of 1848, Girardin was on the verge of being executed for conspiracy, she saved his life with her sharp wit. Approaching Cavaignac, the chief executive officer in charge of Girardin's case, a man who was also a friend, she ridiculed the accusation. "Conspiracy?" she cried. "What nonsense! He can't conspire. No one ever shares his opinions."

Her talent for piercing through illusion had a less happy side. Guimond was cynically practical. Early in her career, she made a small fortune by blackmailing other courtesans with letters she had teased from their former lovers. This perfidy, however, shares a certain ground with the brazenness of her speech. She was determined to survive at all costs. Willpower often comes from an early experience of destitution. Of Esther's life before she became a courtesan very little is known. It is almost as if, before her appearance on the boulevards of nineteenth-century Paris, she did not exist. Still, we do know that she was a *grisette*. Like Duplessis, she would have worked twelve to sixteen hours a day in a sweatshop for wages too meager to keep life and limb together. "Dressmaking," she once said dryly, "didn't suit me."

That one's spirit can be crushed by such a life need hardly be said. The process may be invisible and slow. Faced with such conditions, and little or no alternative, many seem resigned. Given the prospect of being worked to death, one can imagine giving up and at the same time retreating from all that is vivid in oneself. But there are always some who will try to escape this kind of fate no matter how desperate the odds. It is an attempt that requires the summoning of an extraordinary will, strengthened in turn by the exceptional clarity that can arise in response to the many large and small insults, humiliations, and indignities that quickly accumulate in such a life but are so often unnamed or even denied by society.

If, over time, Guimond entered another class, becoming one of the more esteemed women in Paris, the host of a salon that included not only Girardin but Dumas *fils*, Nestor Roqueplan, Saint-Beuve, Guizot, and Prince Napoléon, her past may not have been immediately apparent during her ascension, except that she was quick to perceive an injustice—and even quicker to respond accordingly. In his *Confessions*, the *boulevardier* Arène Houssaye recalls an episode that has become famous. It took place at Longchamps. Breaching protocol, several *grandes cocottes*, Guimond among them, were escorted by a group of fashionable playboys into the grandstand usually reserved for the best families. Outraged, a cabal of society matrons, including the comtesse de Courval, sent the master of ceremonies to tell the courtesans to leave. But true to her character, Guimond stood her ground. She was there by the will of the gentlemen who had accompanied her, she said, and nothing short of bayonets would make her withdraw.

But the story does not end there. Returning to Paris after the races, her behavior became far more incendiary. Paying her driver a louis to race neck-and-neck with the coach of the comtesse de Courval, as they drove along side by side, she tossed the countess flowers and sang her a ribald song that she improvised in thirty-six couplets. It was Houssaye who referred to it as "a masterpiece of impertinence." Soon, all Paris was singing the same song. "That," Esther Guimond used to say, "is how I made my entrance into society."

An Outrageous Proposal

It was in 1906 that the beautiful actress and *demi-mondaine* known as Lanthélme received Misia Sert into her drawing room. Among the many ironies of this meeting, Sert knew that only recently the elegant home on the rue Fortuny, so close to the fashionable Parc Monceau, as well as the eighteenth-century furniture that filled it, had been given to Lanthélme by Alfred Sert, her husband. Misia, a theatrical producer and powerful presence herself, studied Alfred's lover closely. Copying her style of dress, she had rehearsed a dramatic appeal. "You have a woman's heart," she planned to say, before she demanded, "Give him back!" But she was never able to deliver her lines.

That she failed to grasp entirely the worldly ways of her rival is understandable. Born as Mathilde Fossey, Lanthélme, the daughter of a prostitute, was raised in her mother's brothel, where she was put to work at fourteen. All her life she had shown an extraordinary and fierce independence. Rejecting the profession that fate had chosen for her, she applied to study acting at the Conservatoire. When, after a few years, her great talent became evident and she was offered a position at the Comédie-Française, she rejected this, too, choosing instead to perform at the more popular theatres on the boulevards of Paris. She quickly became a sensation, followed by an avid audience especially interested in the fact that she was known to take both men and women as lovers.

Admitted to the salon only after being searched for weapons by Lanthélme's maid, and after waiting in the drawing room under a chic portrait of the stunningly beautiful actress painted by Boldini, Misia was disarmed once again by her rival's entrance. Immediately, Lanthélme showered her lover's wife with compliments, and after brightly discussing the theatre season, asked if she could help Misia in any way. Flustered, Misia simply said she had come to speak about her husband.

"There is nothing at all to worry about," Lanthélme began; "he hardly interests me."

But then she changed her approach.

"My dear, you can really have him—on three conditions: I want the pearl necklace you're wearing, one million francs—and you."

Shocked, Misia removed her necklace immediately and, ignoring the last request, promised that Lanthélme would receive a million francs from her in a few days. But moments after she returned to her hotel, she received a package containing the necklace. Inside was a note written on cyclamen-colored paper, in which Lanthélme proposed, "I have decided to forget the money and return the necklace. I am holding you only to the third condition."

Her Garter Belt

*The spirit of lingerie is fashion and this phenomenon becomes even
more interesting when along with dress codes it reverses received
ideas.*—Marie Simon, Les Dessous

If clothing tells one story, lingerie provides the tale with another layer of meaning. When a woman strips away her outer clothing, lingerie is what remains. Providing an architectural foundation for every erotic facade, the practical structures that hold up breasts, mold hips and bellies, and smooth legs are also signs in themselves. Beneath more muted, somber, modest shades and fabrics, suddenly we find red or black or purple, framing all the forbidden sights with silk and lace. As a woman un-dresses, a froth of sensuousness suddenly appears close to the skin, steamy with sweat and secretions.

No wonder then that lingerie is not meant to be displayed in public. But at the end of the Second Empire, that is exactly what La Belle Otero did. The photograph is sepia-toned yet clear. With both hands she pulls each side of a split skirt apart to reveal her garter belt for the camera. Her expression goes beyond brazenness. As her chin tilts up in the smile of a trickster, Otero has all the *élan* of a pilot in the early days of flying—dashing, daring, impressively insouciant, ready to ascend.

But as if her expression were not enough, what distinguishes her from just another tart showing her wares is the nature of the garter belt itself. Made of precious stones, it was designed by the celebrated house of Boucheron, where throughout the Second Empire and Belle Epoque the titled and the rich came for their jewelry, everyone from Empress Eugénie and Queen Isabella II of Spain to the Vanderbilts. Born illegitimate and poor in a small village in Spain, were it not for her cheekiness, Otero would never have set foot in Boucheron. Thus, the image of her garter belt is doubly insolent, a sparkling effrontery, audacity mingling luxuriantly with seduction.

LA PAÏVA

Arousal
(THE THIRD EROTIC STATION) + + + + + + + + +

*...as the years went by without bringing her either position or
fortune, she firmly resolved that she would win them both.
—comte Horace de Viel-Castel,* Mémoires sur le Régne de
Napoléon III

THE QUESTION BEING, what made her so desirable to all the
men from whom she got finally what she wanted? Especially since,
though Païva was known as "the Queen of Paris," what she inspired in
some was only indignant anger. Jules and Edmond de Goncourt,
habitués and historians of literary and artistic Paris, wrote of her

often, almost always in a disapproving tone. The house she built on the Champs-Elysées, which she promised would be the most beautiful in Paris, was ridiculously ostentatious; the parties she hosted there were overshadowed by her immense pride; and furthermore she was not a great beauty herself, the brothers said. Still, anger, even when elegantly phrased and placed at a neat critical distance, is a strong response. Certainly, in their own way, the brothers were aroused.

Dining at her table one night, both men were especially offended when she described her own climb to wealth and status. "Circumstance means nothing," she said. "One creates the circumstances of one's life through pure will." The magnitude of her willpower is clear in her history. Like so many of her contemporaries who ascended from rags to riches, though she was born poor and untitled, she became a marquise with a great fortune. Her father, who was a refugee from pogroms in Poland, had settled along with his family in Moscow. As the daughter of a weaver, the future Païva was raised with very modest expectations. Following in the footsteps of her mother, she married a tailor when she was just seventeen years old, giving birth to a son soon after. But while working long hours, cutting and stitching in the small basement apartment the three of them shared, she found herself dreaming of escape, until one day, abandoning her spouse and her young son, she fled.

Though we may find it hard to forgive the coldness of her resolve, the force of will evident in this story is breathtaking. Few options would have been open to her. Not educated enough to become a governess, had she become a working woman she would have had to endure a poverty far more severe than the one she had endured with her husband and son. But she did have some resources. Despite the disparaging description of the Goncourt brothers, her figure was thought beautiful and she had what was called a Grecian neck, thick reddish hair, and intensely appealing eyes. But there is also her formidable energy to consider, too—a force that could sustain her while, alone and without protection and penniless, she waited to be chosen at the public balls and cafés she frequented.

Imagining this energy, we can perhaps begin to perceive what must have been almost a kind of tropism that certain men felt in their bodies, as they moved toward the heat of her extraordinary vitality. Let us think for example of the first days that she spent with Henri Herz, the prosperous pianist and composer who was to introduce her to the Parisian world of arts and letters. After searching many great cities—Constantinople, Berlin, Vienna—for the man she needed, she met Herz at the German resort known as Ems. Thirteen years her senior, Herz was perhaps hoping that the country air would act as a kind of tonic, renewing his appetite for life.

In such a mood, her presence would have seemed all the more remarkable. She was not there to rest. Instead of a tired animal put out to pasture, she had more the air of a military horse, all muscle, the air nearly visible with each breath, ready to charge. Cooped up for hours in a small, dark space, she was hungry for life, and no one, nothing would stop her again. Herz would have been able to see this in the way she walked across a room. Through the finished veneer of the gait more fitting to a lady that she had observed and learned to imitate, he must have sensed the blistering pace of which she was well capable, a pace all the more compelling when glimpsed through the veil of her transitory restraint.

Now, as she stands in front of him, he can read the whole story in her posture, the lusty greed she has for everything in life, the indomitable energy, even the inflated estimation she has of herself that moves toward the edge of derangement. Is it at this moment that he begins to see the future? He is perhaps startled for an instant at her directness, when she takes him by the hand, leading him toward his bed. But just as he is startled, his body responds in another way too. He is, after all, used to creating his own circumstances. A musician and composer who established his own piano factory, he is also a successful entrepreneur. Since most often he is the one in command, no one would have guessed, himself least of all, how appealing the thought of this momentary relinquishment would be. As he feels himself yield to the idea, another part of his body grows hard with anticipation.

VERONICA FRANCO

Chapter Four

Brilliance

The bodily eye can scarcely bear the splendor of her brow.
—VERONICA FRANCO, *"By an unknown author in Praise of Verona,*
where Franco is staying"

B ENEATH A THIN veneer of intellectual associations, "brilliance" is fundamentally a sensual word. Whether applied to the taste of vintage wine, a musical performance, a scientific theorem, a witty remark, or a quality of intelligence, the metaphor evokes a particular kind of light—a light that not only reveals whatever lies in its path but is also pleasing, even thrilling, in itself. We think, for instance, of a garden in the late afternoon, when rays of light, alternating with shadow, have a remarkable intensity, one that makes leaves and flowers and vines all seem as if they have been newly blessed.

In this sense, it can be said of almost any successful courtesan that she was remarkably brilliant. Whether entering a grand ballroom or her private box at the opera, she had to shine. Many of the images that have been drawn of her preserve this radiance. Paintings by Titian as well as Veronese and Giorgione, or two centuries later by Boucher and Fragonard, and still later by Manet, have all captured this characteristic luminescence. Not only does the courtesan's hair shine; her eyes are shining, too, and wherever flesh is revealed, whether her breasts, her arms, or legs (or as in Boucher's *L'Odalisque*, her buttocks), her body seems to give off light.

Where her body is not revealed, she is covered with reflective surfaces, adorned with shiny silks and glowing velvet, glittering sequins and beads sewn into the bodice or hem of her dress, a sparkling gem gleaming on her hand or suspended above the intriguingly dark line of her cleavage, lustrous pearls dangling from her ears, a diamond tiara settled on the top of her head, a gold chain circling her ankle. In Nadar's early photographs of Sarah Bernhardt, who, when she was still young and following her mother's plans for her, performed as a courtesan as well as an actress, light ripples over the cloth draped around her bare shoulders. And in almost all the photographic records we have of La Belle Otero, she is dripping in sparkling jewelry.

The courtesan's shine was so bright it appeared to fall on everything around her. The effect was stunningly simulated in the courtesan's drawing room that appears in *La Traviata*, as filmed by Franco Zefferelli; it is suffused with a shimmering light that, reflected off crystal, silver, and as well a seemingly infinite number of mirrored surfaces, bathes the eyes in a warm and exciting brilliance. A similar gleam can be found in the decor of Maxim's, the restaurant made famous by the continual presence of courtesans and their benefactors, where each room is wrapped in necklaces of vibrant mirrors that serve to intensify the incandescence of its patrons.

If the effect of shimmering light is known to inspire desire, perhaps this is because the experience of love often feels filled with light. Accordingly, those who have newly fallen in love are said to glow. Likening this state of mind to the process of crystallization, Stendhal describes a practice in Salzburg in which a tree branch would be thrown into a salt mine and retrieved two or three months later so "covered with sparkling crystallizations" that the original branch was no longer recognizable. In this sense the beloved is not only a source of light; she is also a mirror reflecting back not just her lover's desire but the resplendent beauty of eros altogether.

Eros and Aphrodite came back into fashion during the Renaissance, which was, not coincidentally, the same period during which courtesans rose to prominence. Countless images were painted in this period of Venus, the goddess of love, accompanied by *éclats*—dramatic, rosy bursts of light—surrounding her like aureoles of dawn or misty haloes diffus-

ing into the atmosphere. The men who made these images were the same
great masters who had begun to paint courtesans. Indeed, the likeness of
a courtesan is often preserved in an image of Venus; a figure of Danaë;
as one of the Three Graces; or as Diana or Galatea, for whom she would
have served as a model.

We have pointed out earlier the pragmatic nature of this choice. Unlike a proper lady, a courtesan would have been free to pose without her
clothing, and afterward to let this image of her nude body be publicly
displayed. But the conflation of courtesan and goddess was more than
practical. In this time of transformation, it was through pagan mythol-
ogy that bodily desire was being reclaimed in all its glory.

In the Sala del Maggior Consiglio of the Palazzo Ducale in Venice,
two seemingly contradictory allegories, pagan and Christian, reside side
by side in harmony. On the high ceiling, Veronese has painted Venus as
she assumes her powers, casting and encircled by blazing light. And underneath this image, against the vast wall where the doges sat as they received foreign dignitaries, Tintoretto has painted a flock of saints and
godly Venetian souls floating upward into the soft and luminous light of
heaven. The painters were not from opposing camps. Veronese portrayed his fair share of religious subjects, and though Tintoretto's best
work is religious, he was a friend of Veronica Franco and painted her
portrait as well as his own versions of Venus.

Even so, the reclamation of eros was fraught with conflict. If on the
one hand the Borgia pope, Alexander VI, kept his own courtesan, the famous Vanozza dei Cattaneis (who in turn owned a series of brothels
surrounding the Campo di Fiori in Rome), the painter Raphael rejected
his mistress and model, La Fornarina, on his deathbed and repented the
sin of loving her. In a sense, the courtesan's profession was born of this
ambivalence. Unchaste by definition, she became the unofficial represen-
tative of the pagan world. Yet this did not prevent the representatives of
Christian morality and civic order from chastising her. Forbidden at
times to dress as a lady would dress, she was barred from attending
church during particular hours and even kept from some secular events.

Still, whether seen as divine or luciferous, the light she cast was not dimmed by this ambivalence. It was almost as if she possessed a powerful source of light within her, a light that emanated not from her beauty alone but also from what she knew.

If brilliance is always colored by the metaphorical evocation of light, light in turn is itself a metaphor for knowledge. To shed light on a subject is not only to see it but to understand. It is divine light that brings revelation, a shining light that guides us through dark times, a brilliant mind that can illuminate dark corners of the universe, the light of reason that orders thought.

Certainly, most courtesans had that indefinable light we see in the eyes of many intelligent people. As a group, they were remarkably accomplished. Mogador was both a successful performer and a novelist. Tullia D'Aragona wrote philosophy. Veronica Franco was a poet, Pompadour a respected patron of the arts, Païva an extraordinary businesswoman, Ninon de Lenclos a famous wit. But a courtesan had to have another kind of intelligence, too: an active awareness of what transpires between one person and another during any given moment. She would then be able to read not only French and Italian (and perhaps English, too) but the movements of hands, the slight blush of a cheek, lines around the eyes, a sigh.

We know, of course, that many other women had and still have this skill. But what once made the courtesan exceptional in this regard was that her brilliance was neither concealed nor limited. Rather, she extended her perceptions freely into realms of which proper ladies were supposed to remain ignorant. Imagine the effect then: A man feels a sudden burst of desire, which goes unspoken as if unseen, a source of embarrassment in his own drawing room. But in the presence of the woman he keeps, he is a book which she reads openly and with satisfaction, the knowing look in her eyes filling him with delight.

More and more, we are understanding how critical the need for reflection is to the human psyche. No experience seems complete unless it is witnessed. To have desire as well as feeling recognized and mirrored is itself a desire. This is perhaps one reason why there are so often mirrors in paintings of courtesans. Of course, the mirror was supposed to stand for vanity. But the haunting luminescence of these images suggests far more than the temptations of a minor vice. In one of Titian's greatest paintings, the subject, a beautiful woman, has turned away from the mirror. One senses her lover has surprised her at her toilette, though he is not present in the mirror either. What is reflected back is simply a fragment of light, implying vision itself and the capacity for perception. To be seen by another, especially a lover, is literally enlightening.

The power of the experience is evident in another painting by Titian, too, in which he depicts Venus turned toward a mirror but startled, her hand at her breast, not in modesty but touching her heart, as if she were temporarily shaken by her own image. But of course we are all shaken by what she sees in the mirror, which is after all, since she is the goddess of love, the knowledge of sexual passion.

Carnal Knowledge

. . . if Socrates was so wise and virtuous why don't you make a practice of imitating him? For as you know he discussed everything with his friend Diatoma and learned all manner of wonderful things, especially concerning the mysteries of love.—Tullia D'Aragona, Dialogue on the Infinity of Love

Although it is clear that the courtesan would need to have carnal knowledge, what has not always been so evident is the profound nature of what she knew. The realm of sexual pleasure is also the realm of the psyche. To love or be loved, to touch, be touched, feel pleasure, passion, ecstasy, to surrender and release engages every human faculty, not sensual adroitness alone but intelligence of every kind. As well as being willing to give pleasure, a good lover must be sensitive and aware, registering what kind of touch, for instance, on which part of the body arouses desire, knowing which mood calls for a robust approach, which moment requires gentleness, able to laugh or tease while at the same time probing both the mind and body of the loved one for gateways to greater feeling.

The desire to give pleasure is, however, not the only motive. The deepest ardor of the lover is the desire to know the beloved: to test, feel, see, taste, smell, witness every response, every shade of sensation. In this sense, it is right that Venus as well as courtesans should so often be depicted with mirrors. In recognizing even the subtlest desires of the beloved or in answering these desires with a delicate precision, the lover is providing a mirror for what the beloved feels. The beloved feels known, even ravished, by this intense reflection. And, in turn, the one who is loved feels an echoing need to know, because being a lover as well as the beloved, the desire is to please by knowledge, even know all that can be known at once.

The urge to consume knowledge can be consuming in itself. Though in an afternoon of lovemaking desire may arc and come to fruition, the desire to know is inexhaustible. The wish is for an impossible thoroughness, a complete union between the knower and the known. Yet as Tullia D'Aragona, an Italian courtesan born at the beginning of the sixteenth century, has written, "...Because it is not possible for human bodies to be physically merged into one another, the lover can never achieve this longing."

Respected as an exceptional woman, in 1547 Aragona was cleared of a charge of breaking the sumptuary laws of Florence where, in the mid-sixteenth century, courtesans were required to wear yellow cloaks. It was because she was a poet that the charges were dismissed. As if to prove that her acquittal was just, her *Dialogue on the Infinity of Love* was published later that year, though the substance of her philosophy argues that eros makes everyone exceptional. "Lovers," she says, "entertain both hope and fear. Simultaneously they feel both great heat and excessive cold. They want and reject in equal measure, constantly grasping at things but retaining nothing in their grip. They can see without eyes. They have no ears but can hear. They shout without a tongue. They fly without moving. They are alive while dying."

Erotic desire and pleasure both have the effect of unshackling (or, from another point of view, unhinging) the mind. Received ideas of reality, prejudices, caution, even the restraints of reason, seem to wither, if not vanish, in the presence of the mysteries of love. That a courtesan such as Tullia D'Aragona, who was well trained by her mother, also once a courtesan herself, used beauty, timing, and many other skills to inspire love was thus used by her enemies as a criticism. Thomas Coryat warned British men who traveled to Italy in the sixteenth century that under the influence of a courtesan, they would be liable to temporary insanity.

Coryat's warning had little effect. Perhaps this is because, though the desire would not have been entirely conscious, madness of this kind was exactly what certain men wanted. They were seeing not just physical thrills but mental thrills as well, to go underneath conventional wisdom and reverse the established order of their days, an order which, though comfortable, could also be suffocating.

A certain shine in the eyes of a courtesan would offer a reprieve. That her business was the realm of unreason, folly, foible, indulgence, wild desire, delirium, and disorder was apparent in her expression. Yet the same gaze promised that she would be a trustworthy guide. She was not ignorant of convention. Her knowledge of the deeper order of flesh was mixed with a canny comprehension of the social order. She knew how to read both matter and form; she mixed the understanding of many complex histories artfully with wantonness; those seductive eyes were educated, her misbehavior cultivated.

In this light, it is not surprising that by the mid-sixteenth century, Venice, a city which made its fortune from sophisticated indulgences, should become renowned for its courtesans. These brilliant women were part of a shining panoply of goods, splendid silks, rich velvets, vibrant gems, sharp and intriguing spices shipped from the East, which together with the translucent beauty of the glass blown on the Venetian island of Murano, and the gold leaf in abundant supply that adorned not only St. Mark's but so many private palazzos (covering the entire facade of the Cà' d'Oro, for instance), dazzled the senses. After the visitor gliding in a gondola down the Grand Canal caught sight of the faintly flirtatious image of a palazzo gleaming like buried treasure in the water as he traveled toward St. Mark's Square, the beauty meeting his eyes would seem to multiply beyond any proportions his mind could hold. The cascade of luxurious sights, smells, and sensations that greeted the senses everywhere was almost overwhelming. Strangers encountering Venice, according to one early English writer, would often be "striken with so great an admiration and amazement, that they woulde, and that with open mouthe, confesse, never any thing which before time they had seene, to be thereunto comparable."

But to gauge the entire effect of a visit to Venice during the Renaissance, two other essential ingredients should be included. Mixed inextricably with the luxury of the Ducal Palace, the glorious churches, and all the private palazzos belonging to the great families of Venice was the great art being produced then. Extraordinary figures newly rendered in thread, laid in mosaic and tile, or painted as frescoes by Carpaccio, Giorgione, Palma Vecchio, Veronese, Titian, and Tintoretto embellished ceilings and staircases, entryways and the walls of great rooms. No less impressive to most visitors in that period were the illustrious courtesans of Venice, some so splendid that they must have seemed, like the goddess who looked after the city, as if they had just risen from the sea that shone so seductively at every edge.

It has been said more than once that Venice itself was like a courtesan. Whenever anyone came to the city with whom the Venetians wanted to gain favor, they would supply him with every possible luxury. The visit of the French king, Henri III, provided a chance for exceptional largesse. Isolated by an estrangement from Spain, the doges hoped for the friendship of France. Hence, Henri was wooed with the best of everything the city had to offer. He was brought to the city in a ship rowed by four hundred oarsmen and escorted by fourteen galleys. Then, as his ship crossed the lagoon, it was met by a raft on which, using a furnace shaped like a marine monster whose jaws and nostrils belched flame, glassblowers blew objects that they felt would amuse the king.

Soon another armada joined his ship, decorated in opulent tapestries, adorned with figures of dolphins and gods of the sea. Entering the city, he passed through an arch designed especially for the occasion by Palladio, which Titian and Veronese had embellished with painted figures. The Cà' Foscari on the Grand Canal had been prepared lavishly, his bed sheets embroidered in crimson silk. For the banquet held in the Great Council Chamber inside the Doges' Palace, the sumptuary laws, which ordinarily pressed restraint on the city's ladies and courtesans, were temporarily suspended, so that the women present wore their most extraordinary jewels and pearls, not only around their necks but in their hair and beaded over their cloaks. The meal, served on silver plates, consisted of twelve hundred items, including a serving of bonbons from which there were three hundred different varieties to choose. After viewing the opera written for his visit, Henri was asked to witness the launching of a galley constructed for his benefit during the time that dinner had been consumed. And all this was followed by several other days of splendid sights and pleasures. He visited the aging Titian, posed for a portrait by Tintoretto. And finally he was presented with a heavy book: the *Catalogue of the Chief and Most Renowned Courtesans of Venice*, featuring 210 miniature portraits from which he was asked to choose whom he would like to visit. According to those who witnessed the process, he perused the catalogue intently. After some time, he decided on the courtesan who was at that time the most favored in Venice: Veronica Franco.

We know little of what transpired on the night of their meeting, except that the king must have been pleased. He took a miniature of Franco away with him. And he offered to help her with the coming publication of one of her books. In response, as well as dedicating the book to him and writing sonnets about him, she expressed her gratitude in a letter that overflows with praise for the monarch's "serene splendor."

She was well familiar with splendor; her own was legendary. Her exceptional intelligence alone must have been dazzling. Not only was she bright but she was also educated, an accomplishment rare among the women of her time, when out of any given hundred women in the city, fewer than ten knew how to read, and of these, less than four had received any public schooling. Franco was born to a family of *cittadini originari*, a respected, usually professional class of native-born citizens. In such a family, only the sons would have received an education. But as a girl, Veronica had been allowed to attend the lessons given to her three brothers by their private tutors. Why an exception was made in her case is not known. Perhaps her mother, Paola, who, not unusually among *cittadini* families that experienced financial distress, was a courtesan, believed that her daughter should be properly prepared for this role. Veronica would have no great inheritance to sustain her should the need arise. But if she were to become an honored courtesan instead of a prostitute, she would have to be cultivated.

In hindsight, however, it is easy to see that Franco valued education for other reasons, too. The sheer joy of learning, the love of poetry, the desire to understand, delineate, see beneath the surface were passions which drove her throughout her life. When she reached her sixteenth year, she entered into a marriage that her mother had arranged for her with a doctor named Paolo Panizza. This is virtually all we know about the man, except that since one of several wills she executed over the years requests that her beneficiaries retrieve her dowry from him, we can theorize that he might have been unusually abusive in some way.

Much of what we do know about her life comes either from these wills or from her letters. Elegant, by turns philosophical and decorous, not only do the letters she wrote reveal a shining intelligence but they also make clear how much she took part in the intellectual life of the city. A world closed to most women had opened to Franco when she became a courtesan.

For a short period after her marriage, both mother and daughter were registered with the city. The record shows that they lived together in the parish of Santa Maria Formosa. Neither charged very much for her services. Paola was aging and Veronica was inexperienced. But all that was to change rapidly. Veronica quickly became one of the most sought-after women in her trade. It was in this role, as companion to scholars,

artists, and writers, that she was able to enlarge her education even further. She became a favorite of Domenico Venier, once a protector of
Tullia D'Aragona, and a member of a great Venetian family who supplied more than one doge to Venice. Domenico, who himself had been
a senator, encouraged Veronica, read her poetry, and, equally important,
included her among his regular guests at the salon which was held in his
private palazzo, the Cà' Venier. It must have been through this circle that
she was afforded a brief meeting with the brilliant French essayist Montaigne while he was visiting Venice.

Montaigne knew well that intelligence flourishes from intellectual in-
tercourse. In a famous essay he tells the reader: "To my taste, the most
fruitful and most natural exercise of our mind is conversation." Not
only does discussion provide validation, it also supplies a mirror with
which ideas can be clarified. Even from disagreement, which Montaigne claimed to value, the mind will be illuminated, as sharper edges
are drawn.

And in between accord and discord, there is another space, inhabited
by friends and colleagues, a territory filled with sparks and resonances,
which support and augment any process of creation. As gradually during her mid-twenties Franco became known for her poetry and for the
many anthologies that she compiled, she became a valued participant in
the literary and artistic world of Venice. From her letters, we know that
in this period she was also hosting gatherings of intellectuals and artists
in her own home.

Tintoretto was most probably among the artists who attended these
gatherings. Some scholars of the period believe that the painter and the
courtesan were friends. The thought itself ignites the imagination. Moving back and forth from her poetry to his paintings, one finds an unpredictable but compelling affinity. Besides Franco, Tintoretto painted a
few other courtesans. In one of these, the subject is rendered with beautifully soft degrees of brown. The color, steadfast in her eye, blushes in
the background, rises toward red on her lips, gathers in a filmy tan in the
translucent shawl around her shoulders, shines with a pink luster in the

pearls around her neck, glows with creamy whiteness, rounded by chestnut shadows on her breasts, which she exposes. But though Tintoretto
had a talent for such portraits, clearly he spent his greatest ardor on religious paintings. Indeed, *La Lavande dei Pieti* hangs today in San Moise,
where Franco worshipped later in her life. Certainly the worlds they inhabited converged in casual ways. But where then would the deeper con-
cordance between a religious painter and this poet courtesan be found?

The answer, of course, is in the shine. In every sense of the word,
light is the real subject of Tintoretto's *Paradise*, the great fresco where en-
lightened bodies, free of gravity, rise toward an enveloping incandescence. His painting *The Last Supper*, in the chancel of San Giorgio
Maggiore, presents a drama of light, radiating from the head of Jesus
with such a forceful intensity that it appears to have captured all the
apostles in its path as it splinters the atmosphere of the room. That the
painter was interested in the physical properties of light is undeniable.
The subtlety with which he depicts the phenomenon in all its variations
is impressive. But for Tintoretto, light is both real and symbolic. He has
added a second source of light to the scene, an oil lamp, which, less intense, still burns with a fascinating ferocity of its own, and this light is
surrounded by a choir of angels, as if swimming in the element but also
made visible and even conjured by it.

Though Tintoretto is the true conjuror, simulating light to make visible what, by lesser hands, is seldom depicted—the mystical states that
are experienced by those struck with religious awe. It is this emotion that
seems to fascinate him most and he shows it by showing what the devout
see—a world energized by luminosity.

We find a similar bedazzlement in the poetry of Veronica Franco.
Her subject was, of course, more worldly. But though in some circles
even today sacred and profane love are opposed, the Renaissance was
waking to a certain rapport between the two. What is portrayed in Titian's famous painting *Sacred and Profane Love* is not conflict but harmony.
Together, the writers and artists from this period were reclaiming the
conjoined mysteries of eros.

This was Veronica Franco's subject, what she calls, in one poem, "the supernatural miracles of love." Like Tintoretto, she was drawn to inner states. She explores the awe which lovers feel, an emotion not dissimilar to religious awe. Indeed, she compares Henri III to a god:

> As from heaven down to a humble roof
> Beneficent Jove descends to us here below

Since this king had ascended both the thrones of Poland and France by divine right, the comparison seems especially appropriate. But the practice of depicting lovers as gods was common to an age eager to explore the divinity not only of love but of erotic pleasure. The amorous descent of Jove was often chosen as a subject by painters, among them Correggio and Titian. In these paintings, following the ancient myth, Jove enters the chamber of Danaë as a cloud that empties a golden shower on her. Thus are both semen and sexual pleasure shown as sacramental, the gold here, no less than in the Basilica of St. Mark's, a sign of spiritual illumination.

Franco portrays the king's amatory prowess similarly, but with a more diplomatic delicacy. "He shone such a ray of divine virtue," she writes, coupling luminosity with potency, "that my innate strength completely failed me." Light is everywhere in her poetry. Here, another lover is like a burning sun, there a light more beautiful than the sun. Her own passion is a spark ignited. She herself shines: in fact, the "bodily eye can scarcely bear the splendor of her brow." And also like Tintoretto, the real source of illumination in her work is inward. When she writes that "like snow in the sun you vanished in tears," it is the inner experience of love she is tracking, what we would call today the psychology of eros.

Yet inward as her landscape is, she does not diminish the visceral reality of love. It is her lover's "golden shaft" that penetrates her heart. A viscerality not foreign to the painter, who no matter how mystical his theme, was stunningly accurate as he rendered the turn of a shoulder, the lowering of a head, the raising of eyes, hands frozen in a gesture of wonder. The same devotion to material existence can be seen in the portrait he painted of Franco, her lips redolent with feeling, the lace around her shoulders exquisitely detailed, her reddish hair capturing bits of glistening light in delicate curls, even her beautiful eyelids, brows, finely rendered, her eyes casting an intelligent gaze that, like the painting itself, seems to regard both inner and outer worlds at the same time.

But she herself says this best in the letter she wrote thanking Tintoretto for his portrait: "You concentrate entirely on methods of imitating—no, rather of outdoing—nature, not only in what can be imitated by modeling the human figure, nude or clothed, adding color, shading, contour, features, muscles movements, actions, postures . . . but by expressing emotional states as well."

And this, too, should be added to the background of their friendship. They had both risen to prominence by the same path. A century earlier, when the shared imagination was still turned away from the material world, painters, whose works were often anonymous, were considered no better than craftsmen, and courtesans were hidden. But now that the tenor of the times had changed, the brilliance that each brought to earthly existence made both of them famous. The qualities Franco shared with the artist, a careful attention to the fine points of carnality, a sensitivity to emotional life, the intelligence with which she probed feeling, an attraction to mystical experience, explain why she was not only an honored courtesan but the most honored of her time in a city renowned for this profession. Certainly, mere mechanical pleasures could be found for far less money. The desire she met was instead for the larger dimensionality of pleasure, the spirit within experience. Like Tintoretto, she rendered both the moment and a mirror of the moment.

Imagine, then, the quality of a caress as profound in its own way as any great work of art. It is not just the effect of her touch but of her eyes, too. All your responses, including the ones you are used to hiding from others and at times even from yourself, would be reflected in this regard. Perhaps she notices a slight movement as desire moves into your hand. Thus, knowing that she is your witness, your body quickens as she strokes your fingers. And when, smiling, she sees this, too, the feeling is suddenly so intense that you have the sensation of swimming in the candlelight that shimmers over her body. And now, beyond whatever she knows of you, revelation itself charges the atmosphere. As you take her, you are taken into a mythic realm, as if you yourself had become a god, your body a source of insight now, more alive than you thought possible, though this was all along what you desired. It was what you wanted to know.

Wit

Her contradictions preserve urbanity.—*Louis XIV, speaking of Ninon de Lenclos*

In the realm of intelligence, wit occupies a narrow but nonetheless very effective position. Sometimes kind, it is at other times malicious. At once sly and straightforward, subtle and pointed, polite and rude, sensitive and brazen, it exists on a razor's edge between heretical insight and what is acknowledged to be true. No wonder then that Oscar Wilde, famous for residing between one sex and the other, was a master of an art which, if only temporarily, allows manners and boundaries of all kinds to be transgressed with grace, and while revealing the hypocrisies of the established order, makes those who might otherwise be shocked laugh.

Like the laughter it causes, wit rises; it lightens the mood. Yet it is also true that in order to be witty, one must already have risen, at least to a point sufficiently above the fray to see the humor in the human foibles that lie beneath. As Cupid does, when the witty inflict small wounds to every form of complacency, exciting levity along with love, they send their arrows from aloft. The perspective was indispensable to courtesans, who, living just outside propriety, were at the same time intimate with the most respected members of society.

Ninon de Lenclos was famous for having wit in a witty time. One of the greatest courtesans of any period, she was born in 1620 to a family which belonged to the often impoverished and usually obscure lesser nobility of France. When she was fifteen years old, her father, forced into exile, abandoned Ninon and her mother. Hence, after the death of her mother a few years later, Ninon was left nearly penniless. There were no prospects for marriage, and in any case, from her father she had inherited a distinct lack of enthusiasm for the institution. Thus it was that she decided to take up one of the few professions open to her. She was well equipped for the work. Though she was beautiful, it was her intelligence that made her exceptionally attractive. Not only was she bright, she was unusually well educated for a woman of her time. Her father had given her lessons in philosophy, mathematics, Italian, and Spanish. As a girl, she loved books and read widely, including the work of Descartes. She had even managed to attend one play by Corneille. Highly perceptive even as a child, by the time she reached maturity she had developed a sophisticated sense of humor. All of which, in the early days of the period known as the Enlightenment, made her very popular. As the playwright Paul Scarron was to write of her:

> *Oh beautiful, charming Ninon,*
> *whose wishes no one can decline*
> *so great being the power of one*
> *with both beauty and wit.*

She soon found herself at the center of Parisian society, where she remained throughout her long life. She was admired by the young Voltaire; hosted a famous salon at which Molière first read the manuscript of his new play, *Tartuffe*; and became the lover of countless illustrious men, including two members of the royal family, the duc d'Enghien, eldest son of the Condé branch of the Bourbons, and the duc de Vendôme, natural son of Henri IV, also a prince of the blood.

Some examples of her extraordinary wit are still with us today. It was she, for instance, who said, "We should never speak ill of our enemies.

They are the only people who do not deceive us." She is also famous for having said, "My mother was a good woman with no sensory feeling. She procreated three children, scarcely noticing it." As amusing as these comments are, they give us some insight into the painful circumstances of her childhood, which no doubt contributed, as trials and tribulations often do, to the development of her genius.

Her mother and father's marriage was not made in heaven. It was rather a marriage of convenience made between a man and woman who were, as it turned out, incompatible. Henri, her father, was a freethinker—skeptical, irreligious, worldly; a man of lusty appetites, who loved learning, bawdy talk, music, carousing, all of which his wife, Marie-Barbe de la Marche, timid, devout, and unworldly, disapproved. Ninon, the last child of this unfortunate union, was caught in the middle, the manner of her upbringing a battleground between two parents, both of whom she loved deeply. While her father brought her to the Palais d'Orléans to see a painting by Rubens, introduced her to works by authors such as the skeptical priest Charon, and taught her to play the lute, an instrument considered too licentious for a proper young lady, her mother, taking the opposite tack, made her read sacred books, ordered her to cover her beautiful hair in a scarf, and forced her into dresses made from muted, dark fabrics, the bodices cut so that they would flatten her breasts.

Though she preferred her father's way of life, ultimately choosing to live in a world more like his, when she learned of her father's infidelity, she felt fiercely protective of her mother. Moreover, Henri's affair with a woman who was also married finally led to a violent episode for which, because he had murdered a man, he was forced to leave Paris. Ninon remained by her mother's side, attempting to fill her father's shoes. Though she continued on her own to pursue the liberal education her father had introduced, she did not defy her mother's attempts to raise her as a pious woman, but instead dutifully attended Mass with her (albeit diverting her attention to the beautiful and sumptuous gowns that so many women who lived in the fashionable neighborhood of the Place

Royale wore to services). Somehow, throughout all the tortuous turns of the ill-conceived marriage between her parents, Ninon managed to remain a loving and loyal daughter to both of them. This was a great accomplishment in itself, and more significantly to this history, one that would have required that she be able to extricate herself constantly from battle.

To survive in the atmosphere of hostility that existed for such a prolonged period between the two people she loved most in the world, she would have had to cultivate a certain distance from the passionate recriminations they aimed at each other, as well as from the extremities of passion itself. From this perspective, it is easy to understand how the daughter of a woman betrayed by her husband, a man so in love with his mistress that he risked his own life and took the life of another, would have a jaundiced perspective on the delirium of love. And we can easily see, too, why, given her mother's blind devotion, she would have remained aloof from religious passion. Even the heated political controversies of the period left her unshaken; though sharply discerning, she stayed calmly outside the fires. The fruit of this distance, of course, was the illuminating accuracy of her celebrated wit.

In an age that valued wit highly, the gift was especially advantageous. Not only were the men and women who possessed it considered more attractive, they were also more esteemed, even rising in rank because of it. Louis XIV, called the Sun King, who was born when Ninon was eighteen years of age, was known to favor wit. "You know," he confided to his brother's wife, "I like clever, amusing people." Were he not destined to rule, he probably would have married the niece of the man who had been his regent, the late Cardinal Mazarin. Marie Mancini was known to be very intelligent. But using marriage to consolidate the power of his kingdom, he chose Marie-Thérèse, the not very attractive and somewhat dull Spanish infanta, instead.

Pleased with her submissiveness, he made up for her shortcomings with his mistresses. The beautiful Louise de la Vallière was a lady-in-waiting to his sister-in-law, Henriette, with whom he carried on a scandalous flirtation. He got to know her only after Henriette suggested that, to cover their affair, he pretend to be courting Louise. The pretense soon became reality. He had her declared the royal titular mistress, a custom started by an earlier king, Charles VII, who in the fifteenth century had declared Agnès Sorel his *maîtresse en titre*. But after a while the dewy-eyed and rather elusive ways that once enchanted him lost their charm. Bored again, he turned to Louise's best friend, a woman who often accompanied her at court, the marquise de Montespan. Françoise-Athénaïs, daughter of the marquis de Mortemart, was one of four siblings treasured for their social brilliance. They were fond of laughing and had the gift of inspiring mirth in others. As Nancy Mitford writes, "Their lazy, languishing, wailing voices would bring up an episode, piling unexpected exaggerations upon comic images until the listeners were helpless with laughter." Montespan was, in short, very entertaining.

Amusement was just what the king needed. Though Louis ruled absolutely, his reign was filled with trouble. The conditions of the period in France were not unlike those that Ninon faced in her discordant family life. The realm was divided not only between Protestants and Catholics but also between Jansenists and Jesuits, the Church jostling with the state for power, the rise of secular philosophies that implicitly questioned an order based on divine right; even the royal desire for pleasure was daily pitted against religious values. The only respite was laughter.

In the end, religious drama could not be kept from Louis' court. Though witty and intelligent herself, his last mistress did her best to save him from sin. Following the pattern of his earlier conquests, Louis had met Françoise de Scarron through the marquise de Montespan. Together, both mistresses were prized as being among the liveliest members of court society. Before she became Louis' mistress, Madame Scarron was married to a freethinking and very secular playwright, Paul Scarron, a close friend of Ninon. Often together at the gatherings of writers and philosophers that took place at Scarron's apartment, the two women became good friends. When Françoise was left penniless after Scarron's death, Ninon provided shelter for her in her own apartment. Indeed, because they shared a bed for several months, the rumor was that they had become lovers. But Ninon continued her profession, and in time, saying that she wanted to distance herself from such licentious behavior, Madame Scarron left Ninon's lodgings.

Indeed, in later years Scarron liked to describe her own behavior as above reproach. Her piety only became more exaggerated with time. As she grew closer to the monarch, gradually replacing Montespan, she did her best to convince the king that since Montespan was married, his affair with her was doubly adulterous and hence doubly immoral. Soon Scarron was made the marquise de Maintenon with her own estate, and after a scandal involving poison, Montespan retreated. Then, the queen died. And finally the marquise was free to tell the king that she did not want to live in a state of sin herself. Thus eventually, as most scholars agree, devotion won the day. In a marriage that took place covertly in the alcove of his bedroom, the king's last favorite became his secret wife.

From the distance of time, one might be led to believe that Maintenon's religious scruples were suspiciously self-serving. But even if this were so, it could not have been the whole story. After she married Louis, her zeal only increased. If her growing fanaticism troubled many, none were more affected by this conversion than the hapless students of Saint-Cyr, the school for girls that she had started with Louis' help. In the beginning, this academy was meant to give the daughters of the lesser nobility an education. They were to be prepared with the skills necessary to enter society—cultivation in the arts, including literature and needlepoint—the manners expected at court. The marquise even commissioned Racine to write a play for the girls to perform.

It was the memory of her own circumstances that led her to establish the school. When, as a young woman, Françoise was brought, badly dressed and hardly tutored, to a soirée at Scarron's apartments, she was so aware of her deficiencies that she was reduced to tears by the embarrassment. But Scarron, who was a kind man, took a liking to her. And when he learned that having no means she was to be sent to a nunnery and thus was in despair, he offered to marry her. He was neither physically attractive nor capable of consummating a marriage. Afflicted by illness, unable to walk unaided, he was described by everyone including himself as being shaped like the letter "Z." Yet he fed and clothed her, and just as important, gave her an informal education and an entrance into Parisian society. A scintillating presence, she proved a gracious hostess at Scarron's gatherings and was soon sought and admired by Parisian society in her own right.

Though she never regretted her marriage to Scarron, it was her painful awareness of the terrible choices women were forced to make that had inspired her to establish the school at Saint-Cyr. Yet, reflecting the temper of the times, the conflict shadowed everything she did. Though the school had been established so that girls would not be forced into nunneries, when Françoise saw her students becoming worldly, attracting the attention of the young men of the court, she made the school into a convent. If they wished to stay, the students, most of whom had spent many years at Saint-Cyr and therefore had no other place to go, were forced to take perpetual vows.

It is not hard to imagine what they must have felt. They were by now sophisticated, well read, *au courant* with the latest trends; they had learned to converse eloquently, to argue reasonably. They were habituated to an elegantly sensual life, and through a constant stream of celebrated visitors, for years they had been at the center of a very worldly society. Now all that was to vanish, replaced with the harsh deprivations of their new vows of poverty and the dead silence of the cloister.

Though they were both engaged in the struggle between secular and religious values, the marquise de Maintenon and Ninon de Lenclos eventually landed on different sides of the conflict. Yet they remained friends. It was through her friendship with the former Madame Scarron that Ninon had her only meeting with the king. Hoping Maintenon's influence could win an appointment for a friend, Ninon wrote asking for help. When Françoise brought the matter up to Louis, he said that he had always wanted to meet Ninon and suggested that Françoise arrange a meeting at Versailles. He had heard stories of the famous courtesan since he was a child, and now as her fame had grown, her witticisms and opinions were repeated all over Paris. It is said that whenever the king could not reach a decision about an important matter, he would ask his ministers, many of whom were familiar with the courtesan, "What does Ninon think?"

According to Athénaïs Montespan's journals, Louis hid in a closet in Maintenon's rooms while the two women met. After expressing her dislike of the strictness of court manners, Ninon tried to persuade her old friend to return to Paris, where she promised she would be surrounded "by those delicate and sinuous minds that used to applaud your agreeable stories, your brilliant conversation." When Louis finally came out of his hiding place, he bantered with Lenclos, accusing her in jest of trying to deprive him of his lover. Knowing Maintenon would not be tempted to leave him, he was hardly threatened. Later he said that he liked Ninon's intelligent frankness.

She *was* telling the truth. Though many prominent women envied Maintenon's position at court, for Ninon the sacrifice of "brilliant conversation" would have been too great. From her childhood, Ninon loved learning, books, discourse. Nor would she have been happy to be at the beck and call of the king. Early on, she rejected the passive role women were more often than not required to play. When she was eleven years old, she wrote her father a letter which announced: "I inform you now that I have decided to be a girl no longer, but to become a boy." Thus she requested that he give her "the education needed for my new sex."

Her father, who was clearly charmed by the note, had his tailor make her a doublet and breeches of pale blue velvet, a short riding coat of burgundy velvet, and commissioned a *cordonnier* to make her a pair of riding boots as well as a *chappellerie*, on the Place Royale, to fashion her a beaver hat with one red plume. Dressed appropriately, she learned to ride and fence. Soon becoming the darling of the guardsmen, she quickly picked up the rough slang spoken in the stables, the mastery of which, given the mysterious power language has over the mind, doubtless made her feel as entitled as any of her other accomplishments.

When, many years later, she decided to meet one of her lovers on the battlefield, it must have felt familiar to her to travel dressed as a man, a sword at her side. She was to repeat her vow not to be fettered by the limitations society placed on the members of her sex many times in her life. To one of her lovers, Boisrobert, she wrote: "Men enjoy a thousand privileges which women never have. From this moment, I have become a man." True to her vow, she was reputed by many, including Voltaire, to pray each morning: "God please make me an honest man but never an honest woman."

By the account of "Madame," the wife of the king's brother, who wrote extensive letters (deemed now almost as interesting as the letters of Madame de Sévigné), those who knew Ninon generally agreed that there was "no more honest man to be found than she." And though in one way the achievement is extraordinary for one who has not been born a man, in another sense the integrity and authority of her behavior, including what she said and the brilliant way she said it, would have been fostered by the very fact that she straddled the boundaries between the two sexes.

Wit is an androgynous art. A certain humorous distance from the protocol is required and nurtured by the refusal to obey it. Cross-dressing reveals the absurdity of strict dress codes. Behaving outside the proscriptions of gender makes the comedy of such manners apparent. Moreover, to exist on the edge of disapproval hones the sharpness of observation essential for wit. And that also requires a delicate sense of balance, part of the diplomacy that is the soul of wit—a form of humor that, to be practiced safely, is close to but not beyond the point of outrage. The witty can say exactly what is forbidden and get away with it.

And there is this, too. No less a brilliant conversationalist than La Rochefoucauld, famous for his *Maxims*, said that he preferred the conversation of intelligent women over that of men. "There is a certain suavity in their talk which is lacking in our sex," he said. Putting together the finesse that many women are encouraged to develop with the intelligence fostered in men, we would have an excellent recipe for wit.

In essence all courtesans, no matter how rouged and bejeweled they were, had to have the virtues of both men and women. By turns independent, tough, assertive, courageous, and bold, they were also sensuous. They were not only emotionally aware, but also privy to many intimate secrets, sophisticated in the ways of the heart; and though not always so, at certain crucial moments they could be patient, nurturing, and sensitive. Rather than labor to fit themselves into the constricted roles played by either sex, they censored none of their abilities, developing qualities called masculine or feminine in a complex mix that had to be especially attractive to those bound by social convention.

Yet we should be careful not to deceive ourselves in this regard. Courtesans were by no means entirely free of the strictures that define sexuality. If the terrain at the fringe of acceptability was exciting, it could also be dangerous. As admired, for instance, as Ninon de Lenclos was by many powerful men, even she had her enemies. At the height of her popularity, the Compagnie Générale du Saint-Sacrament petitioned the queen, Anne of Austria, to punish her for ridiculing marriage, as well as for suggesting that women should have the same rights as men. Ninon was confined to a convent in Paris. And when it looked as if Ninon's champions might try to rescue her, she was sent to another convent further off in the countryside. Nevertheless, even outside the city walls, she had a steady stream of visitors. And she was not to be confined for long. After visiting her there, Queen Christina of Sweden obtained her release by writing to Mazarin that by Ninon's absence, "the court lacked its greatest ornament."

This brief imprisonment was the exception in a life that was, for this period, exceptionally unbounded. During the greater part of her existence, Ninon negotiated her freedom with extraordinary success, and in this wit was one of her best instruments. Her diplomatic triumphs in the battle of distinctions between men and women are illustrated by two remarks that have survived their creator by over three centuries. When her friend Boisrobert protested that the talk among a group of men visiting Ninon had become inappropriate for the presence of a lady, she replied that she was too much of a gentleman to mind. She made another famous remark when a lover, called Tambonneau, wished to have his wife hear Ninon play the lute, which he felt she did beautifully. Afraid of exposing his wife to a courtesan, he proposed a solution to the dilemma. Why not hang a tapestry in front of his wife, behind which Ninon, concealed from view, would play, he suggested. On hearing this idea Ninon responded, "Which do you think will give her greater immunity, a Flemish or a Gobelins tapestry?"

Of course, the veil of laughter that protected Ninon was in the end a far less foolish device. Depending on the angle of your vision, it could be considered opaque, translucent, or reflective, but it was always brilliant.

Housekeeping

I am a marvelous housekeeper. Every time I leave a man I keep his house.—Zsa Zsa Gabor

This catalogue would be remiss and certainly unrealistic if still another aspect of the brilliance of courtesans were not mentioned here, and that is the way they handled money. As is true of all the virtues, some were better endowed with this skill than others. But most enjoyed a financial independence that had eluded women of every class until well into the twentieth century. The wealth they acquired did not come to them automatically. Like any successful businessman or -woman, a courtesan had to be able to understand the value of what she offered, to read the climate of the market, to be self-reliant, trusting her own sense of how to proceed; and as with talented investors, have the courage to take certain educated risks in order to realize a larger gain.

The extraordinary story of La Belle Otero affords an example of a brilliant rise from rags to riches. Brutally raped at the age of eleven, after surgery and several months in the hospital, she said good-bye to her mother and left the small village of Valga in Spain at the age of twelve with only a few pesetas in her possession. For two years she wandered in search of handouts, from one man to another, exchanging sex for a place to sleep and something to eat. Eventually, she met a Catalán called Paco who taught her to dance and sing. Acting as her manager and partner, he performed with her in a string of small, sometimes sleazy nightclubs. Like many women who worked in the theatre, she supplemented their small earnings by sleeping with men from the audience who would appear at the stage door after their performances. The possibility of ending this way of life presented itself when Paco, already her lover, wanted her to quit every other liaison and marry him. But she refused. No doubt she did not want to repeat the destitution of her childhood. And from the occasional generosity of the men who followed her off the stage, she had a growing sense of what was possible. She recognized the arrival of this possibility when an American impresario saw her in Marseille and, falling in love with her, asked her to perform at the prominent club he managed in New York.

Just a few years later, having made a fortune from a series of eminent protectors, she owned a beautiful home designed for her by the architect Adolphe Vieil, in the fashionable neighborhood of the Parc Monceau in Paris. Her rooms were filled with luxurious possessions, fine furniture, a wardrobe the envy of royalty, and a collection of jewelry that at the turn of the century was worth 2 to 3 million francs.

She was not as good, however, at keeping her money as she was at acquiring it. A serious vice occluded her financial genius, one that we might describe as the shadow side of her talent at making money: She loved to gamble. Over the many years of her professional life, she made regular and frequent trips to Monte Carlo. When she was young, if she lost more than she won, her income could absorb the deficit. But as she aged and her income began to wane, this vice took its inevitable toll. Perhaps it was a mistake for Otero to retire to Nice, so close to the gaming tables at Monte Carlo. In a short time, she had lost her comfortable villa. But her ending was not as miserable as it might have been. The legend is that when once again, in the last years of her life, having pawned all her jewelry, she was destitute, the casinos where she had gambled and lost most of her money gave her a modest pension, which kept her housed and fed until she died.

Despite Otero's example, many courtesans were very good at financial planning. More than a few were able to end their days on this earth in the style to which they had become accustomed. Some, like Marguerite Bellanger, once the lover of Napoléon III, saved and invested their earnings carefully; some such as the comtesse de Loynes, married well. Others, like Païva, did both. Some were set up in millinery shops by their protectors. Still others relied on the generosity of younger courtesans, for whom they arranged liaisons. And from the fifteenth century through the twentieth, another way existed for a courtesan to face old age with dignity. Like any profession, the art was handed down. If she were fortunate enough to have a daughter, a courtesan could train her in all the necessary skills and thus ensure a means of support in her old age.

If in respect of motherly love this tradition seems wanting, one must remember that, under the weight of the restricted and difficult circumstances that women endured in this period, much of what any mother bequeathed to her daughter was of mixed value. Nevertheless, even if being a courtesan was considered by some as preferable to marriage, there were mothers who did try to avoid passing on their profession.

In fifteenth-century Rome, the famous courtesan named Imperia took care that neither of her daughters would be forced to take up the profession at which she excelled so brilliantly. She had been trained in the art by her mother. Diana Cognati was not notable among courtesans, and probably for this reason Imperia began to supplement her mother's income when she was very young. She gave birth to her own first daughter, Lucrezia, when she was barely seventeen years old. (Who the father of this child was is lost to history now.) Then in the year that Imperia turned eighteen, her mother's undistinguished career came to an end when she married Paolo Trotti, a member of the Sistine Choir. After this union was sanctified, while Imperia's reputation and income grew, Trotti managed her business affairs, investing in property whose ownership was in his name.

But soon Imperia grew to distrust her mother and stepfather. Having gained worldly wisdom of more than one kind, by the time she was twenty-nine, she was shrewd enough to sever her finances from them. Soon after, in a brilliant financial move, she sold a lease of land she had recently acquired to the nephew of Pope Pius IV, Piccolomini. Because the deal was so advantageous to her, he is thought to have been one of her lovers. In exchange for the lease, Piccolomini was to build Imperia a house on the property in which she could live until her death. Furthermore, the terms of the lease required that should she die before her daughter, if Piccolomini asked Lucrezia to leave the house, he would have to pay her 300 ducats, the average price of a home in Rome. Thus, at an early age Imperia ensured that not only herself but her daughter would always have a roof over their head.

Her second daughter, Margherita, born several years later, was the child of Agostino Chigi. Banker to kings, noblemen, and the Vatican, because of his great success in the world of finance, the Sultan of Turkey called him "the greatest merchant of Christianity." Julius II gave him the right to call himself "Chigi Della Rovere," but many called him by the popular title "Il Magnifico." Like Imperia, whom he loved and supported, he possessed the traits of shrewdness and daring, which he employed in a winning combination. Two sites still exist today in Rome that testify to the greatness of his former powers. One is the family chapel designed for him by Raphael in the Church of Santa Maria del Popolo on the Piazza del Popolo. The second is the Villa Farnesina, once the Villa Chigi, the elegant estate that the banker commissioned Baldassare Peruzzi to build.

There is no evidence of the intimacy between Chigi and Imperia in the family chapel; but the villa tells another story. Raphael contributed to the design of the loggia and he painted what is now a famous fresco in the Grand Salon, which depicts Galatea as she rises out of the sea— a version of the goddess said to resemble Imperia. A few still believe it is a portrait of her, but the consensus now among most scholars is that since Raphael wanted his Galatea to possess the characteristics of the Renaissance ideal of beauty, he would have been influenced and guided by Imperia, who was thought to be the best living example of that ideal. In the scenes from the myth of *Psyche and Eros* which Raphael also painted on the ceiling and in the friezes that border the beautiful loggia opening from the Grand Salon, in the personae of Psyche and the Three Graces, a similar face and figure appear: light hair, refined and harmonious features, a body just slightly more corpulent than is fashionable today, sensual, even strong, yet vaguely ethereal and gracefully rounded, as if the painter's brush had glided almost effortlessly over the plaster.

Imperia's presence can be felt throughout the villa, which is as it should be because she was often there. This was not Chigi's principal residence; he used it for entertaining. Thus, though the marriage of Psyche and Cupid floating above the gatherings was meant to celebrate Chigi's marriage, in this villa it was Imperia who presided at the parties attended by business associates, writers, philosophers, painters, dignitaries from the Vatican, and of course courtesans, events which, due to the nature of the evenings, would not have been proper for Chigi's wife to attend.

These occasions must have had an air of excitement. It would have felt as if a pantheon of new pleasures, insights, riches, images, beliefs were rising out of a sea of creation, tumultuous with activity. Even the architecture was daring, the loggia itself opening so that the garden seemed to enter the house in an unprecedented way. These were the first salons—indeed, the French word *salon* would be borrowed from the Italian *salone* in the following century—the ancient antecedents of café society.

That Chigi was a great patron of the arts only partly explains the exciting mixture of guests who frequented the Villa Chigi. His patronage would have sprung naturally from an affinity between those who, in the process of rising to prominence, were inventing a new world with different lines of power, a new vision and its own distinctions. And from a practical perspective, because with the rise of a new bourgeois class there were simply more walls to decorate, along with more men able to pay for the decoration, artists were not only prospering but, as so often happens with monetary gain, rising in esteem. No longer thought of as crafts-men, they were becoming famous. They were not alone in this process. Financiers and courtesans were being similarly transformed.

The resulting alliance was more than practical. Economic change al-most always carries with it, for better or worse, a vision. The locus of meaning shifts. New avenues of thought as well as transaction suddenly appear. In the best of these changes, life seems revitalized. And wherever there is new life, there is also eros. The energy between Imperia and Chigi, two giants of pleasure and profit, would have been as palpable as was the precise and detailed reflection they found in each other.

Business is as much about relationship as it is mathematics. They both knew how intimately conviviality and dividend are related. They under-stood that trust and pleasure engender largesse, that creating a mood of abundance encourages abundance. Chigi was famous for the night that he served his guests dinner on gold and silver plates. Arranging the fes-tivities in a loggia that faced the Tiber, after the dinner was completed, the banker threw his own plate into the water and encouraged his guests to do the same. This was not only a theatrical gesture, it was in itself a drama, symbolic of the liberation from old orders that Chigi and his guests were enjoying.

Nevertheless, both Chigi and Imperia knew that certain earthly laws must still be obeyed. The priceless plates were retrieved the next day from a net Chigi had hidden in the river earlier. Like her protector, though she gave off an air of careless extravagance, Imperia thought of the future, too. It was no doubt at her insistence that Chigi acknowl-edged Margherita as his daughter, and most probably because of Chigi's influence at the Vatican, Pope Leo X legitimized her birth. Eventually she married into the ducal family of Carafa.

Near the end of Imperia's life, once again with Chigi's help, she was able to ensure that her first daughter, Lucrezia, was also married. Despite the unwritten law that whenever a courtesan falls in love, it is at her own peril, Imperia had fallen in love with a man named Angelo del Bufalo. Her admiration was understandable. He was sophisticated, handsome, socially graceful, with an attractively wild streak that did not prevent him from being well respected. But the liaison would prove her downfall. Bufalo, who was married, began to favor another mistress. Imperia felt him pull away from her by degrees, before finally, after telling her that he had fallen out of love with her, he ended the affair. She drank poison.

Her death would be agonizing. But over the several days that she was still alive, she wrote the will that left her property to her first daughter, Lucrezia. Appointing Chigi her executor, as her dying wish she extracted from him the promise that he find a husband for Lucrezia. Thus, ten months after Imperia's death, her first daughter was wedded to a spice merchant from Chigi's native Siena. In the light of the miraculous nature of Imperia's last accomplishment, the salvation of her daughter, the name of the groom, Archangelo Colonna, was suitable. And even more miraculously for this period of history so unfavorable to women, the arrangement proved more than practical. Apparently this newly married couple fell in love with each other.

Her Pink Rabbits

Still one more aspect of the courtesans' brilliance must be mentioned here. They were natural mimics. Though their ability to act did not always translate well to the theatre, off the stage, in what is called real life, they were talented performers. Usually born to either poor or middle-class families, not only did they have to have cheek to travel in upper-class circles, they also had to be able to imitate the manners of upper-class ladies. A performance, we might add, which since in some circumstances they were required to pretend they were not courtesans, while in others they were expected to make it clear that they were, they had to turn off and on at will.

As we have already noted, Emilienne d'Alençon was one of the most celebrated among *grandes cocottes* of the Belle Epoque. Along with Liane de Pougy and La Belle Otero, she was part of a popular trio known in

Paris as *le Grand Trois*. Before her rise to fame she had actually studied acting at the Conservatoire. But probably because classical French drama
hardly suited her, she only lasted for one year. The circus was more her
metier. And it was this career that established her. Eventually, she could
count the sons of more than one aristocratic family among her lovers. In
turn, she was among the many lovers of King Leopold II of Belgium. In
this company there were times when she had to appear well bred even if
part of her attraction was that she was not. For her brief visit to Britain,
she created an entirely fictitious role for herself as the comtesse de Beau-
manoir (translated as the "Countess House Beautiful"). She made a
great impression as this personage, temporarily adopting what Cornelia
Otis Skinner called "crooked little-finger refinement." That she spoke
no English doubtless made her even more admirable.

But by far her greatest performance debuted at the Cirque d'Eté, before eventually she brought it to the Folies-Bergère, in which ostensibly
she simply played herself. The popular act was built around a troupe of
rabbits, which she had dyed shocking pink and outfitted with paper ruf-
fles. Dressed in this way, the rabbits were almost like accessories to their
mistress. Blond, with a rosy, dimpled complexion, she was fond of wearing pink taffeta with lace trimming. The writer Jean Lorrain describes
her as resembling raspberry ice. What she did with the rabbits is unclear
from this distance, though one can easily imagine that they were made to
jump through hoops at her bidding. The whole color-coordinated effect
must have been hilarious.

The humor was not only intended but the result of several comedic
abilities, which, along with the all-important virtue or timing, included
mimicry. In this case, though, what d'Alençon mirrored so brilliantly was
an idea instead of a reality. Molding herself to a classic type in the repertoire of feminine roles, she played the dumb blonde with clever dexter-
ity. Paradoxically, it takes more than average intelligence to play the part
of a bimbo. Imitating life is one thing, but giving lifeblood to a fantasy
is quite another.

Though on one level the act must have been charmingly silly, that there would have been a more complex side becomes evident when one observes any modern comedienne adept at playing this type. Whenever Gracie Allen, Marilyn Monroe, Elaine May, or Goldie Hawn has played an empty-headed woman, as with the invisible wires that hold up a marionette, a quality of intelligence can be felt beneath the masquerade, which gives the performance a subversive meaning, almost opposite to the picture officially presented. That at times, considering the unequal power women have been given, they cannily pretend to be stupid in order to manipulate men is the double entendre of such performances at which everyone, men and women alike, are invited to laugh.

Along the lines of this double meaning, clearly d'Alençon's act was making a comic allusion to the power that courtesans had to commandeer favors from their wealthy lovers. That the rabbits, belonging as they do to a species known for reproductive prowess, seemed eager to please their mistress was part of the appeal. Emerging from the stereotype of a naive young woman, foolish enough to play with rabbits, an entirely different story was told by these obedient animals, tamed and collared by their mistress.

Seduction
(THE FOURTH EROTIC STATION) + + + + + + + + + + +

As THE STORY is told, the young man could not fathom why everyone raved about Ninon de Lenclos. Her fabled powers of seduction would have no effect on him, he boasted to a friend.

"What appeal can a woman of her age possibly have?" he asked.

So it was that his friend, who had been a lover of Ninon, proposed a wager, betting that his friend would not be able to resist her charms.

Ninon, who was delighted to accept the challenge, agreed to a meeting. And of course despite his confidence, once ushered into the courtesan's presence, the young man was disarmed. What was it that she did?

Of course we can only surmise what took place between them, but there is good reason to believe that she began by taking an interest in him. Where were you raised? she probably asked. What beautiful boots you are wearing! she might have said. Or, have you seen the latest performance at the Comédie-Française; what did you think of it? To all his responses, giving him the feeling that she is fascinated.

But if we are to understand the secret of this process, we must take another look. If the interest she focuses on him has an immediate effect, it is because she is not feigning fascination. She is rather, from long habit, studying him closely, with the same intense intelligence she has always turned toward life. And though he has not fallen yet, it is easy to believe that this attention makes him puff his feathers. Why not, perhaps he says to himself, tell his friends one day that the famous Ninon found him very interesting, even though she left him cold.

He begins then to regale her with his accomplishments, trying to reveal everything he believes to be wonderful about himself. She does not stop him. Though there may be a slightly indulgent smile on her face, she listens quietly to everything he says, interrupting only to ask more questions, until finally his bragging begins to slow down of its own accord. There must be something profoundly unnerving to him in the serenity of her composure. In the wake of it he starts, if only slightly, to experience a moment of self-awareness. Perhaps he has gone on about himself a bit too much.

It is with this brief self-reflection, then, that the most subtle expression of embarrassment passes quickly over his face. And though most people would never have seen it, Ninon does. Her smile grows just a bit more indulgent, and seeing that, he feels his embarrassment even more acutely, which in turn causes her to emit a very discreet laugh. The process continues, as with Heisenberg's principle of uncertainty, perception affecting events, in this case intensifying the young man's feelings.

Even if he does not know it, he is already caught. She does not ridicule him. Rather, her interest grows. She is intrigued by what she sees now—not simply an arrogant young man but one in whom intelligence, arrogance, and humility, even a tender vulnerability, are freely mixed. Her response is neither unkind nor maternal. Instead, she allows herself to be touched as well as intrigued. It must have been very early in her life that she realized the way to charm a man is to find him charming. Yet it is not his braggadocio she responds to, but the part of himself he has always tried to hide.

Now, since she makes no effort to conceal the fact that she finds him charming, and since no one else has cared to see what he concealed, much less responded so well, he begins to feel the full force of her fabled seductiveness.

The end of the story, repeated now for over three hundred years, is that the young man lost his bet. Ninon was several years older when the young Abbe Gedolyn began to pursue her with an unmistakable ardor. She put him off for a while and when finally she agreed to be his lover she said he would have to wait for one month and a day. He agreed eagerly, counting the hours until the appointed time. When the day arrived, she was good for her word. Happy in her arms at last, he asked her why she had made him wait for exactly a month and a day.

"Because today is my birthday," she answered, "and I wanted to prove to myself that at the age of seventy, I am still capable of entertaining a lover."

MARION DAVIES

Chapter Five

Gaiety (or Joie de Vivre)

Kiss the joy as it flies.
—William Blake

HE CAPACITY TO take pleasure in life is no less a
virtue than any other. Joy is not as simple as it appears.
There are those who, whether out of fear or judgment, so
habitually resist the feeling that after a while they lose the knack of being pleased altogether. Others, mistaking mastery for pleasure, prefer
conquest to delight and never really taste the spoils of their efforts.
There is an art to enjoying life, to feeling desire and receiving what
comes, to savoring every detail, down to the finest points, of each taste,
sensation, or moment that happens by will or by chance to appear.
The experience requires a subtle courage. Delight, jubilation, elation can
throw you off balance, upsetting the established order of the day (or, as
is more often the case, the night). And because almost all forms of joy
are fleeting, pleasure must eventually lead to loss, no matter how small—
a loss that brings with it the certain knowledge that everything passes.

Abstinence and greed alike provide the means to avoid this knowledge. By shunning pleasure, the loss of it can be avoided. Aesop's fable
of the Ant and the Cricket is one of the more abiding stories regarding
abstinence we have been given. It is a cautionary tale that warns us
against the fate of the hungry cricket, who sang and danced all summer
rather than gathering food as the ant did. Yet, read closely, the story con-
ceals another warning, too. The abstemious ant lacks generosity. When
the cricket asks for food from his industrious neighbor, the ant sardon-

ically suggests that he just keep dancing. There is more than a little jealousy in this response, though in retrospect we can feel some sympathy for him. All summer his attention has been on the winter. But the sight of the cricket must have reminded the poor ant how little he enjoyed the summer.

Aesop himself was not immune to enjoyment. Centuries ago, he supported the courtesan Rhodopis. And La Fontaine, the man who, in the seventeenth century, transformed Aesop's tales into French poetry, was present more than once when Ninon entertained her guests by playing the lute. He must have been transfixed like everyone else. Despite the moral of the tale, his appreciation of music is evident in the beautiful rhymes and rhythms of his telling.

Of course, the story is correct in one sense. The existence of greed alone tells us that the indulgence of pleasure does not always lead to a pleasing end. Yet, though greed seems to be going in the opposite direction to abstinence, it springs from a similar motive. The accumulation of whatever is pleasurable in far greater quantities than can actually be enjoyed creates the illusion that one has escaped the transitory nature of pleasure. The rub is that, as with a gluttony so exaggerated it causes illness, pleasure itself will be sacrificed in the bargain. What is crucial is the intent.

When pleasure itself is the primary motive, excess has a far different effect. In *My Apprenticeships*, Colette describes the experience of taking a meal at Caroline Otero's house on the rue Fortuny. "I have always enjoyed food," she wrote of her taste for hearty meals, "but what was my appetite compared with Lina's." It makes a certain sense that Otero would have a famous appetite. She had been close to starvation many times in her childhood. There is perhaps a certain egalitarian justice in the fact that the women most famous for enjoying pleasure often came from miserable circumstances. Suffering can sharpen appreciation. Knowing that it was useless to worry about how she might be able to eat in the future, even as a child Otero learned to focus her undivided attention on the pleasures of each meal.

A robust dinner of sausages and beef and chicken was served, which both women consumed with gusto. But that Otero was by far the better eater was made abundantly clear. She emptied her plate four or five times. Still, Colette tells us that Otero enjoyed every bite, emanating a mood of "gentle bliss, an air of happy innocence," as she ate, "her teeth, her eyes, her glossy lips" shining "like a girl's." She had not overeaten. After finishing with a strawberry ice, she immediately jumped up from the table, and grasping a pair of castanets, began to dance with a full and intense energy, another pleasure, one that, as Colette writes, "was born of a true passion for rhythm and music." It is fitting that such an evening should end in dance. That pleasure requires an intimate self-knowledge and a refined perception of desire, in turn necessitates that we be present to each moment, bringing to it the full awareness that life is continually moving.

As Colette tells us, it was a joy to see Otero dance. Whenever great pleasure is had, a secondary pleasure arises from being in the presence of the banquet. Pleasure begets pleasure. Of its very nature, joy radiates outward, touching everyone who happens to be in the vicinity where it is had. Accordingly, the capacity to receive pleasure has a magnetic appeal. Wherever a particularly joyous person goes, conviviality is born, excitement is generated, creativity flourishes, and crowds assemble.

There was a reason why Païva was called "the Queen of Paris" or why later Liane de Pougy was known in France as "our national courtesan." The great courtesans were like queen bees around whom countless social worlds developed like so many intricate honeycombs. Whether during the Renaissance or the period of the Enlightenment; the Second Empire, the Regency, the Gay Nineties, the Belle Epoque, the Roaring Twenties; in Paris or Rome, Venice, London, New York, or Hollywood; at balls and parties, salons and cafés, the opera and the theatre, remarkable worlds were woven of wealthy men and aristocrats, artists and writers, around the presence of a few women, who provided an essential and catalytic ingredient to the mysterious alchemy: their gaiety.

Sunset Boulevard

It was a big gay party, every bit of it.—Marion Davies,
The Times We Had

In the midst of the Roaring Twenties, among the most popular parties in Hollywood were those thrown by Marion Davies at a house just above Sunset Boulevard, at 1700 Lexington Road. The white stucco mansion with a large and elegant swimming pool was bought for her by William Randolph Hearst. Davies had been his mistress for several years. Hearst, who was married at the time to another showgirl, met her when she was performing in the *Ziegfeld Follies*.

In the history of courtesans, the promotion from showgirl to kept woman was a common event. Yet, as with Coco Chanel, Marion was not considered a courtesan. By the Roaring Twenties—the age of the flapper—the institution was fading. The liberties that courtesans had enjoyed exclusively were being disseminated. Hence a tradition once built on the premise that proper women's lives were more restricted slowly came to an end. But the lineage of the great courtesans had clearly passed on to the next generation. The art of pleasure was continued with virtuosity by the good-time girl.

In her own telling, Marion was born with a great aptitude for frivolity, an important quality in a good hostess. Though this talent is rarely encouraged in children (at times it is even punished), it is as fruitful a calling as any other, beneficial not only to those who have the ability but to the larger society as well. We have only to imagine an atmosphere dominated by dutiful work, dour expressions, or strict manners to see the necessity.

For parents at the beginning of the twentieth century, Marion's mother and father seemed exceptionally lenient. They were not especially punitive when, on Halloween, she was arrested for throwing a sack of vegetables at the butler who answered the door of a posh mansion. Her mother and father must have felt partly culpable for her actions. While they were out of town they had left her in the care of a maid who, too busy to look after a child, sent Marion by herself to the locked park in the neighborhood below. Very quickly she decided that, as she describes them in her autobiography, "the raggedy looking" children outside the gate were having a better time than those inside. Soon she found herself joining them in a plot to steal vegetables from a grocer on Lexington Avenue in order to throw them at the first person who answered the door of a fancy house in the neighborhood.

Even as a child, the worlds that existed outside the comfortable one in which she was raised seemed more attractive to her. Her father was a moderately successful lawyer in Brooklyn. Yet, in the tape-recorded interviews that document her autobiography, though her grammar is correct, her speech is full of the slang and cadences of a rougher life. On film, Davies seems to be at one moment delicate, and at the next tough and charmingly streetwise. The notion that street life was supposed to be adventurous and romantic was characteristic of a generation that had begun to find the protocols of privilege suffocating. Once, when she was the guest of the socialite Jim Deering, at his villa on Biscayne Bay, after complaining to her mother, "I'm very bored here, what a lot of grumpy people," she escaped over the estate walls and ran off to Palm Beach. Yet again like many in her generation, she was also drawn in the direction of glamour and glitter. If years later she learned that the mansion she and her friends had attacked on Halloween belonged to the man whose mistress she eventually became, the choice was metaphorical as well as accidental. The place she occupied in society would always be equivocal. Lover of a powerful man but not his wife, enjoying a luxury that was not always her own, respected and yet the center of a scandal that lasted for years, Marion Davies eluded definition.

To be free of strict demarcation, uncircumscribed by ordinary expectations, indeterminate and yet determined in another way, loose, spirited, seeking only the definitions of each moment was what she chose. She had little tolerance for anything she found tedious. Since she would not submit herself to the rigors of boredom in school, she was often consigned to the corner. Seldom is the significance of such resistance properly credited. If the wrong path is not refused, the right one may never appear. Though Marion wanted to dance, even ballet school seemed too dull. What she really wanted was to become a showgirl. This tested her parents' patience. But finally, despite her mother's horrified objections, they sent her to Kosloff's, the best among New York's schools that prepared girls to go on the stage. At the age of thirteen she joined the pony ballet, and not much later she became a Ziegfeld girl— a role in which she was able to use her extraordinary gift, a vivid and compelling love for the fleeting joys of life.

Hearst, who sat in the front row of the *Ziegfeld Follies* night after night as she performed, found her irresistibly charming. He pursued her for a period of a year, sending her small offerings, candy, silver, boxes, or gloves. More than thirty years older than Davies, he was not a conventionally attractive man. Pear-shaped and balding, in photographs of the couple he appears like a bloated ghost smiling beside her. But she fell in love with him nonetheless. No doubt the fact that he was so wealthy or that he could help her career with pages of free publicity in his newspapers added to his appeal. But these were incidental details within what was a far more complex attraction. They were both large figures—physically tall, vital, intense, intelligent, forceful in different ways. Like her, though again in different ways, he could be unorthodox. When they did not serve his purposes, he could push conventions aside with ease. Some of the differences between them would have attracted her, too. He was more worldly and better educated than she. That he was focused on future profit as well as present pleasures meant she could be free to dwell in the present without worry. And since he could match her move for move, where he was conventional, he provided her with a measure of safety, a seawall against her own outrageous impulses.

A story she tells from their early courtship evokes the many shades of meaning in the word once used for a courtesan's paying lover, her "protector." One night when Marion was about to go to a party being given by General Vanderbilt for the Prince of Wales, Hearst ducked quickly into Cartier's, bought a diamond and pearl bracelet and ring, and used these to bribe her to stay home. He was afraid he might lose her to the prince, who shared Hearst's enthusiasm for showgirls. Though after she accepted his deal, she planned to climb out her window and go to the party anyway, she found that he had hired detectives to wait outside her house.

But if Hearst could be an almost parental figure, he was also frequently absent. Remembering the parties at 1700 Lexington Road, Charlie Chaplin recalled that the best of them took place when Hearst was elsewhere. Several times a week a group that included Chaplin, Rudolph Valentino, John Barrymore, Mary Pickford and Douglas Fairbanks, Alma Rubens, Harry Crocker, and Tom Ince would gather to swim or play charades, join in masquerades or dance in the incongruously grand ballroom Hearst had added on to the house. There were small dinner parties and larger soirées to which at times over a hundred people were invited, not only actors and actresses but also polo players and senators, chorus boys and foreign heads of state, anyone who interested Marion.

Throwing a good party requires a particular genius. We can get a taste of the quality by watching Davies in her films. In the mid-twenties she had become a popular actress, earning close to half a million dollars a year for her work. She was neither especially good nor bad at acting, but she had an astonishing charisma. In one film she made with Bing Crosby, during a duet they perform together, whenever he sings, it is she who commands attention simply through her smile. When she sings or dances, the tone of her voice and the way she moves have a surprisingly hypnotic effect. Through all her seemingly casual gestures, she radiates an intimate sexuality—loose, authentic, riveting.

It is fascinating to ponder that, though Davies seemed so authentic, she did not always tell the truth about her life. Many of those who are known to have charisma embellish and rearrange their own histories, almost as if they are creating a new past to express the mood of each moment. Any good hostess must have a fierce loyalty to the present. The significance of every other element—elegant food, furnishings, candle-light, atmosphere—pales when compared to her ability to awaken to each guest, every event or remark, thus multiplying everyone's pleasure through her own delighted awareness.

Everywhere She Went

A city, yet a woman.—William Blake, "Jerusalem"

Here is the burning heart of Paris, the high road to mundane triumphs, the great theatre of ambitions and of the famous dissoluteness, which draws to itself the gold vice, and folly of the four quarters of the globe.—Edmondo De Amicis, Studies of Paris

We are accustomed to thinking of pleasure as simple. Yet as much as pleasure belongs to the present, it also belongs to the past. Even the most sensual desires have a complexity redolent with history and tradition. Whether it is a glass of wine or a can of beer, rich coffee and milk taken in the morning with a croissant or perhaps Earl Grey tea with porridge, an embroidered coat designed by Yves St. Laurent, or a pair of blue jeans, a ride down Fifth Avenue in a Jaguar convertible, a ride over the waves on a surfboard, or the glimpse of a certain part of the body that we find attractive, no desire is entirely free of the past. To a great extent, we learn to want what we want.

Like any great tradition, the history of pleasure includes classic forms and revolutionary innovations, influential figures, celebrated movements and times that were especially creative. These famous periods were often centered in particular places, cities that have gradually taken on the aura of sacred sites. During the second half of the nineteenth century, Paris became a mecca of pleasure, as pilgrims from around the world arrived to pay homage and bring back some of the city's wisdom. Florenz Ziegfeld, Jr., who not only founded the *Ziegfeld Follies* but shaped American musical theatre for years to come, was deeply influenced by the music halls he saw in Paris. Indeed, he imported the idea of presenting a spectacular tableau of beautiful women dressed in elegantly revealing costumes from the Folies-Bergère. He was not the only one to be persuaded. Whether it was the Prince of Wales or the king of Prussia, Edith Wharton or Henry James, Stanford White or Eugene O'Neill, everyone fell under the spell of "Gay Paree."

The name is revealing. Long before it was a cypher for homosexual life, the word "gay" had another meaning. Perhaps because its ancestry in Old French includes a word which denoted "licentiousness," the use of the term "gay" during the nineteenth century implied the presence of courtesans. And in truth, it was the *grandes horizontales* who made the city gay. If Paris was a perpetual celebration, the courtesan was the life of the party. Everywhere she went came to life.

Of course, given the mysterious nature of pleasure, this vitality was not spread evenly. Some places were livelier than others. In the center of Paris, the courtesan's paces inscribed an especially legendary geography over an area extending less than two square miles known as the Grands Boulevards. Here the profoundly social nature of pleasure was palpable. The Italian traveler and writer Edmondo De Amicis describes the effect of entering this glittering domain, which began at the boulevard Montmartre and ended at the Place Madeleine. "The horses pass in troops, and the crowd in torrents. Windows, shops, advertisements, doors, facades, all rise, widen and become silvered, gilded and illumined. It is rivalry of magnificence . . . which borders on madness."

That the extremity of this awe-inspiring abundance borders on religious experience does not escape him. Describing the signs on which the names of illustrious fashion houses, shops, and restaurants were spelled out, he writes that "Great inscriptions in gold run along the facades like verses from the Koran along the walls of mosques." But this had to be either a very new or a very old religion, one that worships the fecundity of material life. "The eye," he adds, "finds no place upon which to rest" in this excessive landscape, "full of coquetry and pride, which dazzles and confuses like blinding scintillations," as it expresses perfectly "the nature of a great, opulent and sensual city, living only for pleasure and glory."

Though the last phrase may seem somewhat exaggerated, De Amicis did not invent the hyperbole. The idea belonged to the phenomenon he was observing. It was a momentary illusion, created through an unspoken accord, the crowds not only assenting but each among them doing his or her best to keep alive the glorious feeling that only pleasure lay in every direction. And for a period of several hours, the common consent of the thousands who arrived by carriage or on foot, who strolled past the cafés, entered, drank, dined, danced, flirted, listened to music, laughed at the raucous or ribald words of a song, succeeded in creating a miracle. The pleasure they imagined was conjured into existence.

This extraordinary feat was more than made possible by the fact that it was repeated every night. That certain revelers came again and again, the men called *boulevardiers*, the women known as *demi-mondaines*, was essential. From noon until the early hours of the morning, the region belonged to them. Thus, a courtesan reaching this territory just after rising at noon might head directly to the café at number 22 boulevard des Italiens called Tortoni. Entering by the private door reserved for regular patrons in the back, she would take lunch with a friend or a lover, afterwards most likely indulging in one of the ices for which the café was famous.

After this, she might drop down to the shade of the Tuileries Gardens for a brief stroll before wandering into the passages leading off the boulevard Montmartre, small arcades filled with shops, to look at and perhaps purchase the sumptuous fabrics, the flowers arranged like offerings to the gods, sparkling gems wrested from all over the world, perfumes made from fields of lavender, rose petals, leaves of lemon verbena, and thousands of enchanting objects designed to titillate the eye displayed in the countless windows that lined her path.

Tired then from this brief but richly sensuous tour, she would return to the boulevard des Italiens, stopping now at the Café de Paris across the street from the café where she took her lunch, or instead at the Maison Dorée, next door to Tortoni's, knowing that at this hour, the late afternoon, she will be certain to encounter friends. Perhaps while sitting with a table of *boulevardiers*, journalists, artists, other *cocottes*, she might meet a new protector; then again, if by chance she already has an appointment for the night, she may simply be there to relax.

If it is early fall, when the Paris season is already in full swing yet still not tired of itself, the air that was hot in midday will have a pleasant edge of coolness at this hour, and it is pleasant to sit outdoors as witty remarks fly by, laughter rising and ebbing, and abandon herself to the tide of conversation. Moreover, the relative ease of the hour is needed to revive herself for the larger waves to come.

Soon, she will rise to prepare for the evening. When she returns, she will be dressed far more elegantly and, no matter how nearby she lives, she will arrive in a coach. De Amicis describes the moment "when all the gay life of Paris pours itself out from all the neighboring street," when the odor of musk and flowers and Havana cigars and absinthe mixes heavily in the air, and the carriages stop while "the cocottes, with their long trains descend...and disappear, with the rapidity of arrows through the doors of the restaurants."

Whether she is dining at the Maison Dorée, the Café de Foy, the Café Anglais, Maxim's, the Prévost, Marguery, Viel, Le Cardinal, Ledoyen, or Le Grand Vefour, the meal will be sumptuous, with eight or nine courses, beginning with small, nameless bite-size treats, followed by soup made velvety on the tongue by cream, continuing with fish and then meat, if not game, too, all accompanied by a good champagne, Bordeaux, or Burgundy, a chardonnay, and then perhaps a Charlotte or Croustade d'ananas Pompadour, and finally ices, without of course skipping at the very end a digestif—Armagnac, Cognac, or Chartreuse. She may be dining in a private room upstairs called a *salon particulière*, with just her lover or a small party, or she may be seated in the *grand salon*, the decor of both rooms adorned with velvet and silk brocade, frescoes, gold gilding, lit by dazzling chandeliers in the public room, and quieter, more flattering lamps in the private one. If she is in a salon alone with her lover, they may take another course of pleasure on the couch provided for each private room before descending together at midnight once again into the streets, which are lit now with gas lamps and the thousand lights of every café and restaurant, all of which give the boulevards, against the night sky, a startlingly brilliant illumination.

By contrast to the restaurant in which the air of jubilance is subdued, the streets host a celebration of gigantic proportions: the festivity stretches as far as the eye can see in every direction. Here a perpetual party pulls the couple into a powerful stream heading perhaps toward yet another café, open late at night, the Café de Foy or Paris, or toward the more verdant Champs-Elysées, where singers can be found performing at the *cafés chantants*, their sparkling lights strung like diamonds under the trees; or in the other direction, to the Palais Royale and its gaming tables, which inspire an excitement that makes up for the sordid surroundings, the walls cracking and stained with oil but the spinning wheel seductive.

Yet perhaps they have not dined so early, choosing instead to attend the opera or the theatre first. Before the end of the Second Empire, they will attend the opera on the rue le Pelletier, which is connected to the boulevard des Italiens by a covered passage. Closer to the turn of the century, they will attend the extravagantly decorous Opéra Garnier at the epicenter of the Grands Boulevards where the rue de la Paix, the boulevards des Italiens and Capucines meet. No doubt they will arrive separately, she by coach at the main entrance, mingling for a while with friends in the lower foyer before walking slowly up the grand staircase made of rare marble and onyx so that, appropriately set in this opulent architecture, her own beauty can be admired.

The streets immediately around the Opéra will have prepared them both for this night. Her dress would have been made by a designer headquartered on the rue de la Paix, perhaps the fashionable Paul Poiret or his mentor, Charles Worth (or, in an earlier time, Mlle. Sauvinet on the boulevard des Italiens). And a few steps further west, in the Place Vendôme, her protector would have found the diamond bracelet which he plans to present to her when he visits her private box during the intermission.

Leaving the Opéra, which at this hour would be illuminated by so many lights it appeared almost phosphorescent, they would cross the square to the Café de la Paix, with its pale green and gold gilt interior, designed (as the Opéra had been) by Charles Garnier to be elegant but more intimate, for a late supper together, followed perhaps by a few yet more intimate hours in a room next door at the Grand Hôtel.

Then again, they may have gone to the theatre. The abundance is staggering to contemplate. There were spectacles everywhere. The names are legendary now: L'Ambigu-Comique, featuring the great Frédéric Lemaître, who could milk a laugh from any line; the Théâtre Historique, where Dumas's *La Reine Margot* opened; the Théâtre des Variétés, where Hortense Schneider sang Offenbach's bawdy roles, often portraying a courtesan; the Vaudeville, the Gymnase, the Théâtre de la Porte Saint-Martin—each nightly presenting macabre murders, romance, history, mime, or variety acts filled with gymnasts, clowns, dancers, and singers. There were circuses, too: the Cirque d'Hiver, the Cirque Olympique, and the Hippodrome, established by the Franconi brothers, where Mogador rode bareback and the Frascati brothers clowned.

They might have climbed the hill up to Montmartre, where not far away at the Moulin Rouge the cancan was being performed until the early hours of morning, or gone east on the boulevards to the Folies-Bergère, where one could watch the stage while drinking or eating as tableaux and parades of extravagantly costumed women appeared, some of them legendary. It was here that Colette performed half nude; Liane de Pougy, Cleo de Mérode, and La Belle Otero danced, and Emilienne d'Alençon presented the talents of her famous pink rabbits, all to be followed at the end of the era by performers still fabled in modern memory—Mistinguett, Josephine Baker, Maurice Chevalier, and Charlie Chaplin.

But the performance would be only a prelude to what must have seemed an infinite spectacle. Leaving the theatre, they would rejoin the crowds heading toward the Café Turc, the Café Anglais, the Café des Mauresques, the Café Riche, or Le Napolitain, to drink and dine and continue the party. And of course, they could easily have chosen instead the established center of gaiety, that golden place known as Maxim's, to dine under the glass roof designed by Lalique, drink the best champagne to be had in Paris, and then dance through the early hours of the morning to the music of the house orchestra.

In the Belle Epoque, Maxim's was synonymous with the high life of the *fin-de-siècle*. It was here in a room that held the bar called "The Omnibus," that *demi-mondaines*, actresses, dandies, *flâneurs*, and *boulevardiers* regularly assembled. Courtesans could always be found here. Maxim's was the place for everyone to be seen and where anyone could be seen. Emilienne d'Alençon would come when she finished performing at the Folies-Bergère, leaving her rabbits with Ursula, the caretaker of the ladies' room. Mata Hari and La Belle Otero came, too, and Liane de Pougy along with Cléo de Mérode, both pursued by Leopold of Belgium. His would not be the only royal presence; the Prince of Wales entertained here often. And of course the presiding royalty of the arts could be found here, too, including the playwright Feydeau, Marcel Proust, and Sarah Bernhardt.

More than once, the frivolity reached fevered pitch, as when, for instance, Maurice Bertrand ushered in four pall bearers who were carrying a casket that, when opened, revealed a case of champagne. And whenever in the natural course of a night anyone's capacity for folly began to ebb, the celebrant had only to look in the sinuously beautiful Art Nouveau mirrors that wrapped each room in luminescence to be inspired once more by the sight of someone else laughing, flirtatious, seduced, or all three, and in the process producing delicious gossip.

But there was another kind of reflection which captured the same rooms with ghostly doubles to all the festivities that were produced by artists and writers who took their inspiration from the restaurant. The reputation of Maxim's was so forceful that it migrated into the imagination of an Austrian man who had never been to Paris at all: Franz Lehar set the entire act of an opera in the restaurant he had never seen. Nevertheless, he caught the spirit. "I go off to Maxim's," Prince Danilo sings, "Where fun and frolic beams. With all the girls I chatter. I laugh and kiss and flatter." Thousands of curious visitors, intrigued by *The Merry Widow*, would follow the hero there.

Everywhere along the boulevards the festivities were enlarged and intensified by glittering images and thrilling legends, which danced and sang along with the crowds, calling out like sirens inviting pilgrims from far and wide to join the party. If you strolled in the Passage des Panoramas, Zola's heroine Nana, who loved to look at the fake jewelry in the shop windows there, would be walking beside you. Listening to a concert in the Tuileries, you would be haunted by the painting Manet made of a group of famous *boulevardiers*, sitting where you are sitting. Your expectations of a ball at the Opéra would be heightened by his painting of a masked ball held there; and certainly approaching the bar at the Folies-Bergère, you would be accompanied by another of his luminous paintings.

In the first foyer of the Opéra, the gathering would remind you of the opening scene of Balzac's *The Splendor and Misery of the Courtesan*. In the corridors of any theatre you would remember Flaubert's description of students parading their mistresses during intermissions. Inside the auditoriums, the images continue in intricate layers, as you recall several paintings of ladies and gentlemen in their boxes, as well as Daumier's rendering of the section called Paradise in the upper balcony where the poorer members of the audience are packed.

Entering the street again, your impression would be shaped by Béraud's painting of the boulevard Montmartre in front of the theatre you have just left. Strolling over to a café, the men in silk hats you encounter might have stepped from paintings by Caillebotte, just as so many women you see resemble Manet's *La Parisienne*. And as the next century begins, you would think to yourself that it is here on the boulevard that Colette's character, Chéri, mourning for the loss of the courtesan he loved, spent night after night in drunken dissolution. As when reaching Tortoni's, you would know that Proust's hero, Swann, searched desperately and in vain for the courtesan Odette here.

And all about you while you watch or dine or drink or dance, stories and images are being newly coined. The *boulevardiers*, fond of witty remarks, publish and repeat them. One way or the other, sooner rather than later, everyone has heard Feydeau's famous quip at Maxim's. (After being served a lobster with only one claw, he answered the waiter's explanation, that lobsters often fight and injure each other in the tank, by demanding "Well, then, take this one away and bring me the victor.") And everyone repeats the story of when Caroline Otero, forced to give up her seat at the Comédie-Française to make room for the tsar of Russia and his retinue, threatened: "All right, I'll leave. But I'll never eat caviar again!"

Just as all the stories are being repeated, Nadar is photographing Sarah Bernhardt, Labiche, Dumas and Dumas *fils*, the Goncourt brothers—all principal players in this gaiety. And if now, looking back, the effect of these portraits seems somewhat elegaic, it is perhaps because although the pleasure is multiplied in both space and time, each event mirrored in succeeding reflections yielding the sense of an infinite progression, this moment of eternity will come to an end like any other. It is an inevitability folded into every joy. As is the eventual comprehension, if you glance for more than a moment in the mirror, that what you see there is not just happiness. Each night innumerable catastrophes advance toward the region.

The abundance so evident on the boulevards has a hidden cost. Lives cut short, impoverished, bodies maimed, tortured in Africa and Asia. The violence spent in the colonies will soon come home. The First World War is in the making. Soon French soldiers will be marching along the boulevards on their way to battle. The Dreyfus case, with its thinly veiled anti-Semitism, augurs the terrors of the second war that will follow. The unceasing abundance displayed on the boulevards is matched by a terrible poverty just a few streets away, in the recent memory of many of those who take part in the golden prosperity. And even as the party continues, there are among the celebrants men and women who are dying of the contagious diseases that, fed by poverty, also prosper.

Many, of course, come here only to escape. Drinking or gambling too much, they use pleasure as a path toward oblivion. But pleasure is not by its nature ignorant. During any given moment of delight, the mind starts to expand the circumference of its attention, here taking in the colored glass paperweights in a shop window, there the chestnut tree that has just come into bloom, then the frayed collar and pale face of the young man walking listlessly on the opposite side of the street, together with the look of desperation that clouds the face of a young prostitute as she leaves the notorious bar next door. Among the revelers, there are those who are watching closely, and they leave nothing out.

For gentlemen fleeing the boredom of high society, that this is the meeting place of those who dare to broach forbidden subjects is one of the attractions. It is at the Café Durand that Zola will write *J'Accuse!*, calling the French government's prosecution of Alfred Dreyfus unjust. In these cafés, one can talk openly about subjects banned from polite drawing rooms, not just politics and disease but the ever-fascinating sex and money. "What if instead of these indecent rags," Baudelaire writes of a beautiful girl he observes begging on the street, "the splendid train of a brocade gown rustled at your heels." The air is brisk with forbidden realities.

The perspective can have a prejudicial slant, as when Zola or the Goncourt brothers create a moral distance between their own pleasures and the pleasures of women. Still, as with an ancient carnival, this is a party where the old distinctions dissolve temporarily. Everyone changes roles. Poor women become powerful as rich men beg for favors. And despite every separation, the mood on the Grands Boulevards, shared as it is by multitudes, will inevitably sweep its inhabitants toward union, when for the duration of the vast ritual every fate seems to converge. Hence in the second half of the century, a gentleman and his mistress could pass by the Church of the Madeleine which anchors one end of the Grands Boulevards, where the memory of the large funeral held there for Marie Duplessis still lingers.

And since death anchors every life, subtle signs of this destiny can be found everywhere on the boulevards. Even the most earnest attempts at undiluted frivolity include signs that evoke a vast underworld of meaning. If, between the two world wars, for instance, a man were to take his mistress, one of the last courtesans, to the Folies-Bergère, they may see a fan of feathers crowning the head of Gaby Deslys as she parades the length of the stage, or five diamond-studded fans framing Josephine Baker's face, matching the large diamond spirals hanging from her ears, or a mane of furlike feathers trailing from a golden helmet worn by Edmond Guy, or a python wrapped around Mademoiselle Floriane's arms. Thus, however subtly, on this night of pleasure, Inanna, Isis, and Venus will be evoked, not only inspiring thoughts of love but also revealing the larger mysteries for which pleasure is just one of the stations.

Yet this station is formidable. If, on any given night, the pleasures of Paris have not already, as De Amicis says, "conquered" its visitors, here in the territory of the courtesan they will finally be possessed. Drowning in the strange sensation that past, present, and future have fused, now in this time out of time, while every sensible thought they have is disarmed by a wave of intense tastes, odors, scents, sounds, visions, the pilgrims worshipping here will be subsumed and carried toward abandon by a common stream, rich with the history of desire.

Her Swing

For this and that way swing
The flux of mortal things—Matthew Arnold,
"Westminster Abbey"

When, at the Folies-Bergère or the *Ziegfeld Follies*, a star such as Josephine Baker descended toward the stage perched on a swing, to some the vision would have evoked an earlier image. The original model for this setting can be found in a painting from the eighteenth century commissioned by Monsieur de Saint-Julien as a portrait of his mistress. It was his idea that she be suspended from a swing, and he who asked that his own likeness be placed beneath her where he could admire her legs. At first Saint-

Julien requested that the painter Gabriel-François Doyen to accept his commission; but Doyen, feeling the project too frivolous, passed it on to a younger, more obscure man who, as it turned out, had a strong feeling for the subject matter. When the painting, called Les Hasards Heureux de L'Ecarpolette—*The Happy Risks of the Swing*—appeared, it caused a sensation that made its creator, Jean-Honoré Fragonard, famous.

In the painting, both gentleman and mistress are surrounded by a verdant landscape. It is a pastoral scene, the tree from which the swing is suspended almost mythically beautiful, the gentleman below literally wreathed in a bower of leaves and flowers. Though this background has a unique character, it also partakes of an even earlier tradition—the habit of painting amorous scenes, sometimes with courtesans, sometimes with goddesses (who were usually unclothed), set in the countryside. The *fête galante*, as the form is known, can perhaps most easily be recognized by today's audiences in Manet's *Dejeuner sur l'Herbe*, which when it was painted shocked society by replacing nude goddesses with modern women who sit sharing a picnic lunch with men who are fully dressed. Later, though the version she painted is less famous, Suzanne Valadon took the image into a far more radical dimension when she depicted both men and women at the picnic unclothed.

Next to these examples, *The Swing*, in which both lovers are fully clothed, may appear to be tame. Fragonard can seem foolishly sentimental, except when you understand that his best subject was ecstasy. The vibrant motion of the young woman on the swing, echoed in the billowing pink silk of her dress, which is caught in the light dancing over her, her face, her breasts, and which falls across his face, too, turned toward her, the adoring expression, the joyful ardor of his hand stretched toward her feet, his feeling extended into the tree which also reaches, less with effort than the pure effect of delight, toward a misty, blushing resolution in the deeper landscape—are all expressions of bliss, the frivolous yet nevertheless powerful feeling that merges countryside and lovers together into one buoyant vision.

Of course, the painting captures only one moment in the arc of pleasure. The pendulum will of necessity swing back and away; though the pink shoe that is suspended in midair above him will soon be his, the lover will never seize his mistress's stockinged foot. And yet the feeling of the painting is not one of frustration but rather of a joy that is at that moment being realized. It is as if swing, skirt, trees, blushing sky, taken together were tropes for the nature of sexual passion, which will move through your body like a wave, dissolving your reserve, bringing you to union with forces of life beyond your comprehension, before it recedes, as all things must inevitably do. Though while you are immersed in this motion, you will be too happy to care.

ALICE OZY

Rapture
(THE FIFTH EROTIC STATION) + + + + + + + + + + +

*The real merit of these eyes, their only originality, lay in something
naive and constantly astonished. . . . —Edmond About,* Madelon

ALICE OZY WAS known for combining the wide-eyed innocence in
her character with a fair measure of cleverness and guile. The resulting
mix must have been surprisingly delightful. The duc d'Aumale, son of
the citizen king, Louis Philippe, was devoted to her. The toast of Paris
for decades, she was depicted in novels and poetry by Edmond About
and Théophile Gautier, painted and sculpted by Chassériau and Doré.

Her naïveté could be startling. Once, when she was told in jest that a Gruyère cheese mine had been discovered in Montmorency which would provide employment for the poor, she responded by clapping her hands in joy. But her famous gullibility could not have come from any deficiency of mind. Instead of diamonds, she habitually asked that her lovers give her shares in the railway company. She became a wealthy woman rather early in her life.

As is true for all of us, the source of some of her qualities can be found in her childhood. Her father was not poverty-stricken; he was a jeweler. But both her mother and father had other lovers and, disinterested in each other, they soon became disinterested in her, too. After leaving her with a foster mother for several years, when she reached the age of ten, they decided Alice should earn her own living. Thus, she spent three years of her childhood in the dark backroom of a fabric shop bent over a needle and thread as she executed intricate patterns of embroidery.

Those who have been deprived of a childhood sometimes lack the ability either to be playful or to take pleasure in life. Yet just as often, those who have had their childhoods stolen from them retain an almost childlike joy in life. It is as if at every moment they experience release from a dim prison and are astonished and elated by everything and everyone they encounter.

Ozy's career as a courtesan began in a way that was conventional for the nineteenth century. At age thirteen, she was reprieved from her backroom indenture when her manager, estimating the effect of her beauty, thought she would be better suited to working behind the counter. But considering her innocence, this new position left her vulnerable to a second calamity. Very soon after her promotion, she was seduced by the shop's owner. Now the marriage proposal from a country doctor which seemed imminent could not be accepted.

Her dilemma did not last long. Falling in love with the gifted actor Paul-Louis Brindeau, she eloped with him. And like so many compromised women before her, she entered the theatre, too. At the age of twenty, having made her first appearance in the Théâtre des Variétés, she was already earning 1,200 francs a year. But she was not to stay with Brindeau long. By turn of fate the Variété had been commanded to present the play in which she was performing, *Le Chevalier du Guet*, at the royal palace in the Tuileries. The performance was arranged to honor the return of Louis Philippe's son, the duc d'Aumale, who fell in love with Alice at first sight. Doubtless understanding the fortunate nature of such a connection, and perhaps from a certain restlessness that also must have been engendered by her childhood, she left Brindeau easily. Just as easily as, after a period, she would leave the duke, who since he did not have control of his own money yet, could give her far less than her next lover, the comte de Perregaux.

It is a testament to both the duke and the courtesan that Aumale was not resentful when she left. Still her friend when both of them were aging, he visited her at the château she owned on Lake Enghien in Switzerland, where, it is said, she would take the petals of the roses she grew and scatter them throughout the rooms. Did the scent remind the duke of all the nights he spent with her in her apartment above the Maison Dorée? Many men dreamed of joining her in the rosewood bed encrusted with Sevre Medallions depicting Cupid, and draped in lace. The great womanizer Victor Hugo was very disappointed that he was merely shown her bedroom but not invited to stay. In his novel *Madelon*, Edmond About hints obliquely at what the experience of staying might have been like. "When you saw her," he says, "it was like smelling a bunch of heliotrope or tasting some delicious fruit; you felt something complete and superabundant, which made your heart overflow."

And as if this were not tantalizing enough, he adds a comment that is even more revealing: "She took possession of a man if she touched him with the tips of her fingers." But this, of course, would lead to rapture—the tips of her fingers, fully sensate and fully aware, taking you in and touching you as if her fingers had never touched before, so that you yourself begin to experience touch as something entirely new.

One can imagine the duke being seduced this way, her hand perhaps grazing the side of his leg as they walk side by side down the boulevard des Italiens. By the time they reach her apartment, he has forgotten every worry, every responsibility; even his own expectations and plans for pleasure begin to vanish when her mouth opens into his mouth as she discovers all over again what it is to kiss him.

As he glides his hand around the arc of her hips, over her belly, up the curve of her breasts, she takes her pleasure fully and with a cry of surprise, too, as if this particular stroke were unpredictably pleasurable, fresh. In her intense presence, he feels himself dissolving until, entering her mood entirely, he abandons himself to each ensuing moment of bliss.

MADAME DE POMPADOUR

Chapter Six

Grace

*I learned then that there are no minor roles. They are all major roles
and it's what the dancer does that makes it major.*
—Judith Jamison, *Dancing Spirit*

A LMOST ANY ACTIVITY will be transformed into
something extraordinary when it is done with grace. The
virtue is especially evident in movement. Imagine, for instance, the way that the actress and famous *demi-mondaine* Lanthélme entered a room. The languidly slouching manner of her walk was imitated
by women all over Paris. Or think of Taglioni, the first ballerina to dance
on her toes, spinning across the stage of the Opéra in Paris as if for a
few breathless moments she were more spirit than flesh. Or envision Nijinsky, leaping and then pausing in midair before he descended, only to
bend toward the earth slowly like a serpent.

But if the essence of all grace is movement, the forms of the motion
are manifold. The same virtue, for instance, describes the symbolic gestures we call graciousness, a quality that includes generosity, as well as
the grace of the hostess who puts you at ease. A feeling which can extend into her surroundings, when if they are pleasantly decorated, the
rooms where she receives you will be described as gracious, too.

And then there is also the divine grace, which moves from the mysterious will of gods and goddesses who occasionally favor us with their
blessings. One need not be religious to experience it. Even an atheist feels
touched by a state of grace when, for instance, an astonishing insight
seems to come out of nowhere.

Given the complexity of this virtue, it makes sense that the Greeks would have represented grace with three figures instead of one. The Three Graces are young women, handmaidens of Venus, who share many of her attributes, including beauty, joy, the ability to inspire desire, and an inclination toward games of chance. As well as having the habit of appearing either nude or in transparent clothing, along with the Hours, they helped Aphrodite to change her garments whenever the seasons changed. And there is this, too. Apropos of our subject, they are abidingly associated with love in every aspect, including fulfillment. A fullness which in an earlier aspect of Venus, as a goddess of fertility, was linked to the cycles of earthly life.

Thus it should not surprise us that no matter how weightless the effect may be, this virtue requires a certain earthiness. While grace greases the wheels of almost any endeavor, it is by nature erotic. The way Lanthélme walked, for instance, has been called insinuating. What was insinuated, of course, as she proceeded—limbs loose, movements slow, shoulders curved forward, chest concave (as if she were pausing in a seductive undulation), hips forward—was desire. The thought of a continuing wave, her body softening against yours, would have entered your mind, just as you found your soul caught in the sway of the motion you would have been following so closely with your eyes. For it is difficult to ignore grace.

"The Call of the Wild"

The call of adventure, the call of the wild, was in most of them, no matter what they were doing.—Maud Parrish, dance hall girl

I was never a gold digger. The men threw their gold at my feet when my dances pleased them.—Klondike Kate

Her dance was famous. She would begin in the center of the stage, statuesque and still, with over two hundred yards of gauze wound tightly around her, as if she were wrapped in a cocoon. The audience was made up mostly of miners who came in to Dawson to stake their claims or refill supplies, hopefully taking a night of luxury and leisure before they would return to rough camps in the muddy fields and hills where they worked themselves to exhaustion every day looking for gold. Though with a successful claim a man might become a millionaire, this miracle more often than not eluded him. But here at the Palace Grand Theater, he could be transported to what seemed like heaven for the small price of admission and a few drinks, as somehow with uncommon grace Kate would unwrap herself nightly, suspending two hundred yards of diaphanous fabric in the air while she danced.

"She was forgetfulness of hardship and homesickness," one man said later. Of course, the light, airy image she produced would have erased the memory of dark mine shafts and bodies aching with fatigue for a few hours. It was not just a strip show she offered. Though along with her audiences he found her very appealing, the owner of the theater hired her because she was a good choreographer. And she also had, he said, a "French flair."

She was talented at evoking fantasy. Perhaps the roots of this ability lay in her childhood. Despite the modest means of her parents, her mother a waitress, her father a railroad telegraph operator, she was raised with an air of refinement as well as dreams of a better life. The atmosphere of her first years was permeated by her mother's desire for something more. A larger, more glittering life seemed to beckon her perennially. Already married once earlier, after five years of marriage with Kate's father, she divorced him, too, only to marry her lawyer, a former legislator. When this man became a successful judge and the family moved from Oswego, Kansas, to Spokane, Washington, Kate was swept into a different life, filled with every possible luxury. But the dream did not last long. Soon her stepfather lost all of his money; he died less than a year later, leaving Kate and her mother impoverished once again.

She did not enter her trade by choice. It was to prevent her mother from working in a shirtwaist factory that Kate began to look for employment herself. But at sixteen the only job she could find was in the chorus line at a Coney Island honky-tonk. In the beginning, her mother kept a close watch on her, especially after shows. But when Kate moved back to Spokane, Washington, and began work in a club there, she was taught to induce the customers to buy her drinks after each performance. It was here that, just after she moved her mother west to be closer to her, she heard the first news of the Klondike rush. After sixty-eight miners arrived in San Francisco carrying gold worth $1.5 million and the *Seattle Post Intelligencer* sent over 200,000 copies of a special Klondike edition with the headline "A Ton of Gold!" to newspapers all over the country, thousands of people—including the woman who would soon be known as "Klondike Kate"—began to pour into the Yukon territories.

At first she avoided the saloons where women were expected to take customers to the upstairs bedrooms. But once she became famous and had a private room of her own upstairs, she did not hesitate to accumulate her own fortune this way. And like all the showgirls in northwestern saloons, she would sit and drink with miners after the shows. She excelled here, too. Almost as famous for her sympathetic ear as for her magnetic performances, she was gracious as well as graceful. According to one of her biographers, "she spent many sleepless nights wrestling with the problems of some raw-boned sourdough" down on his luck. On occasion she would even grubstake a miner to a claim.

Here it would serve us to recall that the Three Graces also symbolize the eternal movement of the gift—a movement that, like all of life, is circular. What gifts she gave came back to her. As is evident in the story that a young miner named Ed Lucas has left us, something in Kate's generous nature inspired generosity. After he reached into his pocket to show her the cache of gold nuggets he had worked so hard to obtain, he said that with no forethought he found himself offering one of them to her. She chose the largest. During her first year in Dawson alone, she accumulated $30,000, a small fortune then.

One reason for her popularity must have been that she shared a great deal with the miners. Like them, she had known hard times, and like them, too, she loved the exhilarating mood of the Klondike. Since she arrived before the railway had a line into Dawson, she had come by boat up the five rapids. But because the river was thought to be dangerous for ladies, there was a law against women taking this ride. Thus to avoid the Mounties, she dressed in boy's clothes and jumped just as the boat pulled out, hitting the water before she was pulled aboard. Still, she found the journey, she said later, "perhaps the most exciting trip I ever made." A tomboy as a girl, she loved driving her team of dogs over the frozen snow and in the summer months riding "wildly" on horseback out into the meadows.

From her famous flame dance, it is easy to guess that there was something else Kate must have shared with the miners. The elation that pervaded the Yukon had another cause, more subtle, but still just as powerful as the desire for money. Gold is an old alchemical symbol. Perhaps because of its shine and the labor required for retrieving it, the metal is a metaphor not only for all that is superior but for the process of becoming better. Indeed, even the wish for a fortune is, on one level, the desire for a metamorphosis. Once wealthy, you believe, everything will change. Your spirit finally will glitter, too.

This would have been the vision Kate evoked as the drinking miners, tired from their work but happy to be in town, watched while she emerged from her cocoon, gauze suspended above her like wings, and cheered while they imagined divine grace had coupled with them, their spirits charged by the belief that they, too, were in the midst of transformation, their wildest dreams airborne.

Ecstasies of Elevation

From the stage to the auditorium . . . invisible threads criss-cross between . . . dancer's legs and men's opera glasses, in a network of arousal and liaison.—Edmond and Jules de Goncourt, Journal

Since at least the fourteenth century, dancers in the European tradition have been aiming themselves toward the sky. From the mannered ladies and gentlemen of the court, who often danced on their toes, to the masters of the pirouette and the leap, to Loie Fuller, who, like Klondike Kate, succeeded in floating her cloudlike clothing over her head, the general aspiration of dancers has been, if not to fly, then certainly to appear as if they are in flight.

The resulting illusion is even greater than it seems. For the sense is that the dancer is free not only of gravity but of earthly existence altogether and thus while moving into the more ephemeral realm of air becomes ephemeral herself. Fittingly, as she fuses with the heavens above, she takes on a metaphorical significance, too. Thus, Loie Fuller, who was described in an astronomical simile by one witness as "a sun standing in a shower of stars," was understood by the Symbolist poet Mallarmé to be less a woman than pure force, writing "with her body . . . a poem liberated from any scribe's instrument."

Though graceful movements have been associated with lightness, the idea of the dancer as a vision of purity had its apotheosis in the figure of the ballet dancer Marie Taglioni. It was her role as the Sylph in the Romantic ballet *Les Sylphides* which made her famous. Soon after the opening of this ballet at the Paris Opéra, women all over the city were fashioning their hair as she did in a style called *à la Sylphide*. The story of this ballet, set in what was, to a French audience, the exotic Scottish countryside, appropriately wreathed in mist, appealed to the sensibilities of the times. Seated comfortably before his hearth, the hero is approached by a Sylph who has fallen in love with him. At last, forgetting the woman to whom he is betrothed, he succumbs to the spirit's delicate approaches, and pursues her impulsively into the forest. We can guess at the ending already, as in so many other Romantic tales, his passion will lead to doom. On his way into the woods, he is given a potent scarf by a witch who claims he can use it to capture the Sylph. But the scarf is cursed. When he wraps it around her, the Sylph dissolves sweetly into pure air. And making his tragedy complete, while she dies, the sound of far-off wedding bells can be heard, telling the hero that at this moment, the woman he had abandoned has just married his best friend. He has lost not just one lover but love itself.

The role was created for Taglioni. She was well suited to play a Sylph, who is above all a spirit of the air. Taglioni was famous for lending her movements a light, ethereal quality. When she danced, she seemed, as

Lincoln Kirstein tells us, as if she were enclosed within "an envelope of fairy remoteness and chaste flirtations." That she danced on point only increased the effect. Though dancing on point had been seen on stage several decades earlier, Taglioni succeeded in making the technique as quiet and graceful as it had seemed loud and athletic before. Silent movement was a Romantic preference. One of Taglioni's teachers, the great Coulon, the man who developed what became known as the *style Romantique*, found a way to make noisy pirouettes and jumps silent by replacing the tapping heel of the eighteenth century with satin slippers. To her own graceful execution of this skill, Taglioni added the innovation of the tutu, with its gauzy transparency creating an even greater impression of airiness. Through her dance, she succeeded in creating an impression of purity that was unsurpassed.

Yet nothing on earth will ever be purified of its origins. Though her impressive elevations and the feathery delicacy of her landings were not illusory, her art depended on long hours of experience with gravity. Born to an Italian family that had produced dancers for three generations, Taglioni was trained by her father. By all accounts, he drove her mercilessly. Once the *premier danseur* in Italy, while he performed, composed, and produced ballet in Europe's major cities, he was eager to ready his daughter to follow in his footsteps. The practice which eventually made her appear to be so light in fact required prodigious labor. She would exercise and dance for six hours a day, sometimes collapsing with exhaustion in the middle of a session, only to be bathed by her mother, dressed in clean clothes, and made to return to her exercise. "If I ever heard my daughter dance," her father once said, "I would kill her." Along with her lightness and grace, to produce silence required an uncommon prowess, a muscular strength not usually included in the Romantic picture of feminine fragility.

But such is the nature of life on earth. Whatever exists will usually be coupled with its opposite. Gravity and grace are less antagonists than lovers. And delicacy is not a static state but instead a moment in a continuum that must also include, if one is to survive, strength and daring. During the years when Romantic ballet was prominent, the fragile-looking dancers who twirled about in ephemeral tutus were actually risking their lives. More than one died from burns when their highly flammable costumes brushed too close to the gaslights at the edge of the stage. Taglioni's student, Emily Livry, whom she had been carefully training to take her place one day, died of the burns she suffered in this way.

But there is this, too. The image of chastity that Taglioni emanated was at one end of a pendulum that swung just as often in the other direction. That the dancer Fanny Elssler, who soon rivaled Taglioni's popularity, became celebrated for her sensually suggestive movements was only part of the story. Even while Taglioni seduced her audiences with exulted sighs of motion, backstage, countless scenes of a far coarser nature were taking place. To raise interest in and hence funds for the ballet performances, Dr. Veron, who was the director of ballet at the Paris Opéra, allowed a select group of men to enter the *foyer de la danse* where the dancers practiced, warmed up, and rested after performing. Climbing a staircase installed at the left of the stage, gentlemen from the audience would give their names to an assistant, who had a list of those who were to be admitted. Once inside, they would watch the dancers work, most fascinated less by art than by anatomy, particularly legs. At the end of a performance, many men would leave with a young dancer, sometimes stealing her away from her mother's protective eyes, and at other times bargaining with a mother for the cost of an evening.

As was true for actresses, although ballet dancers were paid more than *grisettes*, the salary was small. It allowed for only the most meager existence. Unless she were a star, after basic expenses, nothing was left to support her mother or save for retirement, which for a dancer comes early. Thus, as also was true for actresses, dancers were often courtesans. The fashion for keeping dancers all through the nineteenth century was so common that the euphemism still used for keeping a mistress, "*Il a sa danseuse*," was coined in this period. Aristocrats and wealthy entrepreneurs, artists and writers, even heads of state shared a passion for dancers. Napoléon III, emperor of the Second Empire, was such a frequent visitor backstage that he kept a private room there. Baron Haussmann, the architect the emperor had commissioned to redevelop the city, kept the dancer Francine Cellier, who, in order to avoid scandal, dressed like his daughter whenever they went out together. A dancer called Finette was kept by the American painter James Whistler. Some, like Cléo de Mérode, were more famous as courtesans than dancers. And a very few such as Lolotte, for instance, who became the comtesse d'Hérouville, were courtesans only temporarily, before they ascended into the aristocracy.

It is fascinating to ponder the irony that a depiction of a woman which implies that she is more spirit than flesh should inspire raw lust. The paradox is an old one. The idea of female purity has had erotic implications for centuries. Young women presented as virgins often command higher prices in brothels than do experienced women. The desire is not only for innocence but for the spiritual renewal that is associated with a chaste body. In the end the two extremes, lust and chastity, belong to each other. Logically, one always implies the existence of the other. Neither can be defined separately. Nor ultimately can they be experienced apart from each other. In the process of preserving chastity, one must continually be wary of lust. Lust is the necessary preoccupation of chastity. It is even easier to understand that anyone possessed by spiritless desire would eventually fixate on chastity, too, as a symbol of the missing soul. Indeed, in a world in which body and spirit were separated and conceived as opposites, to achieve a fully erotic life would be like trying to balance on a narrow precipice. Thus did the ballet dancer, straining to stay aloft for a few miraculously graceful moments, her toes bent painfully back on point, have a titillating appeal, reflecting at once the possibility of ecstasy and the vulnerability of satisfaction.

The Faun

I was poor. I earned 65 rubles a month . . . not enough to feed both my mother and myself.—Vaslav Nijinsky, Notebook on Life

Bartering one's body for financial or social benefits was not unusual among young actors and actresses, ballet dancers or singers. . . .
—Peter Ostwald, Vaslav Nijinsky

Though the dancer has rarely, if ever, been called a courtesan, there are episodes in his life that could easily be found in the biography of a *cocotte*. That he was taken as a lover by several older, wealthy and more powerful men, that his bills were paid by them, that it was through his protectors he was educated and introduced to a more sophisticated world, that eventually he was to be canonized in public opinion as a celebrated object of desire, all speak to the striking resemblance.

Nijinsky met his first protector, Prince Pavel Lvov, shortly after graduating from the Imperial Ballet School, while he was still a dancer at the Maryinsky Theatre in St. Petersburg. As in Paris, it was common in Russia for wealthy men to seek lovers among men and women dancers, both groups underpaid and struggling. With his innovative interpretation of classic roles, Nijinsky was already becoming a sensation. Lvov dressed the dancer in fashionable clothes and furnished him with an elegant apartment, took him to cafés and parties, making it possible for him to mingle with a society far more affluent than he had ever encountered before. It was here that Nijinsky found still other protectors, including a Polish count, whom years later he remembered chiefly because he had bought him a piano. And he met his most famous lover in these circles, too, the man who was to make him famous: Sergei Pavlovich Diaghilev.

When Diaghilev was organizing a ballet company to import to Paris, simultaneously, Nijinsky became both his lover and his protégé. Diaghilev supported him, making sure he dressed well, suggesting what he should read, bringing him to museums, pointing out the paintings he himself admired, as well as introducing him to a set of celebrated and accomplished friends—Jean Cocteau and Marcel Proust among them. And of course, Nijinsky became a principal dancer in his lover's company. The partnership belongs to history now. With music by Igor Stravinsky, choreography by Michel Fokine, and Nijinsky as a principal performer, the company that was eventually to be called the *Ballets Russes* produced a revolution not only in dance but in all the other arts as well.

Along with facing the same circumstances which gave rise to *galanterie*, Nijinsky shared many of the virtues that courtesans had. In the role of a dancer and a choreographer, his timing was astonishing—his erotic beauty can still be seen in the photographs that survive him; the way he moved was at times so brazen that his performances inspired more than one scandal. Although he was known to be somewhat inarticulate, his choreography was brilliantly creative; he celebrated pleasure in his art; and while he was not necessarily famous for his charm, he was astonishingly graceful.

Indeed, whether or not he can be called a courtesan, Nijinsky's particular grace calls to mind an aspect of this virtue in which many courtesans were known to excel. Just as gracefulness shapes and enlivens certain traditional movements, grace also informs and even allows innovations to be made. We might even say that since innovations change our perceptions of what grace is, this virtue continually gives birth to itself. Though for the simple reason that grace is not solitary, this can never be a virgin birth. As with pleasure, grace is always coupled with culture. Thus when a culture changes, so does its estimation of what is graceful.

And there is this to consider, too. The climate of a culture is never itself isolated; rather, it hinges on history. Dance mimics the movements of the body politic. We need only remember that during the French Revolution the rigid balletic positions once required at court gave way to looser, more flowing gestures. Yet the hinge of this doorway moves in two directions. Just as often, dance provides the first signals of social change. When Nijinsky stunned Parisian audiences with an astonishing leap during which he seemed to hover momentarily in midair before disappearing into the wings, did they understand the stunning feat they had just witnessed was symbolic of a future, simultaneously invisible and palpable, a mood whose powerful presence could be felt as if hovering in the atmosphere?

The change was augured in other ways. Through one of the attributes of the Three Graces, the revelation of the body, all over Paris an ancient form of grace was returning to the stage: Lanthélme's slouch, Isadora Duncan's liquidity, La Goulue's cancan, Otero's Spanish dance, the jut of a hip, the lifting of a leg. An erotic vocabulary of movement was reappearing. Yet, as Nijinsky began more and more to explore the dimensions of his own desire, he took the revelation even further.

In the ballet he choreographed to Debussy's *L'Après-midi d'un faune*, the dancer pushed the sensibilities of his audiences to the breaking point. The music he used was composed in response to a popular poem by Mallarmé, a poem that itself had broken convention by describing masturbation. But where Mallarmé achieved his effect by subtle allusion, Nijinsky was shockingly direct. Though his choreography was innovative, the first part of the ballet was more or less acceptable. Following the traditional story, Nijinsky, who appeared wearing a wig of golden curls and horns on his head and carrying a flute and a cluster of grapes, danced the part of the Faun aroused by a bevy of nymphs who flee from all his advances. The end of the ballet, though, was a different matter. Laying on top of the scarf he had stolen from one of the nymphs, Nijinsky thrust his pelvis into the fabric, moving his whole body as if he were having an orgasm.

The dancer's art was provocative in other ways, too. Not only did he challenge the unwritten laws which forbade such a frank display of masculine sexuality, he leaped over the strict definitions that divide men from women. The fact that his body—with its thick thighs, the enormous strength, the darkly beautiful eyes—suggested androgyny made his movements seem even more a mixture of masculine and feminine conventions: here an enormous leap, there the head coquettishly tilted, here ferociously growling, there undulating across the stage like a serpent. The roles he played often accentuated this ambiguity. Cast as slave and lover of his master in more than one ballet, *Pavillon d'Armide*, *Cléopâtre*, and *Schéhérazade*, he was alternately dominant and submissive, ferocious and pliable.

That the way he danced reflected the circumstances of Nijinsky's own life did not escape his audiences, who were fascinated by the love affair between the dancer and his master. Cocteau has made a drawing of the two men, walking down the street, Diaghilev's arm around Nijinsky's shoulders, the older man engulfing the younger. We can see why Nijinsky's feelings for Diaghilev were ambivalent. He felt overpowered, and chafed at the control that the man who was not only his lover but also paid his bills and directed his career exercised over him. Eventually, Nijinsky freed himself, only to marry a wealthy woman who once again provided his support.

It does not seem far-fetched to see a mirror of his own dilemma in the central character of a ballet he created at the end of his career. In *Papillons de la Nuit*, Nijinsky told the story of a courtesan, once beautiful, now "an indomitable spirit in the traffic of love, selling girls to boys, youth to age, woman to woman, man to man." Though it was never performed, the ballet would have been fascinating, once again reflecting what audiences might have preferred to avoid, though it is easy to imagine that the image would have been strangely beautiful.

And is this not the ultimate achievement of grace? To translate difficult circumstances, contradictory demands, ambivalent feelings, painful perceptions into a dance that even as it takes the breath away, moves us in a new direction. Witnessing what we do not entirely understand, we find ourselves suddenly taking an unpredictable leap—a risk of the most dangerous kind, a leap of the imagination.

Her Graceful Curtsies

A king without diversions is a miserable man.—Pascal

Even today the story is being repeated. Long before she met Louis, she would ride at the edge of the royal forest and watch him as he hunted. It is said she cut such a graceful figure, dressed in pink, her coach a complementary blue, the king could not have failed to take note of her. Particularly since she was as agile at driving a coach as she was at riding. We know this last because after she became Louis XV's mistress, the marquise often accompanied him on his hunts, during which she was admired by many for her abilities at horsemanship.

She was not born a marquise. Along with a coat of arms and an estate, the title was given to her by the king a few months after they became lovers. That she was born a commoner would prove to be an obstruction to becoming the royal *maîtresse en titre*, yet hardly an insurmountable one. Though her father, François Poisson, was a steward to the Paris brothers, the financiers on whom both the king and the economy of France relied, no one in the family before her had ever been received at Louis XV's court; apart from the rarely gifted or most celebrated members of society, this privilege was reserved for the nobility.

Yet, despite the odds, Jeanne-Antoinette Poisson, as she was called then, had dreamed of this fate for years. She had wanted to be Louis' mistress since she was too young to have understood exactly what a lover is. It was in the ninth year of her life that her mother asked a fortuneteller to reveal her daughter's future. The ensuing prediction that Jeanne would one day become the lover of the king seemed to have impressed the whole family, who thereafter teasingly called the child "*Reinette*," meaning, in rough translation, "Little Queen."

It has been said by all who witnessed the moment when Pompadour was first presented to the king at Versailles that her curtsies were flawless. Though to a contemporary observer this may seem a minor accomplishment, verging on irrelevance, it was crucial in the eighteenth century, especially at Versailles, where the list of rules for proper deportment was as arcane as it was endless. Every move at court was crusted over with manners whose reason for being had long ago crumbled into invisibility. There was a prescribed way of sitting or rising. Protocol dictated who could and who could not sit on a chair, who could have a chair with a back, who might carry a cushion to chapel, and even at what angle the cushion should be placed (the cushions of princes of the blood could be straight, whereas those of dukes had to be angled). Ladies in court had a particular way of walking, with many short steps hidden under their skirts so that they appeared to glide; the way a woman was greeted, with a movement of the shoulder or a low curtsy, would reflect precisely how wellborn she was, how well married and even whether or not she had employed a good cook. Out of no discernible logic, certain words, *cadeau*, for instance, instead of *présent*, were considered vulgar; only people of a particular rank were allowed to carry *parapluies*, and no matter what misfortune had occurred, nothing but a cheerful expression would ever be tolerated in the public rooms.

Indeed, the separation between private life and public appearances at court was as distinct and impermeable as that between a stage and a dressing room. What resulted was a strange double life in which many quotidian events occurred two times, once ceremonially and a second time in reality. King Louis, for instance, almost always went to bed twice. The first occasion took place during the public ceremony called the *coucher* in his state bedroom, where he never really slept (the fireplace smoked and the location of the room was too public for him). After his boots were pulled off and someone from the royal bloodline, designated with the high honor, handed him his nightshirt, he made the semblance of retiring. But as soon as his courtiers left the room, he rose anew, took off the symbolic nightshirt, put his boots on again, and went out, often to search the small town of Versailles or the city of Paris for some nocturnal amusement, before he finally retired again, this time to the private room he preferred (if not to the bedroom of his mistress).

A similar redundancy took place in the morning. Rising early and working for hours in solitude—he even set his own fire to avoid waking the servants—he had to submit later in the day to a second rising that was ceremonial, called the *levée*, in the same cold and smoky room where he had pretended to sleep, during which he would hand the famous garment back to the lucky prince who had been privileged to give it to him the night before.

Pompadour's presentation to Louis XV at the court of Versailles was equally symbolic. He already knew her well. The king had noticed her on his hunts, but too shy to speak with strangers, he never approached her (though occasionally he would send a gift of game to her house). The opportunity to meet arose at an elaborate costume ball given at the palace to celebrate the dauphin's wedding. Since Louis' last mistress had died, more than one woman at the ball tried to position herself to catch his eye, a difficult task, since it was a costume ball and he entered disguised as one of several yew trees. No one knows exactly when the yew tree turned back into a king. But suddenly everyone could see him laughing with Pompadour, who, dressed as the goddess Diana, was also unmasked. Later in the evening, after Pompadour went to a second celebration at the Hôtel de Ville in Paris, when the king had dispatched his duties, he followed her there and took her into a private room, where they dined and spent the night together.

By the time she was presented to the king at Versailles, she had been his lover for several months. Indeed, for several days she had been settled in her own apartments just above the king's private rooms, to which they were connected by a small staircase and which he must have already climbed, given his reputed appetite, several times since her recent arrival.

Nevertheless, the ceremony had to be daunting for her. When just one low curtsy was a formidable feat for a woman dressed in elaborate courtly attire, protocol required that she execute three. And once the king dismissed her, which he did with a cold nod, she was expected to leave his presence by walking backward, a not wholly unreasonable requirement except for the long train of her dress, an item court fashion dictated that she must wear, and which she had to kick out of her way while receding. Miraculously, she pulled off these difficult maneuvers with a faultless grace that caused some admiration.

Though the achievement must be attributed to her natural virtues, she had received instruction. In preparation for her arrival at Versailles, Louis had dispatched two trusted men to teach her the protocol of the court, the hundreds of rules, manners, gestures, phrases, replies she would need to study and learn over three months. Was the king smiling to himself when he appointed the abbé Benois as a tutor to his mistress? Louis was known not only to enjoy a good laugh but to have a sense of humor along these lines, as when once he read a sermon on chastity aloud to Mademoiselle de Mailly, one of the royal mistresses who had

preceded Pompadour. Benois consulted with another cleric before ac-
cepting this employment, but eventually he decided that since he had not
introduced the lovers, he was not responsible for their union. He spent
three months with his charge and after that remained a lifelong friend.

Though Pompadour's audience with the king was successful, the trial
was not over yet. Her social graces would be put to the test again immediately by her presentation to the queen. Leaving the council chamber, she had to proceed back to the antechamber called *Oeil de Boeuf* and
cross it to reach the queen's chamber, all the while followed by a crowd
of spectators who had been anticipating these events with great relish.
Among all the activities at court—gambling, the hunt, romantic liaisons,
balls, ceremonious events—gossip ranked very high. Everyone, including
the queen, knew that the young woman was Louis' mistress. And knowing that she was a commoner too, many hoped for a memorable mistake.

Contemptuous of the bourgeois, the aristocracy felt threatened by the
rise of a class that was gaining both wealth and power while the landed
nobility, frittering away their riches at court, had allowed their estates to
deteriorate. Those who were not born with titles were regarded as infe-
rior. And to some it was an especially annoying affront to have a member of the bourgeoisie made into the official mistress, or *maîtresse en titre*,
an entitlement never before given to a commoner. Although those who
became close to Pompadour were almost always won over by her considerable charms, some, the duc de Richelieu in particular, would remain
steadfast enemies. The duke's acerbity toward her may well have been
partly motivated by his own insecurity over bloodlines. He had not received his title directly from his father, but instead diagonally through
his uncle. The lineage and hence his blood was thought less than pure,
and thus, as with many whose legitimacy is in some way questionable, he
turned an avidly scornful scrutiny toward the legitimacy of others.

In her first meeting with the queen, Pompadour acquitted herself well,
with only one small mistake; as she kissed the hem of the queen's skirt,
a bracelet fell off her arm. But the queen was kind to her. Instead of
dismissing her with a curt compliment about the style of her dress, as

the crowd had expected her to do, the queen asked after a mutual friend, one of the few aristocrats the Poisson family knew. Understanding the kindness of the royal gesture, the newly titled marquise responded with a warm and grateful ebullience, assuring the queen not only of her love and respect but of her desire to please her. Though Pompadour's exuberance broke an unwritten law against abundant displays of emotion at court, the queen was gratified.

Just as it might be said that Pompadour was able to negotiate the transformation of herself from commoner to favorite with uncommon grace, it can also be said that in bringing a more informal and open manner of expression to Versailles, she foreshadowed what was to be a transformation not only of the court but eventually all of society. Her displays of emotion, her frankness, her loud "forthright" voice, her free laugh, and her familiar language were at odds with standard behavior at Versailles, which according to aristocratic tradition was far more subdued. Ladies only giggled or smothered their laughter and everyone habitually hid or dampened their feelings, even when what was felt was joy. No wonder there was so much intrigue. The atmosphere of constant jockeying for position that surrounds monarchies and indeed every powerful leader was only made more acidic by the fact that anger could not be expressed openly. Hence snide remarks, subtle inferences, small praise, dismissive gestures, indeed every possible form of passive assault characterized the social life of the court.

No wonder that Pompadour's manner appealed to the king. Often laughing, visibly less calculating, liable to burst out with unpredictable enthusiasm, she must have been like a breath of fresh air to him. The painter François Boucher captured her ebullience well. In portrait after portrait, the spirit that enlivens her rose-cheeked face spills out into the room. Rendered with colors that are vibrant and soft at the same time, her dresses appear less to hang than to ripple, and the same vibrant energy seems to bless all that surrounds her; whether it is a brocade curtain, the patterned edge of a chaise-lounge, an elegantly rounded side table, a feathered pen, a clock encased in gold garlands, a compact

filled with rouge, the rose pinned to her bodice, a rose at her feet, a rose
bush behind her, a statue of a woman holding a child in a garden, a
lemon or a beech tree that catches our attention, the eye is dazzled by
exuberance.

That Boucher began to paint the marquise when she was still a child
seems fitting. She was a good subject for him. There was a strong con-
cordance between her way of being and his way of seeing. Not only did
they prefer the same bright pastel colors, they both liked flowers. She was
an avid gardener and he embellished canvasses, tapestries, and vases with
flowery forms. More significant, they shared a precise time and place in
history, positioned between one order and another: the monarchy that
was soon to fall and the bourgeois world already on the rise.

You can see the same contradictory directions, resolved into pretti-
ness, in both her life and his art. As frivolous as both the painter and the
mistress may seem today, together they invented an ingenuous version of
grace, one that allowed them to erase conflicts that otherwise might have
erased them. With a single recognizable style, Boucher has painted the
grand mythic scenes that belonged to the old order, delicate landscapes,
and the more domestic scenes that gently predict a radical shift in values. Similarly, as a young newly married woman, Madame Etioles (as
Pompadour was known before her husband was dispatched with an official decree of separation) hosted her own salon, which the *philosophes*, including Voltaire, attended. For a period even after she was at court, as
well as sponsoring Voltaire, she defended the ideas that would one day
lead to the Revolution. The lightly congenial manner which allowed her
to do so doubtless also made it easier for her eventually to relinquish
these ideas, which were not, understandably, as popular at court as they
were in Paris.

Yet there was much she did not relinquish. Though she learned
proper protocol, she never adopted the rigidly cold manner of court
ladies. And just as Boucher included intimate scenes in his repertoire, she
retained what was then considered a very bourgeois tone of intimacy
with all those who were close to her, including the king. One of the most

revealing portraits we have of her, painted by Alexandre Roslin, seems to catch her in a private moment with her brother, the marquis de Marigny. They both wear ornately embroidered silk, she rose and white, he red and gold, and the same mischievous half smile adorns both faces as if the two siblings had been interrupted in the midst of a game. Marigny, who inherited his title from his father (to whom it was given for obvious reasons by the king), holds an architectural model and a compass, while Pompadour holds a box of jewelry. Though Marigny's model was most probably made to simulate a monumental project they were designing together, the effect of the whole scene, their almost winking expressions, the tea service on the desk between them already used, is informal in an almost modern way.

The air of casual comfort which the marquise exuded must have provided a balm for Louis XV. An intensely private man for a king, he had lost his whole family practically in the space of a week when his mother, father, and brother died suddenly of diphtheria. It is said he was saved simply because his nurse would not allow the doctors, whom she rightly distrusted, to treat him. Growing up unprotected by either a mother or a father in the forbidding court of his great-grandfather Louis XIV cannot have been easy, either. And to make matters worse, after Louis XIV died, there were rumors that the regent, his great-uncle, Philippe d'Orléans, duc de Chartres, had plotted to poison him. Though the rumors were untrue—the regent was always kind to him and the young Louis grew to love him—he was surrounded by those who believed what had been said and cautioned him to be even less revealing than was usual at court.

Now here was Pompadour, who adored him and had stolen his heart, acting in a more intimate manner than anyone dreamed possible at Versailles. When she used affectionate nicknames for the members of her family, it shocked other members of the court; but Louis laughed whenever he heard her call her brother "*Frèrot*" and soon adopted silly nicknames for his daughters, calling Madame Adelaide "*Locque*" as in "rag," for instance, and Madame Victorie "*Coche*" as in "Coach."

Would Pompadour's graciousness have led her to alter her habit of familiarity had the king disliked it? Above all else, she wanted to please him. But this question cannot be answered, if only because it betrays an ignorance of the nature of what passes between lovers who are, as Louis and Pompadour were supposed to be, meant for each other. Each one's idiosyncrasies, as well as virtues, are aligned fortuitously with the other's needs and desires. Thus, even being in the presence of the beloved is a delightful gift. And in the case of Pompadour, who wanted to give more than carnal pleasures to her lover, this alignment allowed her to perceive and respond to the king's needs, at times even before he himself knew what he lacked.

She would, for instance, watch his complexion carefully. Whenever his face grew liverish and yellow, she knew that he was bored. Boredom had to be a serious condition for him. Confined for years to his nursery, he would have associated dullness with the loss of his parents, as well as the danger that reputedly surrounded him. Whenever Pompadour saw this color arise, she was on alert to divert him. Here, too, the lovers' propensities were aligned. She read widely and loved the theatre, painting, and architecture. Though among these literature was the only interest Louis did not share with her, he benefited greatly from what she read. Her library included a wide range of material, everything from history to Voltaire's philosophy to Racine's plays to paragraphs culled by censors from the court's mail to the police reports that were the equivalent of tabloids today. After her death, her brother Marigny sold her library, which contained at her death 3,525 volumes. (He withheld only one book from the sale, *Représentations de M. de Lt. Général de Police de Paris sur les Courtisanes à la Mode et les Demoiselles de Bon Ton* par une Demoiselle de Bon Ton.) She could recite whole speeches from a number of plays she knew by heart, and told Louis tidbits gleaned from less elevated sources with great comedic skill. She was known to be funny.

Let us recall that since those who make us laugh tread a thin line, perilously close to what might offend, humor requires a certain gracefulness. And the other meaning of grace, which is generosity, plays an important role in this respect, too. Witty remarks which proceed from a generous nature are more likely to be well poised, balanced carefully between kindness and candor. The wish is to tell the truth without wounding, or at least without inflicting a wound that is too grave.

Which calls to mind the fact that Pompadour was not always allowed to be funny. Understandably, given the losses Louis suffered during his childhood, he was subject to morbid moods, periods when he brooded on death, which might be sparked off by the slightest stimulus, even the sight of a cemetery from the window of the royal coach as the lovers traveled through the countryside. We can only guess that Pompadour must have tried to divert him from this preoccupation because eventually she was forbidden to try to make the king laugh on the occasions when he was dominated by such a mood. To have the patience to allow her lover to retain his gloominess would be hard for a woman who was by nature giving; yet clearly Pompadour was capable even of this.

Pompadour's generous nature, which above all she aimed at the king, may explain why Louis was known to open his purse strings more graciously with her than anyone else at his court. The gifts that she gave him in return were more than token; it was not only because she understood his nature but because she possessed considerable skills of all kinds that she was able to amuse him so successfully. Using the men and women of the court who had talent as actors or dancers, altogether she organized 122 performances of 61 different plays. And since she herself had been trained to act and sing by teachers from the Comédie-Française, more often than not she also played the major female parts. Once, she even took on the leading masculine role. It was after seeing Pompadour perform the role of the prince in *The Prince de Noisy* that Louis leaped onto the stage and embraced her, saying, "You are the most delicious woman in France."

Because of her theatrical success, plans for a theatre to be built at Versailles were drawn up. Though it was only finished after her death, during the rest of her life, all of which she lived at Versailles, she and the king had many conferences with the architect, the famous Gabriel, over the design. One of the activities that usually proved to keep the king from turning yellow was architecture. He loved to watch buildings as they went up and rooms as they were decorated, redecorated, and then decorated all over again. His interest started young, and perhaps it was also connected to loss. Soon after Louis lost his immediate family, the regent moved the seat of government to Paris, taking the young king with him to the Tuileries Palace. By the time the court returned, Louis was fourteen years old, and so enamored of Versailles that he spent days wandering around the property admiring its architecture and Lenôtre's famous gardens. History has bequeathed us a legendary scene of the young king lying for hours on the floor of the Hall of Mirrors while he focused his attention on the ceiling.

Louis and Pompadour spent a great deal of time making the rounds between one royal palace or another, as well as visiting the many houses that Pompadour had steadily acquired during her reign. Thus, in addition to her hand in the constant building at Versailles, she supervised the redecorations at Fontainebleau, Choisy, and Marly, and she also spent considerable time supervising work at her own houses—among them, the Hermitage at Versailles, her house at Crècy, a house called Montretout, another called La Celle, as well as Province, Bellevue, and the Hôtel d'Evreux, which would one day become the Palais Elysée (currently the official residence for all the presidents of France). She embellished each house with great care, arranging for fifty orange trees here, painted decorations by Loo there; a series of painting by Boucher linked together with garlands of wood carved by Verberckt adorned one room at Bellevue; walls of white and gold or bright pastel enamel in colors invented by the Martin family were everywhere; and all her houses were well ornamented by objects that she chose or even commissioned, an ormolu lantern decorated with flowers of Vincennes china, screens of amaranthus wood, Dresden candlesticks, a dovecote on a column. The list is very long. After her death, it took lawyers one year simply to make an inventory.

The public, understandably angry at the expense, complained. As did various ministers at court, especially Maurepas, who blamed the naval defeats he commanded on expenditures, the cost of which he implied should have gone to buy battleships. But the marquise's appetite mirrored Louis' need for divertissement and so the incessant building continued.

As for what remains from this period of decadence, we can only be grateful, for we have all inherited it. There is, to begin with, the simple matter of a patronage that produced so much. Pompadour was generous in her support of the arts, giving a sinecure to Voltaire at Versailles, and continuing his pension even after, feeling spurned by the king, he wrote verses maligning her; sponsoring a play by Crébillon and making certain not only that it was performed at the Comédie-Française, but that it was a success there. By the time of her death she owned hundreds of paintings, all of which had been paid for, a fact which many in the royal family and the aristocracy could not claim. Perhaps the years when she was young and her father was out of the country, a time during which she and her mother lived in poverty, gave her a sensitivity to the material needs of artists that those who are born to abundance sometimes lack.

In this she had combined two attributes of the Graces, the ability of the muse to inspire art and the generosity to support it. In addition to many other artists, she made certain that Boucher, her own official painter, was well housed and fed while suggesting projects to him and winning him many commissions. At her request, the king established the now famous factory at Sèvres for the production of porcelain vases and china for which Boucher produced many designs. And through her brother Marigny, who by her influence with the king had been made the Superintendent de Bâtiments (or as we would say it today, Beaux-Arts), she saw that Boucher was appointed director of design for the manufacture of Gobelins tapestries.

Working with her brother again, she initiated and supervised many of the monuments that characterize the city of Paris as we know it today, which would hardly be the same without the restoration of the Louvre, or the building of the Ecole Militaire, or Gabriel's designs for the Place de la Concorde and Soufflot's for the Panthéon. And though she died before its completion, it was her vision that gave us one of the prettier buildings at Versailles, the Petit Trianon.

By the light of this legacy, we can perhaps see that within Pompadour's understanding of her lover lies an understanding of human nature. A nature that responds well to what she left us, hungering not only for the bread but for the grace, too, that is our common birthright.

Satiety
(THE SIXTH EROTIC STATION)　✛ ✛ ✛ ✛ ✛ ✛ ✛ ✛ ✛ ✛ ✛ ✛

*N*ow that he's flush and has his own rooms and his own claw-footed tub, he can bathe to his heart's content, before he puts on the shirt he paid to have starched and ironed, and the shiny leather shoes and new wool suit he bought for himself on his last trip to San Francisco. He wants to look his best when he goes to the Palace Grand Theater. He's been planning this night for months, ever since his claim came in. Though he's seen it a hundred times, he does not want to be late for Kate's show. But even so, just as he starts to leave, when he notices a bit of dirt under his thumbnail, he stops to scrub it out. Although she has never complained at all about his grubby appearance whenever he came in tired from the digs and sat drinking with her, she might feel differently now that she is going to take him upstairs.

He is glad to see the show again because it gives him time to anticipate and dream, to build up to a private finale. Though he doesn't fool himself. She has to have known for a while how much he thinks of her, and yet, kind as she always was when he told her all his troubles, he knows she has another regular man, more sophisticated, more of her world. As one more time he watches the extraordinary grace with which she dances, all that gauzy fabric whirling around her, his longing has a different quality now that he knows his desire will soon be met.

He stays in the back of the theatre almost shyly until he sees her nod, and then, looking at the gold watch he has recently bought for himself, he waits for fifteen minutes, just like she told him, before he heads up the stairs toward her sanctuary. The room is as he imagined it, only being real and right there before his eyes—something he can touch and feel and smell—even better. The walls are red and gold; the red bedspread matches the walls, and all the littler things, the picture frames, the vases, the satin-covered chair, show her knowledge of fine things, a knowledge he hopes to have someday for himself. And the way she invites him in is fine, too, making him comfortable and yet at the same time giving him the sense that everything she does is a cut above the ordinary.

What a sense of satisfaction he feels now as slowly she lays her lovely robe over the bedpost. And while he moves across the room to her he marvels at the fine lingerie she is wearing, which she tells him came all the way from France. All the refinement of the room seems to be in her body, the way her skin feels against his. And she amazes him in still other ways. Perhaps he should have guessed at the skills she had. After all, he said to himself when he reflected on it later, anyone who can keep two hundred yards of chiffon flying above her head ought to be able to elevate just about anything. She can tease weight itself past gravity, he thought. But it is not just the mechanics of what she does that has impressed him. He has all he longed for now, even what he never quite understood before that he wanted. It is not just that she had made him happy. He is laughing to find himself lighter than air. And she has given him a deeper pleasure, too; as if reaching into the center of who he is, she has mined the gold that was deep inside.

SARAH BERNHARDT

Chapter Seven

Charm

Some of the wildest men make the best pets.
—Mae West in *Belle of the Nineties* (1934)

THE SEVENTH VIRTUE is enigmatic. Charm, as the dictionary explains, is the ability to please, a definition which may seem simple until, examining the question more closely, we realize almost nothing has been said about its nature. Yet in a sense the mysterious composition of charm is part of the appeal the ability has for us. The virtue seems magical. In fact, as the dictionary also tells us, the word can be used to denote an amulet, an object that possesses magical powers. And the word is also used for certain songs that when recited cast a spell. Thus, when we say that a man has been charmed, we may mean either that he has been pleased or that he has been placed under a state of enchantment. Or, as is often the case, both.

Faced with a charming woman, for instance, you will feel yourself ceding control almost immediately. Suddenly, your body seems to have a mind of its own. Perhaps you sense a spreading feeling of warmth and then an excitement, one that enlivens both body and soul, almost as if you were being reborn. It hardly surprises you therefore that soon you find yourself letting down your guard. You may reveal to her what you never intended to reveal to anyone or laugh at what you never found humorous before. Then you realize you have agreed to what, in different company, you might have found to be rather wild propositions. And all the time you feel looser somehow in your limbs, closer to liquid than substance. Have you become putty in her hands? Even if this were true, the pleasure is too delicious for you to worry about any such consideration. On the contrary, you are more than happy to stay in her hands for as long as it is conceivably possible and by any means necessary.

That despite every impediment to and prejudice against their sex so many women have triumphed through charm has caused alarm among men for centuries. Perhaps this is why the virtue has often been linked to danger and fatality. Ironically, this idea was more dangerous to women than charm ever was to men. In a period when women accused of witchcraft were being burned at the stake, the association between witchcraft and the courtesan's charm was more than etymological. When, in the early seventeenth century, Thomas Coryat warned the traveler to Venice, "thou must fortify thine eares against the attractive enchantment of their plausible speeches," he was not speaking metaphorically. Just as the judges of the Inquisition frequently accused witches of inspiring lust, courtesans were often accused of using witchcraft. Though she was acquitted, even the respected Veronica Franco was tried as a witch.

Nor should we be surprised that a battle would be fought at the nexus between magic and sexuality. The lines of the conflict can be traced back to ancient Greece, where the courtesan was often thought to possess sacred powers. Like the witches who were to come later, the hetaerae practiced healing arts, prescribing herbs or acting as midwives. It was even believed by some that, through lovemaking, these women could initiate men into the mysteries of Venus. Mysteries that are often the source of unpredictable if not tumultuous transformations.

Revelation

... mystery is the visible, not the invisible.
—Oscar Wilde

History has commended Hyperides for understanding the limits of reason. Though the arguments he made in defense of his client, the hetaera known as Phyrne, were brilliant, he knew that even his best powers of persuasion could not win the case. The failure is understandable. The dispute in question centered less on logic than belief. Phyrne, who was not just a courtesan but also a priestess of Aphrodite, stood accused of sacrilege. She had, it was said, invented a god, an act of imagination absolutely forbidden to mortals.

To understand the atmosphere in which this trial was conducted, the contemporary mind must reach back to a time when religion and government were not separated, and hence worship was at the heart of civic life. Under these circumstances, the investiture of a new god could alter the cohesive fabric of society. Thus, the creation of a new deity would give considerable political power to the creator.

Neither the defendant nor the lawyer could dispute the simple facts of the charge; Phyrne had indeed created an original god. All that was left for her defense would be to claim that her right to do so was legitimate. The argument Hyperides made was that as a priestess, Phyrne had been channeling Aphrodite. The goddess herself, he reasoned, was expressing her will through Phyrne. But the argument by itself failed to impress the court.

It is easy to see why mere words would not work in this case. Ordinary discourse grows pale when faced with religious belief. Faith, reverie, prayer, vision, passion, and ecstasy are less the products of reason than of experience. This is why religious teachings are so often rendered through metaphor: the body of Christ eaten symbolically in the ritual of communion, the unleavened bread spread with symbolic mortar during Passover, the fasts and feasts so important to Islamic practice. To be kept alive, a religion must be felt with both soul and body.

Having been raised in a religious culture, Hyperides knew that to win his case, he had to present the court with a revelation. So it was that while Phyrne was standing in the witness box, he asked her to remove her clothing. The strategy worked. According to reports that have come down to us through the ages, awestruck by what they saw, the jurors quickly declared that the presence of Aphrodite was the only possible explanation for such beauty.

In the more secular perspective of contemporary consciousness, Hyperides' strategy appears to have been aimed at carnal appetite rather than the soul. By this standard, the court's better judgment was simply undermined. But this is to ignore the fact that what the jurors declared was correct. Even if we view Aphrodite as an archetype or metaphor for erotic love, it is clear that her formidable force was present at these proceedings. If the jurors' vision was clouded, it was through another means altogether. Though what they thought they were seeing was simply beauty, while they studied Phyrne's body, the jurors were being charmed.

To understand what occurred, it is necessary to state what is obvious, that there are two fundamentally different, if not opposite, categories of nudity. Images of the first kind of nude, in which the body is objectified, are so widely distributed and popular that they often obscure the existence of the second kind, in which the body is a subject, which is to say, aware.

Self-reflection is a desire felt by the body as well as the soul. As dancers, healers, and saints all know, when you turn your attention toward even the simplest physical process—breath, the small movements of the eyes, the turning of a foot in midair—what might have seemed dull matter suddenly awakens. Being a courtesan, of course, Phyrne had a highly refined awareness of her body. That she was fully conversant with her self showed in the way she walked across a room, the movement of her thighs, hips, belly, and shoulders redolent with the body's wisdom. Yet she did not have to move through space for the effect to be felt. Even sitting still in the witness box, it was as if all her flesh, not just skin, muscle, and bone but even the atoms themselves, joined in a subtle harmonious motion. An alchemical dance so in tune with the essence of life that to witness it was to fall into a trance.

This was an art with which she was familiar. As a priestess of Aphrodite, she knew how to induce trance. She was famous, in fact, for using the sight of her own body for this purpose. Once a year, she would immerse herself in the sea from which Aphrodite was said to have sprung. The sight of Phyrne as she emerged must have stunned those who worshipped at her temple. She was not unclothed, but her wet clothing clung to her body so that even the subtlest movement became visible.

Here, of course, the metaphor became reality. But we must remember that metaphor is always real. When Sappho speaks of the purple robes of love, imagining the lush color and the feel of the smooth fabric, those who listen to her words are enjoying a pleasure that is as real as any other. That the meaning is layered only makes the pleasure deeper. So it was when Phyrne arose from the sea. Her beauty, the vitality of her flesh, the flow of the water, would evoke all beauty, all life, all seas, including the waters of our cells and the inner waters of dreams.

And there is the nature of symbolism to consider too. Metaphor itself as a device tends to evoke connection, showing how one thing echoes and evokes another, leading us toward a particularly sensual understanding: knowledge that we are all part of one body. That this spiritual lesson is of its nature erotic belongs to the wisdom of the goddess who is sometimes called Aphrodite the courtesan. Among her many attributes was a golden chain, which she used both to join lovers and to bind all life together. In this lustrous light, Hyperides' argument that Phyrne was expressing the will of Aphrodite when she created a new god seems even more plausible, especially when we learn that the new idol in question was the god of sharing.

The court agreed with Hyperides and acquitted Phyrne of all charges. And so the story ends and we would end here, were we not concerned with charm. On this account, one more observation must be added. It is only possible to grasp the great powers of Phyrne's virtue when we consider the conflict that acquitting her must have stirred among the jurors. Even if Phyrne had been obeying the will of Aphrodite, by this acquittal, the court had decreed that a mortal had created an immortal. Yet, according to the philosophy which at the time must have ordered all their thoughts, mortality was carefully set apart from immortality, an opposite to and even a corruption of the glories of infinity.

But perhaps through her image they were pulled by earlier philosophies, not in private memory so much as inherited from ancient figures and rhymes, part of Aphrodite's own past, when she was known as Astarte or Ishtar, from a time when it was said that eternity is made from mortality through the unending cycles of life in which we all take part.

As if to prove that the court was right in the end, Phyrne herself has received a kind of immortality. The most famous among the many sculptures done by her lover Praxiteles was modeled after her body. Considered the finest sculptor of antiquity, according to testimony, he was able to capture her extraordinary vibrancy brilliantly. Though his *Aphrodite of Cnidus* has been lost, its powers were apparently so great that the sculpture established what was to be the classic form for nude sculptures of women, especially those of Venus, over many centuries. When we think of the realm of Aphrodite today, it is still Phyrne's body that we see, tempting us toward her mysteries.

Bewitched at First Sight

King Louis was bewitched at first sight of that lovely smiling face, so singularly pure and innocent, on which all her sordid experiences had left not a trace.—Joan Haslip, Madame du Barry, the Wages of Beauty

That Madame du Barry had a charmed life is indisputable, though it is also inarguable that in the beginning this outcome would have been nearly impossible to predict. Jeanne du Barry, as she came to be known, had what the eighteenth century called a low birth. Less elevated in station than Pompadour, her family was neither wealthy nor part of the respectable bourgeoisie. There had been, however, a faint brush with nobility. Before he met her grandmother, her handsome grandfather, Fabien Bécu, was married to a countess. But because he was a commoner, when this noblewoman married him, she lost her hereditary privileges. Still, that he remained a commoner did not prevent him from squandering all her money. Thus, after she died at an early age, he was forced to return to his old profession as a cook. It was while he was serving as the chef in a château that he met Jeanne's grandmother, a lady's maid.

The barest hint of a foreshadow can be seen in the fact that as is often the case with those who live a more privileged life for a limited period, Fabien had learned refined manners, and he passed these on to his daughter Anne, Jeanne's mother. She also inherited his beauty. She too would have been taken into the employment of a noble house were it not for her rebellious nature. Even if the cost was a less comfortable life, she preferred her independence. In the beginning luck was against her. She was working as a seamstress in Vaucouleurs, a town at the edge of the Lorraine, when she became pregnant with Jeanne. Seduced and abandoned by a handsome monk called "Brother Angel," who because of the scandal was dismissed from his order and dispatched to Paris, Jeanne and her mother were left to fend for themselves in Vaucouleurs.

Yet, notwithstanding the fact that almost everything in this chapter of the story leans toward a modest if not sad end, when Jeanne was just four years old, Anne's fate took a happy turn. When she gave birth to a second child by another lover, she was not abandoned. Instead, Monsieur Billard-Dumonceaux, who was a man of means, well positioned and somewhat powerful as a paymaster of Paris and inspector of the army commissariats, summoned the small ménage to Paris. He put the family in separate lodgings for a few months, but when the little boy he had fathered died, he decided to move Anne and Jeanne into his own grand and luxurious home.

Here, what was no doubt a misfortune for her mother would, in hindsight, be fortunate for Jeanne. Dumonceaux already had a lover, a woman who lived with him. The identity of this woman can hardly have seemed as auspicious to Jeanne, then just four years old, as it clearly seems to us today. The mistress of Dumonceaux's household was an Italian courtesan, well known in the world of *galanterie* as Madame Frédérique, but known to Jeanne, who came to love her, simply as Francesca.

Francesca, as it turned out, loved the little girl, too. Jeanne was often allowed into her bedroom, which with its velvet chairs, taffeta bedcovers, and scented pillows must have seemed as seductive as the voluptuous courtesan herself. Jeanne loved Francesca's toiletries, the golden brushes and handmirrors, the perfume bottles, her clothing, her jewels; in turn, Francesca loved dressing the very pretty little girl in beautiful clothes. The details have not survived, but small garments of lace and velvet come to mind. She was taught to dance and in other ways entertain the guests who came to the house. And Dumonceaux, who was a bit pretentious where art was concerned, painted her as a nymph in the manner of Boucher.

For two years, Jeanne was the adored center of this unconventional household. But fate took still another turn. Yielding to admonitions from her family to lead a more respectable life, Anne Bécu married a plain man who, because he had a small annuity, was able to provide for her. Any reluctance he might have had over this union was quickly dispelled by the fact that Dumonceaux arranged a lucrative position for him at the army commissariat in Corsica. In the same year, Francesca, perhaps wishing to retain her influence over Jeanne, convinced Dumonceaux to send the child to Saint-Aure's, a convent designed to prepare respectable girls for modest employment in the domestic trades.

The change cannot have been easy. The romantic atmosphere Jeanne had grown used to was absent here. All her pretty dresses were taken from her, replaced with a plain uniform and a plain black veil that completely hid the golden hair so often admired by Francesca. But the child had a basically sunny disposition. And understandably, given the unstable nature of her past, she was good at adapting to different climates. She obeyed all the new rules she had been made to learn, recited her catechisms and prayers, kneeled and rose at the right times, all with an air of insouciance that charmed even the Mother Superior.

Fate, of course, is only one element guiding the course of a life. To every circumstance there are many possible responses. Even at the beginning of what would in the end be a nine-year tenure in the convent,

Jeanne's character had begun to emerge. For the rest of her life, she would be known not only as beautiful but as charming. The alchemy of this virtue can be observed in her early years, years filled, as we have said, with constant change, but also admiration. An effective means to meet, and even at times control, fate was handed to her young. It remained for her to put her own stamp on the ability.

After she left the convent at the age of fifteen, the narrative of her life unfolded swiftly. Francesca, whom she rushed eagerly to meet, was not happy to receive such a beautiful young woman. Jeanne had turned into a potential rival. No further help could be expected now from either Francesca or Dumonceaux. Jeanne was forced to find employment. Her mother's sister knew a hairdresser who needed an apprentice, so the problem of her support seemed, at least for a time, solved. Yet, almost too predictably, she and the hairdresser fell in love. And after they began living together, his mother, who had a better match in mind, threatened to send Jeanne to Salpêtrière, the asylum where wanton women were imprisoned.

To prevent her daughter's imprisonment, Anne took the hairdresser to court with the accusation that he had corrupted a minor. And here we can already find the evidence of an ingredient essential to the charm by which Jeanne would one day win the king of France as her lover. She seemed innocent, far too innocent to the judges to be anything but the victim of a young man's advances. Thus, to avoid prison, her lover had to flee to London.

What followed was a period as companion to the wealthy widow of a *fermier général*,* which ended because of the many intrigues in the household she attracted, the somewhat welcome attention of the lady's two sons, who were both married, and the unwelcome advances of one of the widow's daughters-in-law, who was attracted to Jeanne, too.

Because of the scandal, she was dismissed. But she did not leave empty-handed. Among the wealthy men Jeanne had met in this château, there were some who habituated a shop in Paris so famous for its luxu-

* A collector of revenues.

rious fashions that it was virtually a meeting place for courtesans and libertines. For a brief period she was happily employed at Labille's "A La Toilette," a glamorous place with a heady mix of great ladies, noblemen, officers, courtiers, and courtesans, all of whom came for the painted fans and feathers, ribboned hats, and elegant sword knots. But this too would be just one more way station on her trajectory toward an unlikely destination. Tall and blond, with almond-shaped blue eyes sparkling from a sweetly delicate complexion, Jeanne was a stellar attraction among the *grisettes* working for Labille, most of whom traded their attentions for gifts they received from a clientele that included wealthy bankers, merchants, and government officials. For a period Jeanne lived with various lovers, but though she was offered a shop and house of her own more than once, she kept her independence.

Her resolve did not, however, last for very long. At the public festivities held to celebrate the placement of a statue of Louis XV in the Place de la Concorde, she caught the attention of the comte Jean du Barry. Born to a titled but impoverished family in Toulouse, though the land and manor he had inherited from his godfather afforded him a respectable income, du Barry lived so far beyond his means that soon all he had left was debt. At which point, he abandoned his wife and infant son to cultivate his connections with wealthy men until eventually he arrived in Paris. But despite these connections, he failed to win the diplomatic appointment he sought. Thus, he turned to another way to make his fortune. Possessed of a fascinating charm himself, he became the procurer for a group of men from the most prominent families in France. Searching the city for beautiful women, *grisettes*, shopgirls, and actresses, he could be counted on to provide aristocrats with their mistresses.

In the beginning, he kept Jeanne for himself. She went to live with him in exchange for a sum of money he paid to her parents. Jeanne herself was pleased with the luxuries with which he surrounded her, while for a period he preserved the girl for himself alone. Yet clearly he had other plans. He began almost immediately to prepare her for her debut in higher society. The fine French accent she had learned to speak at Saint-Aure's, and her education there—she had read Shakespeare and was familiar with Greek and Roman classics—and the exquisite sense of fashion she had learned at Labille's shop served her well, and to this du Barry added a certain worldliness. She was presented as his mistress at the Opéra, taken in an elegant carriage to balls and parties, where she mingled and conversed with aristocrats, poets, and writers. And like so many courtesans before and after her, while she was trained to appear as if she were a noblewoman, she also became well versed in erotic arts.

Of the many men to whom Jean du Barry sold Jeanne's favors in this period, probably the most important was the duc de Richelieu. He would be a loyal ally until his own death once she became the king's lover. Yet ironically, it was a meeting with the man who was to become her chief enemy at the court that brought her, almost by accident, into the king's visual range. (For such was her charm that for all practical purposes she won him in a single glance.)

Still hoping for a diplomatic post, and thinking that Choiseul, Louis' minister of foreign affairs, would not be able to resist her, du Barry sent Jeanne to Versailles to plead his case. But Choiseul was not attracted to her. "She was not at all to my taste," he wrote; rightly suspicious of du Barry, he dismissed her.

Disappointed as she may have been, Jeanne must have resolved that the trip she had made not be entirely in vain. The king would soon be leaving mass and going to dine, and like all Parisians, she knew that the public was allowed to watch him as he walked there. Hence she made her way to the state apartments and managed to find a place at the front of the crowd, which was pressed against the royal balustrades, waiting to see their king pass by.

The public was there so often, observing him every time he went to mass or sat down to dine, that the king could easily have failed to turn in her direction. Unless—and this of course is pure conjecture—a certain kind of charm is not only figuratively magnetic but literally so. As absurd as the proposition may sound, it often does appear that very charming people have the power to draw the attention of those in whom they are interested into their own orbits. Whatever the explanation, Louis did turn toward her, and he was immediately struck by what has been described by many of those who knew her as the radiance of her presence.

Three centuries later, we are still speculating what it could have been, once the king turned, that moved him so at the sight of this woman. Of course, she was uncommonly beautiful, but so were many of the women who surrounded him. Like his great-grandfather, the lustful "Sun King," Louis XV was a famously amorous man. He liked to make love with his *maîtresse en titre*, whoever she was, at least twice a day. Moreover, in addition to occasionally spending a night with the queen, he had other, more transitory lovers. While she was still living, Pompadour, who had a more fragile nature and was literally worn out by his appetites, sought to protect him from public scandal by establishing a house called Le Parc aux Cerfs.* His valet, Lebel, picked out the beautiful women who were housed there while they waited for royal visits.

Though he did not bring Jeanne to the Parc aux Cerfs, this must have been the destination Lebel thought the king eventually intended when Louis asked that he bring her to him. Not only was she born a natural child to a seamstress in the provinces, but she was a prostitute living with the notorious Jean du Barry. When finally she came to Versailles as Louis' *maîtresse en titre*, this caused some controversy. Lebel tried to warn him about her past, but Louis was so in love that no one could dissuade him.

In part, his ardor can be explained by what he said to the duc de Richelieu. "She is the only woman who can satisfy me," he told him. Yet this does not solve the mystery so much as locate it. What it was he needed and what it was she gave him are two questions still unanswered. We know that Jeanne was skillful in bed. But skill, especially for a king, used to the best of everything, is never satisfying by itself. Can anything be worse than clinical manipulation where desire is concerned? It was not only her body that he wanted. Apparently long after she had moved into

* The Deer Park.

the palace, he had an almost insatiable wish for her company. True, the king must have been lonely. The queen, who had not satisfied him sexually in years but whom he loved, had recently died. Pompadour, his great friend for years, even after they were no longer lovers, was gone, too. Still there were countless women, noble and otherwise, who would have been happy to accompany him anywhere.

Since love is, of course, mysterious, it would be hubris to pretend to understand the chemistry between these two. If we are tempted to conjecture, it is only because the moment when Louis turned his head has been so well described, a moment that, if it was not love at first sight, certainly contained a powerful premonition of love. Were we to paint the famous scene, the focal point of the canvas would have to be Jeanne's smile. Louis was amazed that she had smiled at him at all. An expression that, under the circumstances, was somewhat brazen.

But where swaying the powerful is concerned, of the two virtues that are most efficacious, cheek and charm, the latter is by far the more important. And Jeanne's smile, as it so happens, was known to be exceedingly charming. In an instant, she managed to convey the impression when she smiled that she was innocent, almost virginal. Yet it was by no means innocence alone that drew the king. At the same time that she seemed fresh, untouched, pure, she made no attempt at all to conceal what in fact she knew. Sexual knowledge is evident not only in bed but in the way a woman carries herself anywhere, the expression in her eyes, her gestures. Jeanne's considerable background in matters of the flesh would have been evident in her least movement, including the subtle shift that occurs as a smile passes over a face.

If this mixture of innocence and experience seems an unlikely achievement to us today, in the eighteenth century it must have seemed miraculous. Yet, looking back at her childhood, the provenance of the mix becomes easier to explain. We have only to begin with the simple fact that her father was a monk. And when we add to this that at the age of four she moved with her mother into the home of her mother's lover, which was shared with his principal lover, a courtesan, the answer becomes almost obvious. Especially when we consider that it was a courtesan, Francesca, who arranged for Jeanne to be sent to a convent school. And that soon after leaving the protection of the nuns, her mother arranged for her to live with a man who planned to sell her sexual favors to the most distinguished members of society.

Not only did Jeanne know the backside of polite society, she was raised to be so familiar with it that nothing of this order shocked her, including her own past. She was, in short, unashamed. Neither her parentage, her upbringing, nor anything she had done to survive in the past embarrassed her. She accepted all that had occurred in her life as if it were ordinary.

That at the convent she attended, she must have heard more than one lecture condemning the way that both her mother and Francesca lived, hardly undermined her convictions but instead must have given her sensibility another level of complexity that would help her in the future. Rather than weep or wonder over the contradictions in her life, Jeanne accepted contradiction as part of the natural order. What was said in church did not necessarily have to apply to what was done outside church. After all, by the time she was a young woman, her father had become a priest ministering to upper-class ladies at Saint-Eustache in Paris.

The ability to ignore conflict must have accounted for her great adaptability. She learned the manners and language of Versailles more easily than had Pompadour. Louis arranged for her to be married to Jean du Barry's brother. Though this may seem odd to us now, the marriage made her seem more respectable, and especially since she was a countess now, eased the way for her move to court. Louis designed a coat of arms for her. And soon she was living above him in the bedrooms once occupied by the late Dauphine.

As they had with Pompadour, many of the king's ministers and courtiers waited for du Barry to make some fatal mistake, but the king only fell more and more deeply in love with her. And in the light of our conjecture, perhaps, finally one can see why. If, for instance, as Louis had implied once to Richelieu, he was suffering in his older age from some sexual dysfunction, Jeanne would have given him just what he needed, not only her skills, but her cheerful, unclouded attitude. The stunning absence of shame she displayed must have relieved the burden of his own guilt, inculcated by years of religious training together with the judgments from many at court, and from the public, too, over his infidelities, a guilt which must have had an inhibiting effect.

Despite, or perhaps because of, Louis' evident pleasure with his mistress, the judgments continued. The citizenry of Paris, angry about how much money Louis spent on her, circulated verses about the countess describing her as a slovenly whore. It was thus more to defend herself than for any other reason that Jeanne became involved in intrigue. Despite the fact that many opposed her, she was also well liked. It was her smile again, which she distributed without prejudice to the highest and lowest born alike. She was known to be kind. The journalist Brissot told the story of her that the day he first visited Voltaire, he encountered her descending the stairs of the great man's house, and because she smiled at him, he took the risk of asking her if Voltaire was receiving visitors. "Very few," she replied; but immediately she escorted him up the stairs and gave him the introduction he needed.

Beginning as the lover of the most powerful man in France, she became a very powerful woman. She was known to have dictated the letter Louis signed asking his brother, the king of Spain, not to risk war with England over the Falkland Islands. She succeeded in bringing down her enemy, Choiseul. Louis dismissed him and he was exiled to the provinces. At her urgings, her good friend the duc d'Aiguillon was appointed minister of foreign affairs. Moreover, once he was in place, she used her influence with him regarding the appointment of ambassadors. At her urging, the baron de Breteuil, whom she felt had snubbed her, was dismissed from his post in Vienna, only to be replaced with the largely incompetent Louis de Rohan, who was among her admirers. At the height of her tenure, her salon would often be crowded with petitioners, including many among the *fermiers généraux*, asking for her help or wanting to tell her their opinions on various affairs of state.

Many men would have been threatened by such potency in a lover. But far from objecting, Louis seems to have been eager to spend even more time with her during this period. A woman who, from her youngest days, was aware of the formidable effect that her beauty and her charms had on others, would well have been able to understand and empathize with the burdens of a king, himself surrounded so much of the time by sycophantic admirers. That the lovers had this experience in common would have made for a strong attraction. The courtesan's charm has often been described as a dangerous form of power. Yet rarely, if ever, has it been admitted how forcefully powerful men are drawn to powerful women.

A Fatal Attraction

I am no more than the shadow of a king.—King Ludwig of Bavaria

Passion is often a weathervane for change in the political atmosphere. As the idea of monarchy came under assault in Europe, the romantic liaisons between kings and their lovers became more tumultuous. A hundred years after Louis XV succumbed to the charms of Jeanne du Barry, King Ludwig I of Bavaria fell deeply in love with a courtesan. Lola Montez had such a disquieting effect on Bavaria and its king that before the affair had ended, she would be forcibly ejected from the country and Ludwig would give up his crown.

Where Madame du Barry was adaptable, Lola Montez was imaginative. Though she claimed to be the daughter of Don Carlos, a Spanish aristocrat killed in a noble cause, this story was only part of an elaborate fable she created about herself. She was, in fact, born in Ireland under the name of Elizabeth Rosanna Gilbert. Her mother Eliza, the natural child of a landed gentleman and his mistress in County Cork, was a seamstress when she met Lola's father, Edward Gilbert, an ensign with the British army.

As with most fiction, however, there was a seed of truth to Lola's story. When she was just two years old, her father successfully petitioned for a post to Bengal in India and thus for three years she lived in a lushly tropical setting. And as in her story, she had witnessed her father's death. Only a few weeks after the family arrived, Gilbert succumbed to cholera.

The mother and daughter stayed on in India, and within a year Eliza Gilbert had married again, this time to an officer named Craigie. Lola's new stepfather, it turned out, would be far more attentive to her than her mother was. But still she felt neglected. While Craigie was out on his command, she was largely left to the care of an ayah who pampered her, bathing her twice a day in the Houghly River, letting her run barefoot in the village. Late in her life, when in her memoir she reclaimed this past, she recalled being fascinated by the parade of exotic birds and monkeys, and by the dancers and holy men who were part of the out-door village life. Was it memories of Southern climates that eventually pulled her to study flamenco dance in Spain?

What is taken away from us suddenly or by force will have a strong appeal for years afterward, stronger than if we had relinquished whatever we loved more naturally, over the course of time. When the child was five, Craigie, who was concerned that Lola was too wild, arranged for her to be sent to England, where she could receive a proper education. The decision was reached and acted upon quickly. She was handed over to friends of Craigie's, Lieutenant Colonel Innes and his family, who were returning to England themselves. The shock must have been great. Her mother and father, the ayah who raised her, the scents of the flowers, the feel of the river, the luxury of bare feet, of moving blithely through warm air, were all suddenly gone. And the manner in which she was raised also changed. The Innes family, who were strangers to her, were kind but far more strict in their habits. As it grew colder and colder and the ship moved further and further away from all she had known, the mood of the child grew more stormy. For the rest of her life she would be famous for a raging anger that could be triggered by even the small-est incident.

She was not to see her mother again until she was fifteen years old.

Her life could not have seemed secure to her. Along with her tumultuous emotions, there were several more moves. For four years, Elizabeth lived with Craigie's mother and father in a small Scottish town, whose inhabitants regarded the manners she had learned in India as exotic. Still another series of moves came when she was ten, at which time she traveled with Craigie's sister and brother-in-law to England, where she stayed with them for a year before being settled for a few months with Craigie's commanding officer, Major General Sir Jasper Nicolls, who, before returning to England, had agreed to find a proper school for her. Elizabeth's temperament could only have been exacerbated by the fact that Sir Jasper did not like his headstrong charge. She was described, even at this age, as having an "iron will." Finally at eleven, she was sent to a boarding school run by the Misses Aldridge in Bath.

It was an excellent school. She had been well provided for, except that she must have still felt abandoned. Sir Jasper, who liked her mother even less than he liked her, complained that when he needed answers to his questions about the daughter's education, Mrs. Craigie failed to answer the letters he sent either often or punctually enough. The failure must have made Elizabeth wonder if her mother cared about her. But this did not stop her from longing to see her family again. At last, when she turned fifteen, the date at which it was generally agreed a young woman should be prepared for marriage, knowing that only she could handle this, Mrs. Craigie arrived in England.

But the long-awaited reunion between mother and daughter did not go very well. After such a long absence, Elizabeth scarcely knew her mother any longer. According to her later memories, when at their first meeting she enthusiastically threw her arms around her mother, Mrs. Craigie withdrew, commenting, "My child, how badly your hair is dressed!" The scene corresponds to the description Montez would write later of her mother as a vain, self-centered woman, who liked parties and balls above all else and was more focused on her own appearance than on her daughter.

According to Lola again, the Craigies had already settled on a husband for her. Was he an older man in his sixties, as she said? As with many courtesans, the truth of Lola's telling cannot be trusted; indeed, the propensity to stretch the truth for the sake of a good story was not a small part of the courtesan's charm. Yet given the humor of the times, during which marriages of convenience were commonly made, this story is not unlikely. In any case, it does not take any great act of imagination for us to understand that after so many years of being moved without her consent from one place and one family to another, to be carried off forcibly to spend the rest of her life with a man she did not know would have disturbed her.

Where Jeanne du Barry was adaptable, Elizabeth was tenacious. In her own account, she felt she was spoiled by her ayah. Though, instead of permissiveness, the factor that corrupted her more may well have been that her caretaker was also her servant. And this, too, should be mentioned. She must have developed her determination not only in response to change but also to counter the effects of neglect, the loneliness that is engendered from feeling unloved. The other happier quality Elizabeth developed in the same period, one that can also be the fruit of loneliness, was an independence of mind extraordinary for a young woman of this period. It was a quality that could only have been augmented by her education, one that was exceptional for girls—she studied history and literature as well as the more usual embroidery and dance—an education that, despite whatever she was told about the proper behavior of a lady, she must have wanted to put to use.

She was, in short, too large for the role in which her mother wanted to contain her. Like the little girl who had seen too much of the world to fit in easily with provincial Scottish life, now her capabilities were too great for her to play the part of a docile bride. The outcome should have been predictable. Tall and willowy, with large blue eyes and raven-colored hair, she was ravishingly beautiful. A lieutenant who had befriended her mother on the journey from India began to take an interest in her. And very soon, they eloped.

The Craigies were so unhappy with their daughter that in the beginning they shunned her. Thomas James, the man she had married, was not a person of means. For her part, along with the first flush of love, she must have looked on this marriage as a way to achieve more freedom. She had evaded her parents' plans by it; she was no longer under her parents' orders at all. But it would not be long before her husband let her know that now he had the upper hand. On the lengthy journey by boat upriver that they made to his station after they returned to India, he busied himself with a notebook where he recorded all her failures as a wife. The marriage did not last long.

After their separation, she may have wanted to stay in India, but this was deemed improper by her stepfather Craigie and her estranged husband. She was obliged to return to Scotland, where it was decided she would live with Craigie's brother. But (and by now this too should have been predictable) she never arrived in Scotland at all. Instead, exciting outrage among the other respectable passengers, she took George Lennox as her lover on the steamship home. After the ship landed, she spent the night with Lennox in a hotel in London. And a few days later, she rented a first-floor suite on Ryder Street in a fashionable neighborhood. The affair continued for several months.

Lennox introduced her to London's high society, where she cut an impressive figure. This was the life she had dreamed of living. The couple attended a round of parties together and enjoyed the city's theatres. But these halcyon days were to end quickly. Word reached her husband of her infidelities, the affair with Lennox ended, and her world started to collapse. Seeking revenge, James took both Lennox and Elizabeth to public court, where he sued them for adultery. With no means of support, and her reputation ruined, Elizabeth's chance for any but the dreariest of futures was too narrow to contemplate. Though she tried to settle quietly with Craigie's brother, even this recourse was closed to her now. She seemed almost without options.

Yet for those who are exceedingly charming, fortune often fails to obey convention. From what must have seemed the insurmountable impasse of her life, Elizabeth Gilbert James reinvented herself entirely. She would, she determined, earn her living as a performer. Since she had shown some talent for dance at school, she decided she would become a dancer. But what kind of dance could she do? Ballet was not possible, of course; she was too old. Then, perhaps drawn even if unconsciously by the warmth of another Southern culture that had to have evoked the early days in India, she settled on the idea of Spanish dance, a style that was particularly popular since it had been introduced into ballet by Fanny Elssler and Marie Taglioni. This was how she would begin a new life.

After studying boleros and chacuchas in Cádiz, the young woman returned to London with an entirely new identity. To everyone she met, she introduced herself as Lola Dolores de Porris y Montez, the daughter of a noble Spanish family, exiled by the Carlist war. The new persona served her in several ways. Given her lack of experience as a dancer, Lola Montez was an infinitely greater draw at the box office than an Irish divorcée named Elizabeth would have been. And by the same transformative stroke, she had evaded, or at least so she thought, the public embarrassment Elizabeth had suffered in the court of public opinion. As Lola Montez, all her past, the pain of the trial, and perhaps everything that had made her suffer, seemed to vanish.

But the reprieve would only be fleeting. Her past continued to haunt her. Her debut at Her Majesty's Theatre, London's most prestigious stage, was triumphant. Though her skill at dancing was minimal, she had a formidable magnetism that held her audience spellbound as she paraded ominously around the stage in her mantilla. But unfortunately she was recognized by several gentlemen who had met her as Elizabeth James through Lennox, and they were quick to inform the manager and later the press of both her duplicity and her indiscretion. Not only was the engagement at Her Majesty's Theatre canceled, but the public controversy continued until finally she resolved to leave England for the continent.

Now she embarked on a labyrinthine journey, filled with many performances, more scandals, and several love affairs, including a brief tryst with the composer Franz Liszt, that was to bring her to Bavaria. In Berlin, after she performed on stage to mixed reviews and at a private party for the king of Prussia, who was entertaining the visiting tsar, an incident occurred which we can read as a foreshadow of the melodrama that would take place one day between Lola and the Bavarian king. The morning after the royal party, during ceremonies in Berlin arranged to honor the tsar, she arrived on horseback alone and tried to enter a section of the parade grounds reserved for royalty and nobility. Since as Lola Montez she had invented a noble family for herself, she must have decided that she was entitled to enter this exclusive compound. When a Prussian policeman ordered her to leave the area, she refused to do so. After he grabbed the reins of her horse, she struck him with her riding whip. It was the first public display of her violent temper recorded by the press. She was forced to leave the city.

Would her temper have continued to escalate no matter what life brought her? There is ultimately no way to second-guess history. Yet it is more than possible that a loss she sustained in Paris only deepened a rage. Though her performances received mixed reviews, she was welcomed in Paris by several celebrated members of the *demi-monde*, including Alexandre Dumas *fils*. The writer Théophile Gautier, who started by being critical, became her fan. She began to establish a viable stage career in the city. And she had fallen in love with a man who returned her love passionately. Alexandre Dujarier was a very handsome Creole, a charming man, a respected journalist as well as publisher of the influential *La Presse*, part of a vital, sometimes glamorous world of Parisian literati. As his mistress, Lola accompanied him to restaurants, theatres, and cafés, and hosted gatherings of his friends. Once again she had the life she wanted.

Yet, as she had experienced before so many times, the sweetness of this moment was to be cut prematurely short. One night, Dujarier did not come to her bed. In the morning a note was delivered to her in his handwriting telling her that if anything happened to him, he wanted her to know that he loved her. He had already left for a duel in the Bois de Boulogne, an event for which Lola knew he was ill prepared. She was a far better shot than he. In vain she tried to find him, hoping to dissuade or help him. Finally, a coach pulled up in the street below her apartment, but when she opened the door, his lifeless body, bloodied by a fatal wound to his face, fell into her arms.

The second death that she suffered must have reminded her of the first loss of her father. For a period, Lola was prostrated with grief. But she could hardly afford prostration. Her engagement at the Thèâtre de la Porte Saint-Martin, which Dujarier had helped obtain for her, was canceled. And perhaps also she could not afford to let feelings continue that may have threatened the sense she had built for herself of a strength impervious to misfortune. Following a trial of Dujarier's assailant, during which she was interrogated roughly, Lola Montez went on the road again.

She decided to stop in Munich on her way to Vienna. Counting on the ability to charm powerful men that was by now famous, she asked to have a brief audience with the Bavarian king to discuss the terms of her appearance at the Royal Court Theatre in Munich. As with seemingly every other decision in his kingdom, Ludwig had the final word in these negotiations. Yet though Ludwig, who was a great admirer of beauty, found Lola beautiful, he was not particularly impressed on the day he met her. Doubtless to get her way, she tried to appear submissive and to flatter the king. But it was not these conventional traits that interested him. Instead, the monarch's fascination for Lola began to grow when, upon inquiring about the nature of the disturbances she had caused in other countries, he learned that she had broken a glass over a man's head when he made unwelcome advances, brandished a whip at a policeman, and made provocative gestures to an audience that had been hissing her performance. It was when finally he saw her dance that he was won over by what he perceived to be her fiery spirit.

Her ferocity, her willfulness, her tempestuous nature, even her violent temper were all qualities that Ludwig shared. A well-loved monarch, he had accomplished a great deal, cutting unnecessary expenditures, establishing a great university in Munich, building the royal library, fostering commerce. But he had a less sanguine side. Hard of hearing, often misunderstanding what was said to him, he would fly easily into a rage if he felt, as he did too frequently, that someone was being disloyal to him. Like Lola, he was known to suspect treacheries where there were none. And like her too, whenever he was opposed, he became even more determined to prevail. He boasted often that he had an iron will.

The natural empathy that occurs between people who are similar would have been enhanced by the fact that they both had charm. Lola's considerable charm must have attracted Ludwig for the simple reason alone that charm is a form of power. Having power over others, Lola could penetrate the unique loneliness that accompanies autocrats in a way almost no one else was able to do. And there was another factor that must have brought them closer. Like courtesanry, more than all other forms of rule, monarchy relies on charm.

With a power that is not elected but conferred, monarchs must constantly convince their subjects that they have the right to rule. In part, they do this through various rituals which put their subjects into a trance. Royal pomp casts a powerful spell. Under this influence, the inhabitants of a nation will relinquish their own power to a ruler who claims that through bloodlines, or because of other signs (such as the pronouncements of august men dressed in impressive robes), this right has been conferred by divine will. The most absolute of monarchs, Louis XIV, understood the importance of ceremony very well, which is why he held so many charming *fêtes* at Versailles. Instead of tending their estates, noblemen who might otherwise have opposed him were kept constantly competing with each other for invitations to the countless splendid events the king hosted. Gilded palaces, flourishes and bows, royal robes, a crown and scepter (recalling a wizard's hat and wand) along with the countless minor rites that punctuated the monarch's day, served to frame the perception that the king's power was legitimate.

But one more enigma remains. How is it possible that a king as strong as Ludwig would have allowed his power to be destroyed by a liaison with a courtesan? To come even close to an answer we must recall that the charm of both lovers was not isolated but, like everything that is monumental, belonged to history. The very qualities that drew the monarch toward Lola alienated the burghers of Bavaria so severely that in the end her very presence incited riots. That she broke all the rules by which society was ordered, that she did not behave as a proper lady should, but instead acted as if she had been given the prerogatives of a man, would have angered the crowds. She would go out unaccompanied or, even worse, accompanied by attractive young men, whom she entertained at her apartment, or later in the house that Ludwig built for her. Rarely modest, she was often arrogant, bragging about her affair with the king, demanding the privileges she felt should belong to an official mistress. She brazenly displayed the expensive jewels Ludwig gave her. Indeed, she often acted as if not only did the prerogatives of nobility belong to her but of royalty, too. At the opera, when he visited her box, she failed to stand when he entered. And then there was the question of her violent temper. She would shout, slap, brandish her whip and was witnessed gesticulating defiantly at the crowds which, in the end, assembled under her windows to protest her presence in Bavaria.

Her behavior, self-destructive as it was, bears all the marks of psychosis. Responding to the loss she had suffered in Paris, repeating the loss of her father at an early age, instead of grieving, she built a citadel of power for herself. It is interesting to note that, as is often the case with mental disturbance, her delusions were strangely prophetic. A hundred years hence, women began to win many of prerogatives once belonging exclusively to men, and the distinctions between aristocrats and commoners had also begun to lose their hold over the public imagination.

But in 1846, these distinctions still mattered. Ludwig's downfall most likely began when he finally assented to Lola's constant pleas to make her a countess. The break in protocol outraged the sensibilities of most Munichers. There is, of course, a contradiction here between the public's complaint against a commoner becoming a countess and the demand for a more democratic rule that was to follow. Yet on an emotional level, the contradiction reveals a deeper logic. Though commoners had been given titles before, Lola did not behave according to the rules. Thus, her elevation would lead to disillusionment. The royal spell had been broken. If once Ludwig's right to rule with absolute power had appeared to be irreversible, a destiny dictated by God, suddenly that fate began to seem less divine. Now as well as seeming arbitrary, it appeared to be eminently reversible.

We might object here that Louis XV took two commoners as his official mistresses and gave them both titles without losing his crown. But here we recall that these actions led to disillusionment too, albeit one that occurred at a slower pace. The royal son, Louis XVI, ultimately paid the price for his father's indiscretions with his head. Of course there were other reasons; the history is far more complicated. And, to be fair to the courtesans in question, they were the symbolic targets for the rage of a populace that, conflicted about monarchy, found it easier to take out its ire on favorites than on kings.

By a strange twist of fate, the queen, Marie-Antoinette, wife of Louis XVI, who had been severely disapproving of Madame du Barry and who herself was faultless according to the strictest standards of chastity and fidelity, was slandered by the Paris mobs, too, who accused her of being a whore nonetheless. In the end, both Marie-Antoinette and Madame du Barry shared the same fate. They were executed in the Place de la Concorde that Pompadour had helped to design, and where the statue of Louis XV she had commissioned was pulled from its pedestal to make room for the guillotine.

So that we do not end these charming stories on such a lurid note, let us add one more observation. Both Louis XV and Ludwig I of Bavaria had fallen under another spell altogether. It was perhaps one of the reasons why the monarchs were attracted to commoners in the first place. They were moved beyond convention by a charm that belongs to none of us in particular but instead to all at once. The charm of new winds, of fresh ideas that can shift fate in an instant with the siren call of transformation.

The Invisible

My very existence was illegal.
—*Quentin Crisp,* The Naked Civil Servant

They were supposed to be invisible. Indeed, according to the conventional wisdom of the American South during the nineteenth century, quadroons were not supposed to exist at all. Perhaps since to speak of these children was to invoke the image of their lineage, they were never mentioned in polite society. Their very existence proved what the principles of plantation aristocracy held to be unthinkable: that unions took place between masters and slaves, which would imply love and desire where it was not supposed to exist. And of course there were other implications, too. Infidelity, rape and how masters, bosses, and all kinds of white men used power.

The children who came of such unions were thus a source of embarrassment. Yet, despite the prohibition against knowledge and perhaps because of the strong passion the mind has for locution, a strange nomenclature developed: categorization by fractions of blood. One black parent: mulatto; one black grandparent: quadroon; one black great-grandparent: octaroon. A system that moved by degrees through a hierarchy whose crowning achievement would be the erasure of any hint of scandal.

But as is often the case with the vocabulary of injustice, an irony soon developed. The words "mulatto," "quadroon," "octaroon" took on a power of their own. To pronounce them at all was to conjure a powerful fascination. That these words were allied with all that was forbidden gave them a certain inalienable force (such is the justice of language).

Thus the same words that were used to pinion and shame children into invisibility also made for a narrow opening, a door through which a few could escape the harsh conditions of the times. In New Orleans, for instance, sometimes right next to the debutante dances, an event would be held called the Quadroon Ball. Here, just as at the Bal Mabille in Paris, a young woman born to difficult circumstances and designated quadroon might meet a wealthy man who would keep her in a very fine style.

Accordingly, a neighborhood came to exist in New Orleans that, like a region of the mind kept separate from waking thoughts, was, if not as invisible as its inhabitants, in disguise. The area of the city where the highly educated African-American mistresses of wealthy men were kept by white southern gentlemen had a fancy name, one that only regular visitors would be able to understand. It was called the Marigny Quarter. By using her brother's name, the term made a sly reference to the most famous of all the courtesans, La Pompadour.

Here a woman might live in her own cottage. When she went out, dressed in the finest clothing, of course, she would be driven in her own coach with a splendid pair of horses. And though the sum must be large, no one has counted all the friends and members of her family who, along with being better fed, were saved from unnamed cruelties when she did what she could to influence fate through her not inconsiderable charms.

Do with Me What You Please

Though Marie Duplessis gave the impression of belonging to a more elegant tradition that was waning, she was also a harbinger of what was to come. Looking back, we can see that her famous charm was comprised of the complexities that characterized the times, the fourth decade of the nineteenth century, a period in which the ruler of France, Louis Philippe, was known paradoxically as the Citizen King. Her beauty, grace, wit, and enthusiasm for life were all wrapped in a remarkably supple style. To her lovers, she gave the impression that she was the opposite of willful. It was said of her that if Lola Montez could not make friends, Marie Duplessis could not make enemies. One drawing made of her in this period captures the vaunted impression. She is rendered with such softly contoured lines, it seems as if she would bend to the wind of any man's desire.

This was, in the end, the way Dumas *fils* portrayed Marie, first in the novel, and then in the play that would make her, if not immortal, at least a fixture in the European mind for over a century as the character Marguerite. Those of us who attend the opera still encounter the same character today as Violetta Valéry in Verdi's *La Traviata* and filmgoers will recognize her in the character Greta Garbo portrayed in George Cukor's *Camille*. But in order to create such a compliant character, the playwright had to change the narrative of Duplessis's life.

It is true that after they met one night at the Théâtre des Variétés, the two had a torrid affair. This was one of those liaisons for which courtesans did not charge. Marie claimed to be in love with Dumas *fils*. He was in love too and wanted her for himself alone. He resented the evenings when because she was entertaining one of her protectors the door was locked against him. But they both knew he could not afford to support her in the style to which she had become accustomed. And most likely she understood that he would never marry her. Not because, as in the play, his father would have objected. The playwright's father, Alexandre Dumas, was a famous womanizer (a lover briefly of Lola Montez). Rather, it was the son's own ambition that would not have allowed such a marriage to take place. When he did finally marry, it was to an aristocrat.

Duplessis did not sacrifice herself, as Marguerite does in the play, leaving her lover Armand in order to preserve his reputation. Rather, because Dumas *fils* was tired of sharing her with others, and since she refused to sacrifice her only income, it was he who left her. Nor did Duplessis pine for him the way Marguerite does so movingly. Instead, after he left her, motivated in no small part by her own ambition, she married her longtime protector, comte Edouard de Perregaux. Because his family never accepted the marriage, it was annulled and they never lived together. But this did not prevent her from retaining the title of countess. She had her stationery and a set of china embellished with the Perregaux family crest.

Far from languishing in grief over either Dumas *fils* or Perregaux, Duplessis took one more lover still before she died, the composer and pianist Franz Liszt. What was to be the last was probably also her most passionate affair. An offer she made to him has been cited as evidence of her acquiescent nature. "Take me, lead me wherever you like," she said. "I will be no trouble to you. I sleep all day, go to the theatre in the evenings and at night you can do with me whatever you please." Yet here we can see the great effect of her particular charm at work. While asking for what she wanted, she was able to create the illusion of suppliance.

Reading more closely, we can see that reversing the roles assigned to men and women in courtship, she is the one to suggest that they go off together. Though protesting that she will be no trouble, she gracefully suggests that she will not change her own eccentric habits while she is with him. And since she had already experienced what Liszt liked to do with her at night and indeed seems to have liked very much, what seems a generous offer is in reality a graceful expression of her own desire.

Yet, if those who loved her were encouraged to feel that it was they rather than she who were in control, there was a seed of truth to the illusion. She had relinquished control in an area where many of us never choose to succumb. Chronically ill from tuberculosis, though she sought the best medical advice, including that of Liszt's own doctor, and made the rounds of several spas more than once, she had the sense that she would not live long. She seemed to accept this verdict with a kind of equanimity. She was not bitter. Her only complaint was boredom. She found it intolerable to be bored for any length of time. A suitor who failed to interest her would be treated with open yawns or banished from her presence. Not only regarding sexual desire but in this sense too she was a harbinger of a new order. Where before men demanded that the courtesans they supported be entertaining, now she demanded to be entertained by her lovers.

She was kind, it is true, giving money generously to women less fortunate than herself, but she did not contort herself to try to please her lovers. It is also true that she made up stories about her life which made her slightly more glamorous. But her intent was not to hide her past. She was remarkably frank about her origins: the poverty she had endured as the daughter of an itinerant salesman, her father's brutal attacks on her mother, the fact that he sold her into prostitution when she was barely thirteen years old. She concealed none of this. She once said, "Lying keeps your teeth white," a remark that gives us a clue to a deeper motive. She was entertaining herself.

It was something else that made her so extraordinary: her awareness of mortality. Passionately in love with life, exuberant at times, by turns free of constraints and yet well trained in all the manners of polite society, exquisitely refined, she possessed the composure that can only come from detachment. Was this what Dumas *fils* was aiming for in his portrait of her? It is a quality that saints share with the dying, a sense that artists have only when they are practicing their art. This must have been what Liszt meant when he wrote that being with her put him in the vein of poetry and music.

The Blue Angel

Moreover she will endeavor to enchant thee partly with her melodious notes that she warbles out upon her lute . . . and partly with that heart-tempting voice of hers.—Thomas Coryat, 1608

*In the ancient world all flutes were halfway to being magic ones.
—James Davidson,* Courtesans and Fishcakes

A few years before the film called *The Blue Angel* appeared in 1930, the old codes had already begun to lose their power. Here and there, more and more women born to respectable families were going out alone, daring to show their legs and smoke, and among them was the young actress whom the world would one day know as Marlene Dietrich. Seen often on Berlin's Kurfurstendam at night, she moved from one cabaret to another, studying the techniques of showgirls as she partied. Soon she was appearing as a showgirl herself, and then in minor parts of plays.

She is not called a courtesan, though in an earlier age she might have been. Years later at dinner parties given by her friend, the director Billy Wilder, she would entertain his guests by listing all the lovers, both men and women, she had had as a young woman in Berlin. In 1924, at the height of her revels, she married Rudolf Sieber and lived with him for more than five years; yet she continued her affairs. In the meantime, Sieber, who was a casting director for UFA film studios, was able to get her several small roles in movies.

Then, like Pompadour, who left her husband for Louis XV (or Alice Ozy, who abandoned hers for the duc d'Aumale), though Dietrich remained married to Sieber until he died, she left both him and Berlin for the man who made her famous, the director Josef von Sternberg. Before bringing her to Hollywood, Sternberg cast her in a film about cabaret life. She became an overnight success in the role of a singer who lures a man to his doom.

In the fading imagery of the old film, we watch as a story that reflects the downfall of an old order is told. An ageing professor hectors his students, lecturing against the seductive powers of a popular nightclub singer. This voice will lure you to damnation, he warns them. Thus we know he is making a mistake when he decides to witness her for himself. Especially since the club is called the Blue Angel. "Blue," the word for drunkenness in German, is also the color of moonlight, of the waters over which the siren's voice wails, of nighttime thoughts and haunting melodies. Will she enchant him with her throaty voice? How could it be otherwise? Eventually, he will even consent to dance with her on the stage.

We have seen this story many times before. The same tale has been told for millennia. The thrilling powers of the Queen of the Night; the insinuating charm of music. As far back as ancient Greece, the same powerful lure was used by Dionysus and the Furies and by the sirens, too, and the auletrides, the flute-girls who played and danced at feasts, beguiling all those who listened (including the great warrior Alexander who, according to legend, under the influence of music so lost his bearings that he ran for his sword). A music continued by the courtesans of Venice, by Ninon with her lute, and still going strong two hundred years later as charming women sang in the music halls that lined the boulevards of Paris. What is happening here in this little café in Berlin is nothing new.

Though we are glad even now to see the self-righteous professor fall, we are saddened by the humiliation into which enchantment has led him. But this does not prevent us from listening. The low and alluring tone of the singer's voice summons a mysterious mood in the mind, a dangerous but also oddly familiar place that lurks between one thought and another. As this woman, in her top hat, with a voice like a man, sings a song about love, we ourselves are drawn away from the straight course we had charted. We cannot help it. We are falling in love again.

Her Golden Voice

Bernhardt could turn the utmost banality into Homeric poetry with her famous Golden Voice which seemed to float about her.
—*Cornelia Otis Skinner,* Elegant Wits and Grand Horizontals

Together with nuances too subtle for words, a great speaking voice manages to express what is so often concealed by language, the unspoken thoughts, secret histories, and even censored desires which, carried by intonation, can make any utterance far more truthful than it appears to be. We can only imagine the effect Sarah Bernhardt's famous voice had on her audiences when she played Marguerite in *La Dame aux camélias*. She made her first appearance in this role on the New York stage. Astonished by the performance, Henry James wrote that the play was "all champagne and tears—fresh perversity, fresh credulity, fresh passion. . . ."

Though *Camille*, as it was called in England and America, was almost forty years old at the turn of the century, it was new to American audiences. Since the original play that had opened in Paris at mid-century was viewed by American promoters as too scandalous, another script, called *Heart's Ease*, had been performed in its stead, one which, to avoid shocking audiences in the United States, substituted the courtesan with a flirt.

By the time Bernhardt brought the uncensored version of the play to New York, the Parisian audience, used to the brazen atmosphere of the approaching fin-de-siècle, found the play somewhat old-fashioned. As early as 1880, the comte de Maugy had declared that Marguerite Gautier "would only provoke a smile of incredulity among the bon viveurs" of his day. Yet, by one of those delicious ironies with which history often surprises us, the great success of Bernhardt's performance in the New World revived an interest in it in Paris, where the play became a great success once again. And, as opposed to the relative innocence of the American public, here audiences were able to appreciate the fine points of a performance that reflected a knowledge that, in the words of the critic Sarcey, "only a . . . worldly woman, born and bred in Paris," would have. To say Bernhardt was uniquely qualified to play the role is an understatement. As she faithfully spoke the lines Dumas *fils* had written, she would have been able to layer the script with countless memories.

She was born in 1844, just three years before the real Marguerite, Marie Duplessis, died. Like Marie, Sarah's mother, an unmarried immigrant from Amsterdam named Youle Bernard, had started life as a seamstress. Demanding work at a grueling pace for long hours and little pay, it was the kind of profession that shortened many women's lives, a fate Youle was determined to escape. At night she attended the public balls of Paris with the intent of meeting men who might give her an entry to another life. She hoped against hope that like a fortunate few before her, she might edge her way into the *demi-monde*.

With a small daughter to support and a low-paying job, little money

for fancy clothing, and only a smattering of education, neither proba-
bility nor circumstance was on her side. Yet her determination must
have been great because, against all odds, she reached her goal by the
time Sarah was six years old. It was no small accomplishment that
eventually Youle's salon was regularly attended by Alexandre Dumas
père, Rossini, the duc de Morny, and the baron Dominique, once
Napoléon's military surgeon. Sarah, however, did not enter this ribald
atmosphere until she was older. Sent as an infant to a wet nurse in Brit-
tany, she pined after her mother, who on her rare visits seemed like visiting royalty to her.

One day, after a visit from her aunt, overcome by despair, the child
hurled herself out of the window. That her arm was broken by the fall
hardly mattered to her: she knew her fate was changed. Yet, though Youle
took her home to Paris, the time with her mother was to be brief. Before
the year had ended, Youle, who found her daughter too willful, had en-
rolled Sarah in a fashionable boarding school for girls known as the In-
stitute Fressard, where for two years she learned to read and write,
embroider, and practice all the manners expected of refined women.
Then, at the age of nine, she was moved again. And this time, despite
the fact that Youle was Jewish, she sent her daughter to a convent.

The choice was well considered. Grandchamps was the school where
the daughters of all the best families in Paris were sent to be educated.
Sarah protested the move almost violently, climbing a tree to avoid
capture and then throwing herself in the mud, but she was to come to
love the convent. It was the Mother Superior, Mère Sainte-Sophie, who
wisely won her over, giving the child a little plot of ground to garden,
treating her with tender solicitude. At first Sarah distinguished herself
as the class clown, imitating the gestures of the bishop as he gave a
solemn funeral oration, laughing at the lessons the girls were given
in how to remove a glove or carry a handkerchief. But finally she
embraced the dramatic mysteries of the church—the flickering candlelight, the haunting incantations, the awesome presence of the tab-
ernacle, at whose feet she dreamed of throwing herself in sacrifice, to

be covered, she fantasized, by a black velvet cloak embellished starkly with a shining white cross.

Her reverie soon came to an end. By the age of fifteen, Sarah had decided to become a nun; but her mother had different plans for her. She had not sent her daughter to the convent for religious training, but for the upper-class refinement she would receive. Now it was time for Sarah to contribute her share to the household. Once again Sarah rebelled, this time against her mother's attempts to initiate her as a courtesan. Because Sarah's resistance most likely had the same strength her mother had displayed years earlier, as she had fought her way out of poverty, the two soon had reached what looked like an unsolvable impasse. But the duc de Morny came up with a brilliant compromise. Sarah had played the role of an angel in a play at the convent with great success. Perhaps her powerful moods and her talent at self-expression would serve her best in the theatre. Hoping to turn her in the direction of the stage, Alexandre Dumas took Sarah and her mother to see a play at the Comédie-Française. The plan worked. Sitting in his box, Sarah found herself moved to tears and laughter, won over, enthralled. As she wrote in her autobiography: "When the curtain went up I thought I would faint. It was the curtain of my life that had risen before me."

Although there are many elements contained in this story that mixed with the right magic helped to create Sarah's golden voice, the concept of *duende* may help us to better understand the process. The term is used in the tradition of flamenco to describe that quality of a singer's voice which rather than range or amplitude depends on an understanding of the nature of life that can only be gained with experience. Put simply, the singer must have suffered. But suffering is seldom simple. Even if what we have suffered is loss, the feeling will be tinged with the inevitable conflict between desire and circumstance. Though conflict itself is a form of suffering, too.

In the fifteen years of her childhood, Sarah experienced both loss and conflict—the repeated loss of her mother, her departure from the Institut Fressard, her rejection of the convent, followed by her decision to be a nun, and the conflict she felt with her mother's plans for her. Pulled in two directions, between Mère Sainte-Sophie and her own more worldly mother, devoted as she was to the theatre, her ambivalence was only mitigated by the choice she made to be an actress. She could not have discarded her earlier devotions so easily. And as the modern Polish director Jerzy Grotowski writes, "the words 'actress' and 'courtesan' were once synonymous." What was true for many others in this career held for Sarah, too. Even after she became famous in Paris, until in fact she had made a fortune with her tours to the American continent, she supplemented her relatively small salary with income from a retinue of protectors.

But the work an actor does on the stage, what Grotowski calls a "penetration into human nature," offered another solution to the conflict. Along with her loneliness as a child, her tantrums and her rages, her powerful will and her bitter knowledge of defeat, each conflict she had suffered only made her performances more faithful to reality. All that she witnessed, all that she felt—her mother's transgressions, the passion of the nuns, her dreams of piety, her great talent for seduction, the triumphs of her spirit together with its humiliations, all the pleasures of her body and the purity of her soul—could exist side by side, undiluted and uncompromised, in her voice.

As an actress, she had extraordinary powers. The incantatory powers at her command redolent with the liturgies of church and boulevard alike, gave a new life to the role of the dying courtesan. As Marguerite flirted and laughed, cynically dismissed Armand's proposal of love, then succumbed, fell more deeply in love, and finally sacrificed herself for him, Sarah's great voice would have conjured the real story that lay beneath the sentimental narrative. Had we been in the audience, we might have heard it all: the ferocious strength of a young woman trying to survive, the odds arrayed against her, the fate of all those who had failed to escape, worked to an early old age, begging in the streets, carted off to a prison or an asylum for indigence, her defiance, and all she saw as she fought to live, the backsides of the grandest men, the betrayals of others and herself, audible in the undertone, along with the unexpected kindness she encountered, and the tenderness, even her own, would have been there too as all the while the voice would have wooed us, taking us deep into the territory of desire, so that as we listened, we would have known for certain that the sound of all we heard was, in its own inexorable way, holy.

Afterglow
(THE SEVENTH EROTIC STATION) + + + + + + + +

When he thought of Ellen Olenska it was abstractly, serenely, as one might think of some imaginary beloved in a book or a picture; she had become the composite vision of all that he had missed.—Edith Wharton, The Age of Innocence

THE REVERIE COMES later. Perhaps he has left her sleeping so that he can walk home through the park in the cool morning. Or perhaps a few years have passed. Either way, the shadows under the trees are fresh with memory. More than once, he strolled with her here. They came to the edge of these trees after their first lunch in the café under the arcade. Even then he must have known, without being able to say it in words, what it was he wanted. He was so taken with the hem of her skirt and the froth that curled at its edge as she walked. That and the playful rhythm of her gait, the intense green of the braid lining her collar, the blush in her cheeks that was nearly unacceptable, the shock of her frankness, the dazzling speed of her responses, and the way her hand would gesture with countless small enthusiasms, all swept him past reason. He was charmed. But now as he hears the sound of a slight breeze carrying a leaf to the ground and is reminded of the way her voice whispered in his ear, he is beginning to understand his own desire. Remembering the way the soft vibrations of her whisper moved through his body, he suddenly knows. The petals of the flowers in the beds here, still wet with the morning dew, the way they open now to the sunlight, remind him. It was this that drew him, not just to imagine how she felt but to feel what she did, as her body responded, opening like ruffled petals, like a sea creature widening in a wave.

The water of the fountains beginning to arch, and ripple, the waiter's low laugh as he places the first table outdoors, the sudden flap of a bird's wings, all converge on the desire he is startled to claim as his own, though it makes him laugh too because he cannot help but see now that the feeling is reflected everywhere—in the gardens, the clothes of the ladies strolling here, the curling ornaments on the columns, the splendor in the shop windows—all spreading a sweetness through the atmosphere along with a subtly raucous invitation to move past boundaries which, he knows now, are only imagined as real.

ALICE OZY

In the End

ITH A COARSELY wrought tale, the end of the story often serves as a simple morality lesson. Those who are good, the narrative seems to say, will die well, just as those who have been bad will meet a bad end. But, as with a well-told story, reality is far more complicated, filled with surprises and ironies, rises and falls, sudden turns, descents and ascents that seem to occur somewhat independently from justice. If in the nineteenth century working-class girls were warned that the life of a courtesan ended in sorrow, the truth is that in the end *cocottes* seem to have flourished or floundered at about the same rate as anyone else. Yet the dire prophecies of the self-righteous could at times be self-fulfilling.

BEFORE MOGADOR MARRIED Lionel de Chabrillan, he had already lost his own fortune and been disowned by his family. To save his estate, he planned to marry a wealthy woman. But instead, still in love with Mogador, he sailed to Australia to join the gold rush when he lost what little he had left. After he returned to Paris to marry Mogador, the couple sailed together to Australia, where this time Lionel would serve as the French consul general. Yet his salary was meager. Though the couple were not destitute, they faced severely reduced circumstances. Thus in order to supplement their income, Mogador took up a new career; in the course of four years she wrote three best-selling novels. Severely ill, however, she was forced to return to Paris. After Lionel joined her in Paris, he tried to obtain a diplomatic posting in Europe. But the scandal of their marriage shadowed them both. When he sailed for Australia again, stricken with a sudden illness, he died.

Penniless and mourning for her husband, she revived her career on the stage. Though the first night was a brilliant success, the show was terminated when a series of articles appeared, reminding the public of her notorious past. But calling once more on her formidable determination to survive, she took the play that Dumas had based on her novel *Les Voleurs d'Or* on tour, making a small fortune. And once again she took up writing, producing altogether twenty-six plays, twelve novels, and seven operettas. Always generous, she moved her mother to her châlet at Vesinet, founded a women's ambulance corps during the Prussian War, and no doubt remembering the terrors of her own childhood, offered to build a home for war orphans on her land. But because of the scandal that followed her until her death, she was forced to hide behind a tree as she watched the girls at the orphanage hand bouquets of flowers to the more respectable patrons. Finally, after moving to an old people's home in Montmartre, she died at the age of eighty-five.

WHEN CORA PEARL faced a different kind of scandal, the consequences were far worse. Shunned by the *demi-monde* as well as society, she was eventually financially ruined, too. She had become an object of scorn after a former lover, Alexandre Duval, son of a famous restaurateur, wounded himself severely. He had intended to aim his bullet at Cora but the gun went off in his hand instead. While he hovered for several days between life and death, the story of what transpired between them circulated through the city. He had spent all of his fortune on lavish gifts for her. But when the money was gone, she dismissed him coldly.

Neither the fact that he had planned to murder her, nor his subsequent return in full health to his old life on the boulevards, mitigated public opinion. No longer able to find protectors, slowly all Cora's resources dwindled. Once known for receiving as much as 10,000 francs a night, she was grateful now for 5 louis. Yet she never lost her spirit. Before she died at the age of fifty-one from stomach cancer, she spent time promulgating an invented universal language, and she wrote and published two versions of her life story, books that are still being read today.

MARIE DUPLESSIS DID not die as utterly alone as *La dame aux camélias* portrayed. Though the crowd of suitors thinned considerably, her maid stayed with her until the end, as did some loyal friends, among them her erstwhile husband, Edouard Perregaux. She died well cared for, in the comfortable surroundings of her luxurious apartment. The physician, whom Liszt had sent to care for her, was the doctor most highly esteemed among society women of the day. Yet ironically he probably hastened her death by giving her experimental doses of arsenic. The loyalty of her maid came as much from friendship as from employment. Having been born to the working class herself, Duplessis was known not only to be kind but also inordinately generous to working women. Her estate was auctioned after her death. Even after all her bills were paid, there remained a considerable sum, which she gave to her sister in Normandy.

ARETINO DID NOT depict the death of his character, the first fictional Nanna. We only see her as she grows older, passing on her knowledge to her daughter Pippa. The Nana we know best now, the heroine of Zola's novel, was supposed to be based on the life of Blanche d'Antigny. After seducing and ruining a string of lovers, Nana dies of smallpox alone in a room at the Grand Hôtel in Paris. Describing her suffering vividly, Zola gives the impression that she is getting a just reward.

SUPERFICIALLY, BLANCHE D'ANTIGNY, whom Zola used as a model for Nana, suffered a similar death. Some say she died of smallpox, some typhoid, some tuberculosis, which she would have caught while nursing Luce, the man she loved. But due to the kindness of another courtesan, Caroline Letessier, Blanche was well cared for when she died. And in stark contrast with Zola's cold and unfeeling heroine, since Blanche's spirits as well as her economic health had been broken by her lover's illness and death, it is not unreasonable to say that she died of love. After her death, Théodore de Banville, who had always admired her, wrote touchingly: "Blanche d'Antigny has taken with her one of the smiles of Paris."

APOLLONIE SABATIER WAS thirty-eight years old when her chief benefactor, Alfred Mosselman, suffered financial ruin. He offered her 500 francs a month, but she declined, trusting her independent efforts instead. She took up painting—four of her miniatures were shown in the Salon of 1861—as well as restoring the paintings of others. Unable to make a living doing this, she auctioned some of the valuable objets d'art she had been collecting for years, raising 43,000 francs. Moving to a smaller apartment, she began to do her own cooking. Yet we would be mistaken here to think that because she was aging, Sabatier's career was over. Beauty was not her only asset. Even in reduced circumstances, she was spirited. As Judith Gautier described it, she sang as she cooked. In the same year she began a new liaison with Richard Wallace, natural son of the marquess of Hertford, who promised that if ever he became wealthy, he would take care of her. True to his word, when at his father's death he inherited a fortune, he gave her 50,000 francs and a monthly income. She spent her last years at Neuilly, in very comfortable surroundings. Having outlived many of her companions, she was lonely for them. Yet this is always the price for having had many beloved friends. She died peacefully on the last day of 1889, at the age of sixty-seven.

JEANNE DUVAL HAD many other lovers in addition to Baudelaire, one of them a woman who lived with her for many years. Over several years she held a lively salon in her own rooms. But she struggled with a degenerative illness, which eventually paralyzed her. After they parted as lovers, she and Baudelaire remained friends. During the last years of her life and through her hospitalization, he continued to support her.

FLORA, A VERY successful and wealthy courtesan in ancient Rome, was eventually made into a goddess and as such is still alive and well today.

THE DAUGHTER OF an army officer, Liane de Pougy married a naval officer herself. When, because she was unhappy in this union, she left him, he shot her; she had two bullets in her thigh until her death. For a short period she taught piano, but her life as a courtesan was launched when she appeared in an open carriage with the marquis de MacMahon at Longchamps. Her career as an entertainer was launched when the Prince of Wales became her fan, introducing her to his friends who were members of the Jockey Club. During her years as a courtesan she had many protectors, including Prince Strozzi in Florence, Maurice de Rothschild, Roman Potocki, Baron Bleichroder in Berlin, and Lord Carnarvon in London. In her thirties, she retired from this life to enter a Dominican order of nuns in Lausanne. As a postulate, she took the name of Sister Anne-Marie Magdalene. But she was back in Paris again after a year.

One of her lifelong friends was Jean Lorrain, the acerbic critic, known to be gay, who went about the boulevards wearing rouge, his hair dyed blond. Because he had given her a bad review, when they met by coincidence in the Bois du Boulogne, she went after him with a horse whip. But he admired her fortitude and they became good friends. For many years one of her most ardent supporters in the press, finally he wrote a play for her. That they were both gay must only have deepened their rapport. When the American heiress Natalie Barney came to court Pougy dressed as a Renaissance page, the two women became lovers, and remained amorous friends for many years.

Along with Emilienne d'Alençon, who was also at one time her lover, Pougy spent much of her time in the informal society that surrounded Barney, women who loved women or poetry or art. And usually all three. The circle included Renée Vivien, Anna de Noailles, Lucie Delarue-Mardrus, Marcel Proust, Dolly Wilde, niece of Oscar, and Colette. Along with her extensive journals, she wrote and published several popular romans à clef about her amorous pursuits, including the popular *Idylle sapphique*, a novel whose heroine is based on Natalie Barney. Barney hoped to rescue her from courtesanry, but instead, at the age of 39, Pougy became the lover of Prince George Ghika of Romania, who was at the time 24 years old. Within two years they were married, and except for a short separation when George had an affair with his secretary, the prince and princess lived happily together until his death. Known for her good works in the later part of her life, she never forsook her religious feelings. At the age of seventy-three she joined the third order of Saint Dominique (a lay order) as Soeur Anne-Marie de la Pénitence and began to devote much of her time to good works. After Georges died, she spent hours in her rooms at the Hotel Carlton in prayer, prompting her spiritual guide, Mère Marie-Xavier to comment, "*La soeur à pénitence a devenu la soeur à prière*" (The sister of good works has become the sister of prayer). She died in 1950 at the age of eighty.

+ + +

By the time she was in her forties, having lost her beauty, and since doubtless her audacity was less becoming in maturity, Harriet Wilson had fallen from her position as a favorite of high society. No longer able to make her living as a courtesan, she became a writer instead. Yet she was reaping profits from her former trade. Before the publication of her memoirs as well as several subsequent works, she would blackmail former lovers with the material she had written about them. Though she herself must have turned a good profit, apparently her last novel, *Clara Gazul*, suffered so much from the resulting cuts that it was too boring to sell more than a few copies. After 1832, history records almost nothing about her; she is said to have died in England, in 1846, at the age of fifty.

Esther Guimond kept entertaining way past her prime, giving her dinner guests ample portions of wit along with their food. She is said to have served as an unwitting inspiration for *La Dame aux camélias*. Having known kindness from Guimond as a child, Dumas *fils* was sitting by her bed while she was suffering from an episode of typhoid, when suddenly he jumped up, declaring, "Now I have my fifth act!" But unlike his heroine, Esther did not expire. She died several decades later, of cancer. The day after her death, her good friend Girardin, who along with many of the men she knew feared exposure from the extensive papers she kept, spent hours alone in her library. It is thought that he destroyed the eight hundred letters she had preserved. Given that she tried to blackmail him with these letters, we cannot blame him. Nevertheless, it is unfortunate for us that his own history as well as hers is now lost.

Lanthélme went off with Misia's husband. But the affair did not last long. While on a pleasure cruise, she either fell or was pushed from the open window of her stateroom. Her body was recovered hours after she had drowned.

SINCE LA BELLE Otero blew her fortune at the tables on the Riviera, she would have been destitute had not the owners of the casinos where she lost all her money given her a pension. But then again, if we were to make a list of all the disasters that might have befallen her during her lifetime, it would be very long. She lived simply but comfortably in Nice until her death. She never lost her style. Even in an altered, elderly shape, when she entered a room, heads turned.

AFTER PAÏVA HAD her marriage with the penniless marquis who had given her a title annulled, she married one of the wealthiest men in Europe, Henckel de Donnersmark. The ostentatiously resplendent Hôtel Païva, which still exists today on the Champs-Elysées (now the home of an exclusive men's club called the Players), was a gift from him. He also bought her the Château de Pontchartrain, situated on the route from Paris to Dreux, the palace made famous two centuries earlier by the amorous visits of Louis XIV and his favorite Louise de la Vallière. Since Henckel was a Prussian count, however, with the advent of the Prussian War, the couple was forced to leave France and settle instead on a family estate in Silesia. When Païva died at the age of sixty-one, she had amassed the largest fortune ever owned by a courtesan.

IT HAS BEEN supposed by some that Veronica Franco repented late in life, but most scholars agree that the evidence for this is slim. In a letter she wrote to a friend who was considering turning her daughter into a courtesan, Franco wrote: "You can do nothing worse in this life... than to force the body into such servitude... to give oneself in prey to so many, to risk being despoiled, robbed or killed. To eat with someone else's mouth, to sleep with the eyes of others, to move as someone else desires, and to risk the shipwreck of your faculties and your life—what fate could be worse?"

In fact, the impassioned tone of her letter does not contradict the passionate defense she made of courtesanry, but instead outlines the perils courtesans faced, especially when they were not among the most successful. In the end, she herself was to join the ranks of the less privileged in her profession. The last years of her life, during which she was supporting her brother's children as well as her own, were not prosperous. Circumstances took their inevitable toll. She died of fever at the age of forty-five.

In 1531, when she was barely twenty years old, Tullia D'Aragona was the reigning courtesan of Rome. But by 1535, she and her mother, the courtesan Giulia Campana, moved to Adria, perhaps to conceal the birth of a daughter, Penelope, officially listed as Giulia's child but widely thought to be Tullia's. In the ensuing years, in several different cities, including Venice, Ferrara, and Florence, Tullia flourished both as a courtesan and as an intellectual. Her friendship with the respected philosopher Benedetto Varchi furthered her career.

As Tullia entered her late thirties, she tried to fashion a new life, free of her most profitable vocation. She founded an academy in Florence, where she organized debates and provided musical entertainment on the lute, at which she was famously skilled. When her academy achieved great success, she became one of the most notable figures in Renaissance Florence. But this glory was interrupted after potentially scandalous charges of violating the sumptuary laws required for courtesans were brought against her. The law would have prohibited her from wearing silks or jewels, at the same time requiring that she wear the scarf with a yellow border used to identify prostitutes. Along with Varchi, Eleanora de Toledo, the duchess of Florence, came to her aid, and Tullia was acquitted and freed from the sumptuary requirements. And hence she began a flurry of writing and publishing, which included the *Dialogue on the Infinity of Love.*

But her intellectual pursuits did not pay her bills. She was forced to leave Florence, a man she loved passionately, and her patron Varchi. In Rome, Tullia, her mother, and Penelope rented small lodgings in a fashionable part of the city, probably hoping to finance their household when Penelope, nearing fourteen, was presented as a courtesan. But the child's career as well as her life was short. She died in 1549. Tullia's history is lost to us now. We find her again only in 1555, as she writes her will in a room, in the Trastevere, which she rented from a former maid Lucrezia and her husband, Matteo. What little she had to leave—furniture, jewelry, clothing—was carefully apportioned to a son, Celio; Lucrezia and Matteo; her young maid, Christofara; and the percentage that the church required from courtesans when they died. Apparently devoting herself to good works at the end of her life, she had made her peace with the church. She requested that no one attend her funeral except members of the Company of the Crucifix, to which she belonged at the time of her death.

NINON DE LENCLOS remained uncertain about religion all her life, though this uncertainty did not prevent an abbé from falling in love with her when she was eighty years old. In her inimitable fashion, she continued to enjoy life and inspire admiration until her last breath at the ripe old age of eighty-five. True to her lucidly honest character to the end, just before her death, asking for pen and paper, she wrote:

> Let no vain hope be held out to make my courage waver.
> I am of an age to die, what is there left for me to do here?

After which she closed her eyes and died.

+ + +

WE HAVE ALREADY described Imperia's death. But we have not yet told the famous story of what happened to her daughter several years later. Lucrezia was known to be as beautiful as her mother. Probably for this reason, when Cardinal Raphael Petrucci, accompanied by troops, arrived in the town in Tuscany where Lucrezia and her husband lived in 1522, he had Archangelo arrested on trumped-up charges. His plan was to bargain for Lucrezia's sexual favors with Archangelo's freedom. But when his messengers summoned her, saying simply that she wanted to change her clothes, Lucrezia, as her mother once did, took poison. This story however has a happier ending. Lucrezia recovered, and the tale of how she saved her honor was repeated for generations throughout Italy.

AFTER AN ESTIMABLE career as an entertainer and courtesan, Emilienne d'Alençon married an aristocratic army officer and thus like many courtesans before her gained the title of countess. From this new position, she hosted a literary salon and wrote a book of poems herself, called *The Temple of Love*. But the marriage was short-lived. Soon after, she became the lover of the famous jockey, Alec Carter. After he was killed in World War I, she became part of the circle that gathered in Natalie Barney's rooms on the rue Jacob, where she devoted herself to the love of women and poetry, as well as experimentation with drugs. Earlier the lover of Liane de Pougy, she was also the lover of the poet Renée Vivien, who had been Barney's lover, Valtesse de la Bigne, and Madame Brazier, the proprietress of the lesbian bar Le Hammaton, with whom she was depicted sitting in a box in the theatre by Toulouse-Lautrec. She was last sighted in 1940 at a casino in Monte Carlo, at age seventy, still looking good.

MARION DAVIES CONTINUED to act, sing, and dance in film until she made her last movie in 1939. After the death of Hearst's mother and his separation from his wife, Hearst and Davies divided their time between San Simeon, the older estate at Mount Shasta called Wyntoon, and Southern California. They continued as lovers for thirty-nine years, until Hearst died in 1951 after an extended illness. In a codicil to his will, he had left his longtime lover thirty thousand shares of preferred stock, yielding her an annual income of $150,000. Six weeks after his death, when she was fifty-four years old, Marion married Horace Gates Brown III, an old friend of her sister, and frequent visitor to San Simeon, a man who was said to bear a remarkable resemblance to Hearst. They remained married for the rest of her life.

She augmented her already considerable real estate holdings with several purchases. But though more than comfortable, her last years were quiet. That she was still a hard drinker did little to mitigate the fact that gaiety is harder to summon in isolation than in a crowd. Many of her fellow revelers gone, in a sense there was no one left to party with, though her old friend Joseph Kennedy did what he could. She attended the wedding of Jacqueline Bouvier to John F. Kennedy and she was an honored guest at Kennedy's inauguration. Three years later, a life of heavy drinking having caught up with her, she suffered a minor stroke, and soon after at the age of sixty-four, she succumbed to cancer.

PROSPEROUS TO THE end, Alice Ozy multiplied her resources several times by investing successfully on the Bourse. Of her talent to make money grow, Gautier once said, "If I had a sack of diamonds I would trust them with Alice Ozy. She would soon give me back more than I had left with her." Gustave Doré was her last lover. At fifty years of age, with a fashionable apartment on the boulevard Haussmann and her own château facing Lake Enghien in Switzerland, she was able to say, "I am growing old with dignity." By sixty-five, having changed her name back to Madame Pilloy and become respectable, she had grown somewhat stout and unhappy in her aging solitude; but at least she understood what she was missing. And she must have remembered the hard times of her childhood, too, when, before she died at seventy-two years of age, she wrote a will leaving all of her fortune, 2,900,000 francs, to a society for the nurturing and education of the children of impoverished actors.

WHILE SHE WAS building and maintaining a successful career as a performer, Klondike Kate fell in love with the businessman, Alexander Pantages, whose name would later become a household word due to the string of vaudeville and movie houses he owned. After she invested in his first theatre, she went on tour, only to find that in her absence he had married a much younger woman. She sued him for breach of promise but won only a small settlement.

Kate returned briefly to the stage before marrying a cowboy, but the marriage did not last long. Then she suffered a decline for a period, making money by bootlegging and possibly also procuring. But a few years later, when Pantages was sued and convicted for raping a seventeen-year-old actress he employed at one of his theatres, Kate gained some notoriety by testifying against him at his trial.

Her former lover was sentenced to fifty years in prison, which must have improved her mood, because shortly thereafter her life took an upward turn again. Still attractive and lively at fifty-seven, when she decided she wanted to marry, she found she had two choices. She fixed on Johnny Matson, a successful miner who had worshipped her from a distance during the old Klondike days. Reading of her in the newspaper accounts of the Pantages trial, he looked her up and began to court her. They were happily married for thirteen years, until his death in 1945.

Two years later, at the age of seventy-two, she married the second man who had been courting her, William L. Van Duren. During the ceremony, her seventy-one-year-old groom commented, "Time is of the essence." Kate replied, "I was the flower of the North, but the petals are falling awfully fast, honey." The last petal fell eight years later. She died peacefully and, as she had told a reporter a year earlier, "with no regrets." A portrait of her remains with us in the character of Cherry Malotte, the heroine of Rex Beach's *Silver Horde*.

ONLY A MONTH into a shipboard romance, Nijinsky precipitously married an admirer and fellow ballet dancer, Romola Pulszky. His former lover, Diaghilev, felt betrayed and eventually responded by dismissing the dancer from the Ballets Russes. After a hiatus, Diaghilev brought the dancer back into the company, with which he continued his legendary work. Psychologically fragile, his despair and irrational rages began to worsen, undermining his work, his marriage, and finally everything he did. Creative even in madness, he wrote an extraordinary diary that records his state of mind. Though Romola had other erotic liaisons, she remained loyal to him for the rest of his life. Nijinsky's illness prevented him from performing as a dancer or a choreographer ever again. After years of breakdowns and attempts at recovery, he died at the age of sixty-one.

ALWAYS OF FRAGILE health, La Pompadour was cast into mourning by two deaths in the royal family, those of Madame Infante and the ten-year-old duc de Bourgogne. Her mood had already been dampened by the Seven Years' War, which she feared would tarnish the king's glory. "If I die," she said, "it will be of grief." Thus, at the end of her life, she and the king reversed roles. Now it was Louis who tried to cheer her up. Hoping that time spent in a more intimate space away from the worries of the palace might revive her spirits, he commissioned the Petit Trianon. But it came too late. By the time she died, only the outer walls had been raised.

No doubt she was worn out, too, by what she called her "perpetual combat" to keep the king's affections. She had not been his lover for years, and now his attention was straying toward a Mademoiselle Romains, who bore him a son and whom he had set up in a house in Passy.

He soon wearied of the young woman, however, and Pompadour was not replaced. When, in 1763, she made her last public appearance at the ceremonies held to celebrate the placement of an equestrian statue of Louis in the center of the newly designed Place de la Concorde, for which she had been responsible, the woman who would one day take her place, the young Jeanne du Barry, was in the crowds. But Pompadour would not live to see another *maîtresse en titre* enter Versailles. In the following year while she was at Choisy, she had an attack of illness so severe it became clear she would die soon. She was just forty years old.

Despite the rule that only royal family members were allowed to die in the rooms of Versailles, the king brought her back to her rooms at the palace where, because her lungs were filled with fluid, to make her breathing easier, she sat up a chair and received the last visits of her friends. The king stayed by her side for days, until, because her doctors said that she was dying, a priest was sent for so that she could give her confession. The king could not be in her presence after this, and thus the priest was alone with her when she died. Her last words were addressed to him as he prepared to leave the room. "One moment, M. le Curé," she said to him. "We'll go together." And then she died.

For propriety's sake, the king could only follow her funeral cortège with his eyes. As her body was borne off to Paris, he watched from his balcony until she had left the range of his vision. When he turned away, tears were seen pouring from his eyes. *"Elle avait de la justesse dans l'esprit et la justice dans le coeur,"* "She had rightness in her spirit and justice in her heart," wrote Voltaire. "We shall miss her every day. . . . It is the end of a dream."

WE DO NOT know exactly when or how Phyrne died. We do know that her image was sculpted more than once by Praxiteles, and by that Botticelli took this image as inspiration for his *Birth of Venus*. She became so wealthy that after the Macedonians destroyed the city of Thebes, she offered to pay for the walls to be rebuilt, providing they bore the inscription: "Alexander may have knocked it down, but Phyrne the hetaera got it back up again."

BETWEEN THE DEATH of Louis XV and her own, Jeanne du Barry lived several lives. Her story recalls the wisdom of certain folk tales meant to show that fortune, which is never predictable, often turns out to be the opposite of what it seems to be at first. Risking exposure to smallpox, she sat faithfully by the king's bedside for days as he grew more ill; but just before he died, in an act of repentance for his sins, he asked that his mistress leave Versailles. She spent several nights in a château belonging to the duc d'Aiguillon before the king died, when she was ordered to enter the Abbaye de Pont-aux-Dames. She never learned that it was her own lover who had decreed this fate. To be banished to this decrepit convent, which was dark and damp, must have felt like an unjust punishment. But reverting to the modest demeanor she had before she became the king's favorite, the countess soon won the friendship of the abbess, Madame de la Roche Fontenelles, with whom she spent many hours in conversation. When, after a year, she was allowed to leave the convent, the other nuns wept at her departure.

Slowly she regained some of the wealth she had accumulated at Versailles. With her collection of jewelry, said to be the most valuable in Europe, the properties she owned, and the rents she received from shops in Paris, in addition to the annual income left to her by the king, she was not poor. After living for a time in a newly acquired, very large estate, Saint-Vrain, she was able to move the extraordinary paintings by Greuze, Fragonard, Vernet, and Van Dyke, and the elegant furniture she had acquired under Louis' patronage, back to her estate at Louveciennes. Soon she became the lover of her neighbor, Lord Henry Seymour, nephew of the Duke of Somerset, but this affair ended badly. Henry, who was married, was given to jealousy, and objected to her friendships with other men. Though she tried unsuccessfully to regain

Seymour's affections, he steadfastly snubbed all her attempts, peavishly sending back her miniature portrait with the words "Leave me alone" written across it.

But good luck often disguises itself as misfortune. It was because Seymour was so rejecting that Jeanne became the lover of the duc de Brissac. With his wife seemingly indifferent to his conduct, Brissac and du Barry became a devoted couple, dividing their time between her estate at Louveciennes and his hôtel on the rue de Grenelle. Wealthy himself, Brissac supported her in the style in which she had been indulged as the king's favorite. And paradoxically, as his mistress, she was more acceptable to the aristocracy than she had been as the king's favorite. She became a beloved figure in aristocratic society. Over time, she even gained the approval of the royal family.

Though Brissac was loyal to the crown, it was under his influence that she began to read the *Encyclopédistes* and to entertain liberal ideas. Because of her generosity, du Barry was well liked in the village near her estate, but to revolutionaries the king's favorites were symbols of royal corruption. And in the end, as the Revolution unseated the king and proceeded toward more and more violence, both Brissac and du Barry sided with the royalists. In the chaos of change, her great collection of jewelry was stolen from her. But this, as it turned out, was to be the least of her losses. After Brissac was arrested, he was killed by a mob who rushed to Louveciennes with his head on a stick to parade in front of the comtesse's windows. We might suppose that fortune finally favored her again when her jewels were discovered in London. But just as good fortune arrives disguised as bad luck, the reverse is also true. She made several trips to England—first to identify the collection and then to appear in court—and it was during these trips that she began to lend support to royalist émigrés in London.

It is supposed that she fell in love with one of Brissac's old friends there, because after he returned to France, despite evident dangers, she returned to France, only to be arrested, accused of treason, and after several months in prison, condemned to death. Over a lifetime she had

showed remarkable courage on many occasions, but at the end her bravery deserted her. Perhaps her pluck came from an intense love of earthly
pleasures. Somewhat portly now, her hair gray, clearly aging, still she did
not go quietly, but rather wept and struggled as she was carried to the
guillotine. Perhaps it was because at this moment she so little resembled
the popular picture of her as an arrogant whore that crowds in the Place
de la Concorde did not cheer at her death.

LOLA MONTEZ EVENTUALLY landed in America, where she
toured in a play based on her life called *Lola Montez in Bavaria*. She settled
for a while in Grass Valley, Nevada, where she was well liked. But though
she had mellowed somewhat, her life was still tumultuous. While on
tour, when her company was sailing to South America, one of her lovers
disappeared into the Pacific Ocean. Later, though the American press re-
ported that she had married an Austrian prince during a tour of Europe,
it was he who jilted her. She covered the damage, however, with her own
version of events, claiming that she left him because he had taken up
with a singer.

In her last years Montez shifted her profession from actress to lec-
turer, including among her topics "The Comic Aspects of Love,"
"Wits and Women of Paris," and "Gallantry." The publication of
her letters proved so successful that she followed this with *The Arts of
Beauty, or Secrets of a Lady's Toilet, with Hints to Gentlemen on the Art of Fascinating.* Prosperous for a while, at her home in upper New York State
she hosted a small salon, masterfully inciting and guiding witty conversation while she smoked cigars. Though her disregard for the truth
continued unabated, in her last years she tried to become what was
then called "a good Christian." But financial need forced her onto the
lecture circuit again. For the first time since her childhood, she returned to Ireland, and later spoke in Britain as an expert on America.
Returning to America, she lectured throughout the country on England.

Finally she had earned enough respect and success to feel certain of her future. Yet within a few months, on a very hot day in New York, she suffered a stroke. With her formidable will, she struggled back to health, even walking again with a cane. She seemed on the road to full recovery and spent some time at the New York Magdalene Society counseling women who were trying to give up prostitution. But on Christmas Day, a walk in the cold windy air proved fatal. Stricken with pneumonia, she did not recover. She was forty years old when she died, listening as, at her request, a friend read her passages from the Bible.

THE GREAT SARAH BERNHARDT was able to give up *galanterie* after she made millions from her tours in the New World. Her leg had to be amputated, yet she continued with her brilliant career, carried onto the stage, seated in a chair or propped up. She traveled to the front to entertain soldiers during World War I, and performed in the theatre through her late seventies. One of her last appearances was organized to benefit Madame Curie's laboratory. When her failing body forced her to give up the stage, she appeared in a film. "There was nothing left of her," the young actress Mary Marquet wrote. But when the director shouted "Camera!" suddenly she rose from her torpor. As Marquet remembered it, "her face lit up, her eyes were shining, and she demanded, 'What should I do?' in a voice that seemed suddenly strong and young. She had just dropped thirty years." A few months later, at the age of seventy-nine, her health finally failed.

Colette has given us a portrait of her at the end. "I record here one of the last gestures of the tragedienne approaching her eightieth year: a delicate faded hand offering a full cup; the cornflower blue of her eyes, so young, caught in a web of wrinkles; the laughing interrogative coquetry of the turn of her head. And that indomitable, endless desire to charm, to charm again, to charm even unto the gates of death."

As if proving the truth of Colette's words, on her deathbed she asked her son Maurice to make certain that her coffin was covered in lilacs. As the funeral cortège, followed by one of the largest crowds ever seen in modern France, moved from the Church of Sainte-Françoise-de-Sâles to Père Lachaise, the mourners stopped for a moment of reverent silence in front of the Théâtre Sarah Bernhardt, transfixed by the memory of her golden voice.

Glossary

les abonnés: subscribers to the ballet, and also men who pursued dancers and courtesans

Accademia: gatherings of men and women in Rome, Venice, and Florence during the Renaissance who met to share a meal and discuss art and ideas; occasions which wives could not attend but at which courtesans often were present

les agenouillées: literally, the kneeling ones, slang for courtesans who did have occasion to kneel at times

les amazones: the word used for the masculine riding costume women wore and for the women who wore it; also a code word for courtesans who, even if they were not always androgynous in manner, took the prerogatives of men

auletrides: young women who played the flute for hire at banquets for men in ancient Rome. In addition to playing the flute at the beginning of the evening, they would often engage in prostitution at its end

le Beau Monde: literally, the beautiful world; fashionable society, which included courtesans

les belles petites: term for courtesans

les biches: a term for courtesans and *lorettes;* using the image of a doe, the term expresses and projects the animality that men associated with courtesans

le bon ton: good taste; the fashionable crowd

le boulevard: "The Paris of the Parisians," wrote Cornelia Otis Skinner, "began at the Madeleine and ended at Tortoni's. . . ."

boulevardier: "The term boulevardier was now invented to describe men whose principal accomplishment consisted in appearing at the proper moment in the proper café," writes Roger Shattuck. As Roger Moréas described, this moment went on for hours. "In the old days, I arrived around one in the afternoon . . . stayed until seven and then went to dine. At about eight we came back and didn't leave until one in the morning."

camélias: another code word for courtesans, derived from the play by Alexandre Dumas *fils, La Dame aux camélias*

cocodès: in English in the 1920s and 1930s, the translation would have been "swells"—men out for a good time who were willing and able to pay for it

cocodette: a déclassé society woman, excluded from high society because of scandal or divorce, who lived the life of a courtesan while preserving her upper-class manners. Thus, according to Philippe Perrot, helping to blur the demarcations between "zones of social hierarchy"

cocotte: literally, hen; a slang term used for both prostitutes and courtesans

coquette: a flirt

cortigiana: Italian term originally coined in Rome to mean courtesans who learned many of the skills of courtiers; it came to apply to prostitutes as well

cortigiana oneste: in Italy, particularly Venice, an honored courtesan as distinct from a prostitute

cortigiano: Italian for courtier

courtisane: French for courtesan

dames galantes: see **femmes galantes**

dégrafée: unhooked, unclasped, unbuttoned; another term for a courtesan

demi-castor: a word for a particular kind of courtesan, a middle-class or bourgeois woman, often unmarriageable due to scandal, who instead of being supported directly would be given expensive gifts by her lovers. Laure Hayman, the mistress of Marcel Proust's uncle, whom Proust used as a model for Odette Crécy in *A la recherche du temps perdu*, was considered a *demicastor*

demi-mondaines: women in the *demi-monde*, not all of whom were courtesans. KiKi of Montparnasse, for instance, was a *demi-mondaine* but not a courtesan

demi-monde: the alternative world of gentlemen, artists, writers, social rebels, actors, courtesans, and *lorettes* which existed in Paris throughout the nineteenth century. The word was coined by Alexandre Dumas *fils* in his play *Le Demi-Monde*, though the definition changed

demi-reps: British term for wellborn women who became courtesans

deshabillés: literally, undressed, partly undressed, or undressing; a term for courtesans

diseur de mots: a witty man, usually to be found in a café on one of the Grand Boulevards

the fashionable impure: since purity meant chastity in a woman, the impure were women who were not chaste but were fashionable. Usually but not always courtesans

favorites: the women chosen or "favored" and kept by French kings and emperors

femmes galantes: most often courtesans, living a life of *galanterie*; the seventeenth- and eighteenth-century analogue of the *demi-mondaines*

femmes honnêtes: respectable women; but the term *honnête* came to mean authentic in the seventeenth and eighteenth centuries, and as such was applied to both Ninon de Lenclos and Jeanne du Barry

femmes légères: women who take moral lessons lightly; courtesans

fille d'amour: a young woman who was either a courtesan or a potential one

filles de marbres: courtesans and *lorettes*; taken from a popular play of the nineteenth century, *Les Filles de Marbre*

galanterie: the sensual and amorous life led by aristocrats in France in the seventeenth and eighteenth centuries; also used for the pursuit of pleasures, especially amorous and especially with courtesans in the nineteenth century

galants: men who were well mannered and elegant, often pursuing women while they led fashionably debauched lives

garde-robe: wardrobe, an essential word in the lexicon of the courtesan

gay: the word now used for homosexual once implied the presence of courtesans, hence gaiety

Gay Nineties: the Belle Epoque, famous for its courtesans and their wild behavior, whose epicenter was Paris, and within Paris, Maxim's

"Gay Paree": the risqué world of courtesanry, artistic rebellion, and general mischief that attracted initiates and tourists from around the world

grandes horizontales: a term for courtesans that was especially popular in the Belle Epoque and the fin-de-siècle

les Grandes Trois: Liane de Pougy, Caroline Otero, and Emilienne d'Alençon, the three most sought-after courtesans of the Belle Epoque

le grand monde: high society, the upper classes; **le petit monde:** the working classes

les Grands Boulevards: the great boulevards in Paris that run from the eleventh arrondissement to the first, from the Bastille to the Madeleine, including boulevard des Italiens, boulevard Montmartre, boulevard Haussmann, boulevard Bonne-Nouvelle, boulevard du Crime, boulevard du Temple, etc.

le Grand Seize: the private room reserved for royalty and the courtesans they invited upstairs at the Café Anglais

grisette: literally, milliner's assistant, but the word applied to seamstresses and shopgirls too. Since these women were paid so little and had few prospects, many engaged in casual prostitution, hence the meaning: a woman of "easy virtue." Madame du Barry began as a *grisette*, as did Marie Duplessis and Alice Ozy

hetaera: courtesan in ancient Greece; sometimes also a priestess of Aphrodite

high life: in French, as taken from English, "le high life" (pronounced to rhyme with "fig leaf"). It meant an elegant good time filled with almost constant revelry

honnête homme: one of several names by which Ninon de Lenclos was called in Paris—*Il n'y a point de plus honnête homme que Mlle Lenclos* (There is no more honest man than Mademoiselle Lenclos). Among other names, she was known as *la belle courtisane* and *la vieille courtesan*

impure: not chaste; courtesan

Jockey Club: the club, founded by Lord Seymour, father of Richard Wallace, Alice Ozy's famous protector, whose aristocratic members shared an enthusiasm for the British custom of racing horses. They were also famous for their enthusiasm for courtesans

jolies filles: beautiful girls—applied to *grisettes, lorettes,* courtesans, and *demi-mondaines* alike

joyeuse: blithe and gay; also the term for a courtesan

libertinage: philosophically, the attempt to reconcile Epicureanism with Christianity, led by Pierre Gassendi; also refers to the activities of libertines, who indulged freely in sensual pleasure

libertine: a man who practices libertinage, the equivalent of sex, drugs, and rock and roll during the Ancien Régime

lion: as in social lion, for whom, at least in Paris, keeping a courtesan was de rigueur, and belonging to the Jockey Club almost equally obligatory

lionne: pursued, chased, and kept by one or more *lions*

lorette: a kind of minor league courtesan, part of the gay life along the boulevards, supported but not in the grandest style, usually hoping for advancement. So many lived in the neighborhood of the church called La Dame des Lorettes in the ninth arrondissement that the *boulevardier* Nestor Rocqueplan christened them "*lorettes.*" "A marvelous lorette of the tall sort," Delacroix wrote in a letter to George Sand, "all clad in black satin and velvet . . . when alighting from her cabriolet let me see up her leg to her belly, with the nonchalance of a goddess"

maîtresses en titre: the semiofficial mistresses of French kings, who were presented at court and entertained at various royal palaces

mangeuse d'homme: the direct translation would be man-eater, but in French *mangeuse* connotes a woman with a large sexual appetite, hence a term for a courtesan

monde entier: the whole world, but also society (as in tout Paris)

mot juste: as with *bon mot*, a witty remark or response

"notre courtisane nationale": "our national courtesan"—Liane de Pougy

précieuses: aristocratic women of the seventeenth and eighteenth centuries who cultivated romantic love in a highly refined way, so refined that they shunned its more bodily expressions

restaurant discret: a restaurant that provides *salons particulières*, where private meetings or parties can be held with courtesans. Famous among such restaurants was the Café Anglais, which had a room, *le Grand Seize*, often reserved for royalty and their friends. The Parisian restaurant Lapérouse has retained its *salons particulières*

ruelle: intellectual gathering in eighteenth-century Paris

salon: writers, artists, and philosophers gathered with their friends in the *grands salons*, or great rooms of private residences, to discuss their work, listen to performances, hear music. A number of these salons were conducted by courtesans—notably, Ninon de Lenclos, Marion Delorme, Sabatier, Jeanne Duval, and Alice Ozy. The custom was earlier practiced in Renaissance Italy

salone: Renaissance Italian word for salon

salon particulière: a private room in a restaurant where gentlemen could dine and spend much of the evening with the courtesans they escorted

souper et galant: to dine with a *femme galante*, followed by *galanterie*, often conducted in the *salon particulière* of a *restaurant discret*—a tradition initiated by Philippe d'Orléans, regent of France after Louis XIV

tendresses: yet another euphemism for courtesans and *lorettes*

the Three Graces: aside from the mythological figures who assisted Aphrodite both sartorially and with the seasons, there have been two sets of famous women given this name in the French history of courtesanry:

the three Mailly sisters, daughters of the marquis de Nesle, all lovers, sequentially, of Louis XV; and the trio celebrated during the Belle Epoque—Liane de Pougy, La Belle Otero, and Emilienne d'Alençon

vigna: villas in Renaissance Rome and outside Venice in whose beautiful gardens gatherings of artists, writers, philosophers, and courtesans were held. "Oh when I think back to those times gone by," Jacobo Sadoleto writes, "how often I recall those suppers and our frequent meetings . . . how after our homely banquets, spiced more with wit than gluttony, we used to recite poetry and make speeches. To the great satisfaction of all, because though they revealed a lofty spirit, they were delivered with gaiety and grace."

voluptuary: one whose life is devoted to sensual pleasure

Bibliography

Adler, Laure. *La Vie Quotidienne dans les Maisons Closées, 1830–1930.* Paris: Hachette, 1991.

Anderson, Jack. *Dance.* New York: Newsweek Books, 1974.

Anon. *An Englishman in Paris.* New York: Appleton & Co., 1892.

Apraxine, Pierre, and Xavier Demange, eds. *La Comtesse de Castigione par elle-même.* Paris: Editions de la Réunion des Musées nationaux, 1999.

Aretino, Pietro. *Aretino's Dialogues,* trans. by Raymond Rosenthal. New York: Stein & Day, 1971.

Atwood, William G. *The Parisian Worlds of Frédéric Chopin.* New Haven: Yale University Press, 1999.

Bach, Steven. *Marlene Dietrich, Life and Legend.* New York: Da Capo Press, 2000.

Balzac, Honoré de. *A Harlot High and Low,* trans. Rayner Heppenstall. London: Penguin Books, 1970.

———. *Les Boulevards de Paris.* Paris: Le Cadratin, 1994.

Baral, Robert. *Revue. A Nostalgic Reprise of the Great Broadway Period.* New York: Fleet Publishing, 1962.

Barbier, Patrick. *Opera in Paris, 1800–1850. A Lively History,* trans. Robert Luoma. Portland: Amadeus Press, 1995.

Baring, Anne, and Jules Cashford. *The Myth of the Goddess. Evolution of an Image.* London: Viking Arkana, 1991.

Barrot, Olivier, and Raymond Chirat. *Le Théâtre de Boulevard, Ciel mon mari!* Paris: Gallimard, 1998.

Baudelaire, Charles. *Intimate Journals,* trans. Christopher Isherwood. San Francisco: City Lights Books, 1990.

———. *Les Fleurs du mal,* trans. Richard Howard. Boston: David R. Godine, 1983.

————. *Paris Spleen*, trans. Louise Varèse. New York: New Directions, 1970.

————. *The Painter of Modern Life and Other Essays*, ed. Johnathan Mayne. New York: Phaidon Press, 1995.

Baudot, Françoise. *Fashion, The Twentieth Century*. New York: Universe Books, 1999.

Beauvoir, Simone de. *The Second Sex*, trans. H. M. Parshly. New York: Alfred A. Knopf, 1957.

Benjamin, Walter. *The Arcades Project*, trans. Howard Eiland and Kevin McLaughlin. Cambridge: Belknap Press, Harvard University, 1999.

Benstock, Shari. *Women of the Left Bank, Paris 1900–1940*. Austin: University of Texas Press, 1986.

Bernhardt, Sarah. *My Double Life. The Memoirs of Sarah Bernhardt*, trans. Victoria Tietze Larson. Albany: State University of New York Press, 1999.

Bigne, Yolaine de la. *Valtesse de la Bigne*. Paris: Perrin, 1999.

Blackmer, Corinne E., and Patricia Juliana Smith, eds. *En travesti. Women, Gender, Subversion, Opera*. New York: Columbia University Press, 1995.

Boudet, Micheline. *La Fleur du Mal. La Véritable Histoire de la Dame aux Camélias*. Paris: Albin-Michel, 1993.

Bourguinat, Elizabeth. *Les Rues de Paris au XVIII siècle. Le regard de Louis Sébastien Mercier*. Paris: Museé Carnavalet, 1999.

Boussel, Patrice et al. *Dictionnaire de Paris*. Paris: Larousse, 1964.

Bowers, Jane, and Judith Tick, eds. *Women Making Music. The Western Art Tradition, 1150–1950*. Chicago: University of Chicago Press, 1987.

Boyle, Kay, and Robert McAlmon. *Being Geniuses Together, 1920–1930*. New York: Doubleday, 1968.

Bressler, Fenton. *Napoleon III, A Life*. New York: Carrol & Graf Publishers, 1999.

Briais, Bernard. *Grandes Courtisanes du Second Empire*. Paris: Tallandier, 1981.

Bricktop with James Haskins. *Bricktop*. New York: Welcome Rain Publishers, 2000.

Brown, Frederick. *Zola, A Life*. New York: Farrar, Straus, Giroux, 1995.

Brownstein, Rachel M. *Tragic Muse. Rachel of the Comédie-Française*. Durham: Duke University Press, 1995.

Bruson, Jean-Marie, et al. *L'ABCdaire de Madame de Sévigné*. Paris: Flammarion, 1996.

Callan, Georgina O'Hara. *Dictionary of Fashion and Fashion Designers*. London: Thames & Hudson, 1998.

Carter, William C. *Marcel Proust, A Life*. New Haven: Yale University Press, 2000.

Castiglione, Baldesar. *The Book of the Courtier*, trans. George Bull. London: Penguin Books, 1976.

Chalon, Jean. *Liane de Pougy, Courtisane, princesse et sainte*. Paris: Flammarion, 1994.

Chartier, Roger. *A History of Private Life. Passions of the Renaissance*, trans. Arthur Goldhammer. Cambridge: Belknap Press, Harvard University, 1989.

Childers, Caroline. *Haute Jewelry*. New York: BW Publishing Associates with Rizzoli, 1999.

Choulet, Jean-Marie. *Promenades à Paris et en Normandie avec La Dame aux Camélias*. Condé-sur-Noireau, France: Editions Charles Corlet, 1998.

Christiansen, Rupert. *Paris Babylon. The Story of the Paris Commune*. New York: Penguin Books, 1994.

Clark, T. J. *The Painting of Modern Life. Paris in the Art of Manet and His Followers*. Princeton: Princeton University Press, 1984.

Clarke, Mary, and Clement Crisp. *Ballet. An Illustrated Story*. New York: Universe Books, 1973.

———. *The History of Dance*. New York: Crown, 1981.

Clébert, Jean Paul. *La Littérature à Paris. L'histoire, les lieux, la vie littéraire*. Paris: Larousse, 1999.

Cole, Bruce. *Titian and Venetian Painting, 1450–1590*. Boulder, Colo.: Westview Press, 1999.

Cole, Toby, and Helen Krich Chinoy, eds. *Actors on Acting. The Theories, Techniques and Practices of the World's Great Actors, Told in Their Own Words*. New York: Crown, 1970.

Colette. *Chéri and The Last of Chéri*, trans. anon. New York: Ballantine Books, 1987.

———. *Gigi* and *The Cat*, trans. Roger Senhouse. London: Penguin Books, 1958.

———. *Lettres à Marguerite Moreno*. Paris: Flammarion, 1994.

———. *Mitsou and Music-Hall Sidelights*, trans. Raymond Postgate and Anne-Marie Callimachi. New York: Farrar, Straus & Giroux, 1958.

———. *My Apprenticeships and Music-Hall Sidelights*. London: Secker & Warburg, 1957.

———. *Recollections. Poignant Memories by the French Writer*, trans. David le Vay. New York: Collier, 1972.

————. *The Pure and the Impure*, trans. Herma Briffault. New York: Farrar, Straus & Giroux, 1967.

————. *The Vagabonde*, trans. Enid McLeod. London: Penguin Books, 1960.

Colombani, Roger. *Les Belles Indomptables, Les Grands Destins*. Paris: Flammarion, 1999.

Conner, Randy P. L. *Mirror of My Love: Jeanne Duval and Baudelaire in the Cosmos of Voudou*. Unpublished manuscript.

Croutier, Alev. *Harem, the World Behind the Veil*. New York: Abbeville Press, 1989.

Damase, Jacques. *Les Folies du Music-Hall. Histoire du Music-Hall à Paris du 1914 à nos jours*. Paris: Editions Spectacle, 1960.

La Dame aux Eventails. Nina de Callias, modèle de Manet. Paris: Musée d'Orsay, 2000.

D'Aragona, Tullia. *Dialogue on the Infinity of Love*, ed. and trans. by Rinalda Russell and Bruce Merry. Chicago: University of Chicago Press, 1997.

Davidson, James. *Courtesans and Fishcakes. The Consuming Passions of Classical Athens*. New York: St. Martin's Press, 1998.

Davies, Marion. *The Times We Had. Life with William Randolph Hearst*. New York: Ballantine Books, 1990.

Day, Lillian. *Ninon, A Courtesan of Quality*. London: Jarrolds, 1958.

De Amicis, Edmondo. *Studies of Paris*, trans. W. W. Cady. New York: G. P. Putnam & Sons, 1897.

Debriffe. *Madame de Pompadour, Marquise des Lumières*. Paris: Le Semaphore, 1999.

Degaine, André. *Guide des Promenades Théâtrales à Paris. Histoire des Théâtres Parisiennes sous forme de Cinq Promenades*. St. Genouph, France: Nizet, 1999.

Delorme, Jean-Claude, and Anne-Marie Dubois. *Passages Couvertes Parisiennes*. Paris: Parigramme, 1999.

Dion-Tenebaum, Anne, and Marie-Nöelle de Grandry. *L'Art de Vivre à l'Epoque de George Sand*. Paris: Flammarion, 1999.

Duchêne, Roger. *Ninon de Lenclos ou la manière jolie de faire l'amour*. Paris: Fayard, 2000.

Dumas, Alexandre. *Charles VII at the Homes of His Great Vassals*, Introduction, Dorothy Trench-Bonett. Chicago: Noble Press, 1991.

————. *Filles, Lorettes et Courtisanes*. Paris: Flammarion, 2000.

Dumas *fils*, Alexandre. *La Dame aux Camélias*, trans. David Coward. Oxford: Oxford University Press, 1991. Paris: Calmann-Lévy; Paris: Le Livre de Poche, 1983.

————. *Théâtre Complet*. Paris: Calmann-Lévy, 1898.

Eisler, Riane Tennenhaus. *Sacred Pleasure*. San Francisco: Harper San Francisco, 1996.

Filles de Joie, The Book of Courtesans, Sporting Girls, Ladies of the Evening, Madams, a Few Occasionals and Some Royal Favorites. New York: Dorset Press, 1966.

Flanner, Janet. *Paris Was Yesterday, 1925–1939*, ed. Irving Drutman. New York: Harcourt Brace Jovanovich, 1972.

Flaubert, Gustave. *Sentimental Education*, trans. Robert Baldick. London: Penguin Books, 1964.

Fleetwood-Hesketh. *The Hôtel Païva*. Paris: Association de Sauvegarde de l'Hôtel Païva, 1990.

Fontaine, Gérard. *Palais Garnier, Le Fantasme de l'Opéra*. Paris: Editions Noêsis, 1999.

Foucault, Michel. *The History of Sexuality*. Vol. I, trans. Robert Hurley. New York: Pantheon Books, 1978.

Franco, Veronica. *Poems and Selected Letters*, ed. and trans. Ann Rosalind Jones and Margaret Rosenthal. Chicago: University of Chicago Press, 1998.

Frederich, Otoo. *Olympia. Paris in the Age of Manet*. New York: Simon & Schuster, 1992.

Frey, Julia Bloch. *Toulouse-Lautrec: A Life*. London, Phoenix, 1995.

Gallet, Danielle. *Madame de Pompadour, ou le pouvoir feminin*. Paris: Fayard, 1985.

Garber, Majorie. *Vested Interests. Cross-Dressing and Cultural Anxiety*. New York: HarperPerennial, 1992.

Garelick, Rhonda K. *Rising Star. Dandyism, Gender, and Performance in the Fin de Siècle*. Princeton: Princeton University Press, 1998.

Gascar, Pierre. *Le Boulevard du Crime*. Paris: Atelier Hachette/Massin, 1980.

Gerlini, Elisa. *Villa Farnesina alla Lungara Roma*. Rome: Istituto Poligrafico e Zecca della Stato Libreria dello Stato, 1990.

Godeau, Jerôme, ed. *Le Promeneur de Paris. 10 promenades de la Rive Droite*. Paris: Actes Sud, 1999.

Goffen, Rona, ed. *Titian's Venus of Urbino*. Cambridge, U.K.: Cambridge University Press, 1997.

Gold, Arthur, and Robert Fizdale. *Misia. The Life of Misia Sert.* New York: Alfred A. Knopf, 1980.

———. *The Divine Sarah. A Life of Sarah Bernhardt.* New York: Random House, 1991.

Goncourt, Edmond de. *La Fille Elisa.* Paris: Fleuron, 1996.

Goncourt, Edmond and Jules de. *The Goncourt Journals, 1851–1870,* ed. and trans. Lewis Galantière. New York: Doubleday-Anchor, 1958.

Groetschel, Yves. *Village Opéra, Chaussée-d'Antin, Faubourg-Montmartre.* Paris: Village Communication, 1997.

Grotowski, Jerzy. *Towards a Poor Theatre.* New York: Simon & Schuster, 1968.

Haslip, Joan. *Madame du Barry, The Wages of Beauty.* New York: Grove Weidenfeld, 1991.

Hauser, Arnold T. *The Social History of Art. Vol 2.* New York: Vintage, 1960.

———. *The Social History of Art. Vol 3.* New York: Vintage, 1958.

———. *The Social History of Art. Vol 4.* New York: Vintage, 1958.

Haye, Amy de la, and Shelley Tobin. *Chanel. The Couturière at Work.* London: Victoria and Albert Museum, 1995.

Haynes, Alan. *Sex in Elizabethan England.* Thrupp, Stroud, Gloucestershire: Sutton Press, 1997.

Hutcheon, Linda and Michael. *Opera, Desire, Disease, Death.* Lincoln: University of Nebraska Press, 1996.

Ingamells, John. *Mrs. Robinson and Her Portraits.* London: Wallace Collection, 1978.

Jamison, Judith, with Howard Kaplan. *Dancing Spirit. An Autobiography.* New York: Doubleday, 1993.

Jarasse, Dominique. *La Peinture Française au XVIII Siècle.* Paris: Terrail, 1998.

John, Nicholas, ed. *Violetta and Her Sisters. The Lady of the Camellias, Responses to the Myth.* London: Faber & Faber, 1994.

Jowitt, Deborah. *Time and the Dancing Image.* Berkeley: University of California Press, 1989.

Kirstein, Lincoln. *Four Centuries of Ballet, Fifty Masterworks.* New York: Dover, 1984.

Kluver, Billy, and Julie Martin. *KiKi's Paris. Artists and Lovers 1900–1930.* New York: Harry N. Abrams, 1989.

Koestenbaum, Wayne. *The Queen's Throat. Opera, Homosexuality and the Mystery of Desire.* New York: Poseidon Press, 1993.

Ladurie, Emmanuel Le Roy. *The Ancien Régime. A History of France, 1610–1764.* Oxford: Blackwell, 1991.

Laver, James. *Costume and Fashion. A Concise History.* London: Thames & Hudson, 1996.

Lehnert, Gertrud. *Fashion. A Concise History.* London: Laurence King, 1998.

Leider, Emily Worth. *Becoming Mae West.* New York: Da Capo Press, 2000.

Lessard, Suzannah. *The Architect of Desire. Beauty and Danger in the Stanford White Family.* New York: Dial Press, 1996.

Lewis, Arthur H. *La Belle Otero.* New York: Trident Press, 1967.

Lipton, Eunice. *Alias Olympia. A Woman's Search for Manet's Notorious Model and Her Own Desire.* Ithaca: Cornell University Press, 1992.

————. *Looking into Degas. Uneasy Images of Women and Modern Life.* Berkeley: University of California Press, 1988.

Loliée, Frédéric. *Les Femmes du Second Empire, La Cour des Tuileries.* Paris: Jules Tallendier, 1954.

Loomis, Stanley. *Du Barry, A Biography.* New York: J. B. Lippincott, 1959.

Louÿs, Pierre. *Mimes des Courtisanes.* Paris: Editions Albin-Michel.

Ludlam, Charles. *The Complete Plays of Charles Ludlam.* New York: Harper & Row, 1989.

Lyonnet, Henry. *La dame aux camélias de Dumas fils.* Paris: Société Françaises d'Editions Littéraires et Techniques, 1930.

Madsen, Axel. *Chanel, A Woman of Her Own.* New York: Henry Holt & Co., 1991.

Mann, A. T., and Jane Lyle. *Sacred Sexuality.* Shaftesbury, U.K.: Element, 1995.

Markale, Jean. *The Great Goddess. Reverence of the Divine Feminine from the Paleolithic to the Present.* Rochester, N.Y.: Inner Traditions, 1999.

Masson, Georgina. *Courtesans of the Italian Renaissance.* London: Secker & Warburg, 1975.

Maupassant, Guy de. *The House of Madame Tellier and Other Stories.* London: J. M. Dent & Sons, 1991.

Maurceley, Charles Baude de. *La Vérité sur le salon de Nina de Villard.* Paris: Librairie La Vouivre, 2000.

Maurois, André. *Les Trois Dumas.* Paris: Hachette, 1957.

McCarthy, Mary. *Venice Observed.* New York: Harcourt Brace Jovanovich, 1963.

Miller, John, ed. *Beauty.* San Francisco: Chronicle Books, 1997.

Miltoun, Francis. *Dumas' Paris*. Boston: L. C. Page & Co., 1904.

Mitford, Nancy. *Madame de Pompadour*. New York: Dutton, 1984.

————. *The Sun King*. London: Penguin Books, 1994.

————. *The Water Beetle*. New York: Atheneum, 1986.

Mogador, Céleste. *Mémoires*. Paris: Librairie Nouvelle, 1859.

Moncan, Patrice de. *Guide Littéraire des Passages de Paris*. Paris: Editions Hermé, 1996.

————. *Les Grands Boulevards de Paris, de la Bastille à la Madeleine*. Paris: Editions du Mécène, 1997.

Montaigne, Michael de. *Four Essays*, trans. M. A. Screech. New York: Penguin Books, 1991.

Morgan, Lael. *Good Time Girls of the Alaska-Yukon Gold Rush*. Fairbanks, Alaska: Epicenter Press, 1998.

Morris, Jan. *The World of Venice*. New York: Harcourt Brace, 1993.

Murray, Venetia. *An Elegant Madness. High Society in Regency England*. New York: Viking Press, 1999.

Nasaw, David. *The Chief. The Life of William Randolph Hearst*. Boston: Houghton Mifflin, 2000.

Neave, Christiane, *Ombre et Lumière. Alexandre Dumas fils, 1824–1895*. Marly-le-Roi, France: Editions Champflour, 1995.

Néret, Gilles. *1000 Dessous. A History of Lingerie*. Cologne: Taschen Books, 1998.

Norwich, John Julius. *A History of Venice*. New York: Alfred A. Knopf, 1982.

Oberthür, Mariel. *Montmartre en liesse 1880–1900*. Paris: Paris Musées, 1994.

Ostwald, Peter. *Vaslav Nijinsky. A Leap into Madness*. New York: Lyle Stuart, 1991.

Ovid. *The Art of Love*, trans. Rolfe Humphries. Bloomington: Indiana University Press, 1963.

Panofsky, Erwin. *Renaissance and Renascenses in Western Art*. Stockholm: Alquist Q. Wiksell, 1960.

Paquet, Dominique. *Miroir, mon beau miroir. Une histoire de la beauté*. Paris: Gallimard, 1997.

Paris, Ginette. *Pagan Meditations. Aphrodite, Hestia, Artemis*. Dallas: Spring Publications, 1986.

Pastori, Jean-Pierre. *La Danse 1/Du ballet de cour au ballet blanc*. Paris: Gallimard, 1996.

Pearl, Cora. *Grand Horizontal, The Erotic Memoirs of a Passionate Lady*, ed. William Blatchford. New York: Stein and Day, 1983.

Perrot, Michelle, ed. *A History of Private Life, From the Fires of Revolution to the Great War*, trans. Arthur Goldhammer. Cambridge: Belknap Press, Harvard University, 1990.

Perrot, Philippe. *Fashioning the Bourgeoisie. A History of Clothing in the Nineteenth Century*, trans. Richard Bienvenu. Princeton: Princeton University Press, 1994.

Pevitt, Christine. *The Man Who Would Be King. The Life of Philippe d'Orléans, Regent of France*. New York: William Morrow, 1998.

Phelps, Robert. *Belles Saisons, A Colette Scrapbook*. New York: Farrar, Straus & Giroux, 1978.

Pichois, Claude. *Baudelaire*, trans. Graham Robb. London: Hamish Hamilton, 1989.

Pineau, Gisèle, and Marie Abraham. *Femmes des Antilles. Traces et Voix, cent cinquante ans après de l'esclavage*. L'Outre Mers, France: Stock, 1998.

Poiret, Paul. *En Habillant l'Epoque*. Paris: Bernard Grasset, 1986.

Pougy de, Liane. *Mes Cahiers Bleus*. Paris: Plon, 1977.

Prendergast, Christopher. *Paris and the Nineteenth Century*. Oxford: Blackwell, 1995.

Prévost, Antoine-François. *Manon*, trans. Helen Waddell. London: Soho Book Company, 1986.

Proust, Marcel. *The Remembrance of Things Past*. trans. C. K. Scott-Moncreiff and Terence Kilmartin. Vol I–III. New York: Vintage, 1982.

Raczymow, Henri. *Le Paris Littéraire et Intime de Marcel Proust*. Paris: Parigramme, 1997.

Redmond, Layne. *When the Drummers Were Women. A Spiritual History of Rhythm*. New York: Three Rivers Press, 1997.

Reyna, Ferdinando. *A Concise History of Ballet*. New York: Grosset & Dunlap, 1965.

Richardson, Joanna. *The Bohemians. La Vie Bohème in Paris, 1830–1914*. South Brunswick, N.J.: A. S. Barnes & Company, 1971.

———. *The Courtesans. The Demi-monde in Nineteenth-Century France*. New York: World Publishing Company, 1967.

Roberts, Nickie. *Whores in History. Prostitution in Western Society*. New York: HarperCollins, 1992.

Rosand, David. *Painting in Cinquecento Venice. Titian, Veronese, Tintoretto*. New Haven: Yale University Press, 1982.

Rosenthal, Margaret F. *The Honest Courtesan. Veronica Franco, Citizen and Writer in Sixteenth-Century Venice.* Chicago: University of Chicago Press, 1992.

Rudorff, Raymond. *The Belle Epoque. Paris in the Nineties.* New York: Saturday Review Press, 1973.

Samuels, Steven, ed. *Ridiculous Theatre, Scourge of Human Folly. The Essays and Opinions of Charles Ludlam.* New York: Theatre Communications Group, 1992.

Sanders, Barry. *Sudden Glory. Laughter as Subversive History.* Boston: Beacon Press, 1995.

Scarry, Elaine. *On Beauty and Being Just.* Princeton: Princeton University Press, 1999.

Schama, Simon. *Citizens. A Chronicle of the French Revolution.* New York: Alfred A. Knopf, 1989.

Schenkar, Joan. *Truly Wilde. The Unsettling Story of Dolly Wilde, Oscar's Unusual Niece.* New York: Basic Books, 2000.

Seigel, Jerrold. *Bohemian Paris. Culture, Politics and the Boundaries of Bourgeois Life, 1830–1930.* Baltimore: Johns Hopkins University Press, 1999.

Seymour, Bruce, *Lola Montez, A Life.* New Haven: Yale University Press, 1996.

Shattuck, Roger. *The Banquet Years. The Origins of the Avant Garde in France, 1885 to World War I.* New York: Doubleday-Anchor, 1961.

Simon, Marie. *Les Dessous, Les Carnets de la Mode.* Paris: Editions du Chène, Hachette, 1998.

————. *Mode et Peinture, le Second Empire et l'impressionnisme.* Paris: Hazan, 1995.

Skinner, Cornelia Otis. *Elegant Wits and Grands Horizontals.* Boston: Houghton Mifflin, 1962.

Souhami, Diana. *Mrs. Keppel and Her Daughter.* New York: St. Martin's Press, 1996.

Spencer, Charles. *Erté.* New York: Clarkson N. Potter, 1970.

Sperling, Jutta Gisela. *Convents and the Body Politic in Late Renaissance Venice.* Chicago: University of Chicago Press, 1999.

Steele, Valerie. *Paris Fashion. A Cultural History.* Oxford: Berg, 1998.

Sterling, Dorothy, ed. *We Are Your Sisters. Black Women in the Nineteenth Century.* New York: W. W. Norton, 1984.

Stortoni, Laura Ann, ed. *Women Poets of the Italian Renaissance. Courtly Ladies and Courtesans,* trans. Laura Ann Stortoni and Mary Prentice Lillie. New York: Italica Press, 1997.

Terkel, Studs. *The Spectator. Talk About Movies and Plays with the People Who Make Them.* New York: New Press, 1999.

Thirkell, Angela. *Tribute to Harriet. The Surprising Career of Harriet Wilson.* Pleasantville, N.Y.: Akadine Press, 1999.

Thurman, Judith. *Secrets of the Flesh. A Life of Colette.* New York: Alfred A. Knopf, 1999.

Tingali, Paola. *Women in Italian Renaissance Art. Gender, Representation, Identity.* Manchester, U.K.: Manchester University Press, 1997.

Traugott, Mark, ed. and trans. *The French Worker. Autobiographies from the Industrial Era.* Berkeley: University of California Press, 1993.

Turner, James Grantham, ed. *Sexuality and Gender in Early Modern Europe. Institutions, Texts, Images.* Cambridge, UK: Cambridge University Press, 1993.

Valois, Thirza. *Around and About Paris. The 1st, 2nd, 3rd, 4th, 5th, 6th and 7th arrondissements.* London: Iliad Books, 1995.

———. *Around and About Paris. From the Guillotine to the Bastille, the 8th–12th arrondissements.* London: Iliad Books, 1996.

———. *Around and About Paris. The 13th–20th arrondissements.* London: Iliad Books, 1997.

Voillot, Patrick. *Diamants et Pierres Précieuses.* Paris: Gallimard, 1997.

Wallach, Janet. *Chanel, Her Style and Her Life.* New York: Nan A. Talese-Doubleday, 1998.

West, Mae. *Goodness Had Nothing to Do with It.* London: Virago, 1996.

Wharton, Edith. *The Age of Innocence.* New York: Macmillan, 1993.

———. *The House of Mirth.* New York: New American Library, 1964.

Wickes, George. *The Amazon of Letters. The Life and Loves of Natalie Barney.* New York: Popular Library, 1978.

Wickham, Glynne. *A History of the Theatre.* 2nd ed. Cambridge, U.K.: Cambridge University Press, 1992.

Zola, Emile. *L'Assommoir,* trans. Leonard Tancock. London: Penguin Books, 1970.

———. *Nana,* trans. George Holden. London: Penguin Books, 1972.

Art Credits

Grateful acknowledgment is given to the following sources for the art used throughout this book: page iii, Erich Lessing/Art Resource, NY; page xiv, Art Resource, NY; page 18, ©Harlingue-Viollet; page 47, ©Harlingue-Viollet; page 52, Réunion des Musées Nationaux/Art Resource, NY; page 75, ©Harlingue-Viollet; page 78, ©Collection Viollet; page 90, ©Collection Viollet; page 94, *Portrait of a Lady (Veronica Franco[?])*, by Follower of Jacopo Tintoretto, 16th Century, oil on canvas, 61.5 cm x 47.2 cm, Worcester Art Museum, Austin S. and Sarah C. Garver Fund, photograph ©Worcester Art Museum; page 128, Musée de Bruxelles/©LL-Viollet; page 132, The Birchard Collection; page 153, Giraudon/Art Resource, NY; page 158, *Jeanne-Antoinette Poisson, Marquise de Pompadour*, 1758, by Francois Boucher, oil on canvas, 82.2 x 64.9 cm, courtesy of the Fogg Art Museum, Harvard University Art Museums, Bequest of Charles E. Dunlap, Photographic Services, ©President and Fellows of Harvard College, Harvard University; page 184, MacBride Museum Collection, Whitehorse, Yukon; page 188, Brown Brothers; page 227, Erich Lessing/Art Resource, NY; page 230, Bibliothèque Nationale de France.